Mass Revision

JIMMY AKIN

Mass Revision

*How the Liturgy Is Changing
and What It Means for You*

CATHOLIC
ANSWERS

SAN DIEGO
2011

Excerpts from English translation of *The Order of Mass I* © 2006, 2008, 2011, International Committee on English in the Liturgy, Inc. (ICEL); excerpts from *Documents on the Liturgy, 1963–1979: Conciliar, Papal, and Curial Texts* © 1982, ICEL; excerpts from the *Ceremonial of Bishops* © 1989, ICEL. All rights reserved.

Excerpts from the *General Instruction of the Roman Missal Including Adaptations for the Dioceses of the United States of America* © 2003, 2011, United States Catholic Conference, Inc. (USCC); excerpts from the *Appendix to the General Instruction of the Roman Missal for the Dioceses of the United States* © 1982, USCC; excerpts from *This Holy and Living Sacrifice* © 1985, USCC. All rights reserved.

The section titled "Roman Missal Translation Highlights: 1963–2010" was prepared by Adoremus Bulletin (© 2010 by Adoremus). Reprinted by permission.

Summorum Pontificum and the letter of Pope Benedict XVI accompanying *Summorum Pontificum* are © 2007, Libreria Editrice Vaticana. All rights reserved.

Published by Catholic Answers, Inc.
2020 Gillespie Way
El Cajon, California 92020
888-291-8000 U.S. orders
619-387-7200 international orders
619-387-0042 fax
www.catholic.com

Cover design by Devin Schadt
Typesetting by Loyola Book Composition

Printed in the United States of America
ISBN 978-1-933919-45-4

Contents

Bonus Materials

Abbreviations

AAS   *Acta Apostolicae Sedis*

AGI   U.S. Bishops, "Appendix to the General Instruction for the Dioceses of the United States." Citations taken from *The Sacramentary* (Collegeville, Minn.: Liturgical Press, 1985)

BCDW   United States Conference of Catholic Bishops Committee on Divine Worship (formerly the BCL)

BCL   Bishops' Committee on Liturgy (see also BCDW)

CB   *Ceremonial of Bishops* (Collegeville, Minn.: Liturgical Press, 1990)

CCC   *Catechism of the Catholic Church* (San Francisco: Ignatius Press, 1994)

CCEO   *Codex Canonum Ecclesiarum Orientalum—Code of Canons of the Eastern Churches* (Washington, D.C.: Canon Law Society of America, 1992)

CDS   Congregation for the Discipline of the Sacraments

CDW   Congregation for Divine Worship

CIC   *Codex Iuris Canonici—Code of Canon Law* (Washington, D.C.: Canon Law Society of America, 1983)

CMRR   *Ceremonies of the Modern Roman Rite* (San Francisco: Ignatius Press, 1995)

CSDW   Congregation for the Sacraments and Divine Worship

D   Denzinger's *Enchiridion Symbolorum*

DC   John Paul II, *Dominicae Cenae* ("On the Mystery and Worship of the Eucharist"), February 24, 1980

DMC   "Directory for Masses with Children." Citations taken from *The Sacramentary* (Collegeville, Minn.: Liturgical Press, 1985)

DOL   *Documents on the Liturgy* (Collegeville, Minn.: Liturgical Press, 1983)

DS   Denzinger and Schönmetzer, *Enchiridion Symbolorum*, 36th ed. (Barcelona: Herder, 1976)

EM   *Ecclesia de Mysterio (Interdicasterial Instruction on Certain Questions Regarding the Collaboration of the Non-Ordained Faithful in the Sacred Ministry of the Priest)*, issued by the Congregation for the Clergy, *et al.* (*Libreria Editrice Vaticana* translation)

FC   CDS, *Fidei Custos*, April 30, 1969 (citations taken from DOL)

GIRM   "General Instruction of the Roman Missal"

GNLC   *General Norms for the Liturgical Year and the Calendar*

HLS   U.S. Bishops, "This Holy and Living Sacrifice: Directory for the Celebration and Reception of Communion under Both Kinds" (citations taken from LD)

IC   CDS, *Immensae Caritatis* (citations taken from DOL)

ID CSDW, *Inaestimabile Donum*

LD *The Liturgy Documents: A Parish Resource*, 3rd ed. (Chicago: Liturgy Training Publications, 1991)

LFM *Lectionary for Mass for Use in the Dioceses of the United States of America*

MD John Paul II, *Misericordia Dei*

NDRHC United States Conference of Catholic Bishops, *Norms for the Distribution and Reception of Holy Communion under Both Kinds in the Dioceses of the United States of America*

NCCB National Conference of Catholic Bishops

PS CDW, *Paschales Solemnitatis* ("Preparation and Celebration of the Easter Feasts")

RS CDW, *Redemptionis Sacramentum*

SC Vatican II, *Sacrosanctum Concilium* (citations taken from LD)

SCT Benedict XVI, *Sacramentum Caritatis*

VC2 Austin Flannery, O.P., gen. ed., *Vatican Council II: The Conciliar and Postconciliar Documents*, vol. 1 (Boston: St. Paul Books and Media, 1992)

Introduction

The original edition of this work was published as *Mass Confusion: The Do's and Don'ts of Catholic Worship* in 1998, a time of great upheaval in the liturgy. Though it had been almost thirty years since the Mass had been revised and translated into English, the "liturgy wars" were still underway.

Roughly speaking, three major groups were involved. One group wanted to keep tinkering with the liturgy—pushing beyond what was allowed in the Church's liturgical books, introducing new elements and prayers, changing traditional wording, striking references to the male gender, and other similar things. Opposite them on the spectrum were those who disapproved of the liturgical reform in its entirety and wanted to restore the liturgy to the form it took prior to the Second Vatican Council. In the middle were those who could accept the form of Mass that was introduced after the Council but who wanted it celebrated properly, according to the liturgical books, without unapproved innovations, deviations, and abuses.

Mass Confusion was written primarily for the middle group —to let them know what the Church's liturgical law actually was. Frequently they had been lied to in parish settings, told by a liturgy director or even priest that something was acceptable when in fact it was not. As a result of this pattern of deception, many people became suspicious of anything they were told about the liturgy. It seemed advisable to produce a book that quoted the Church's liturgical law so that people could see for themselves what was and was not allowed.

In the years since 1998, matters have changed. The three

groups still exist, but the liturgical situation has substantially improved.

In the pontificate of John Paul II, the Holy See began a slow but steady application of pressure to rein in liturgical abuses. This effort involved a series of steps that each closed off an avenue of liturgical dissent and nudged the liturgy back toward its correct celebration. The most important of these was the release of a third edition of the *Missale Romanum* (the *Roman Missal*) in the early 2000s. The full translation of this work —which includes the prayers used at Mass—was still years in the future, but its *General Instruction* (the part that contains the main rules for celebrating Mass) was translated and implemented early in the decade.

The question of the "old Mass" versus the "new Mass" was also dealt with. In 2007, Pope Benedict XVI issued a *motu proprio* (a document issued on the pope's initiative) in which he clarified the status of the older form of Mass and provided wide and generous opportunities for its celebration. He also expressed the hope that the two forms of Mass could enrich each other over time.

The year 2010 saw the approval of the full translation of the *Roman Missal*, an event that was bound to cause another outburst of controversy. Even before it was released, liturgical dissidents were gearing up to resist its implementation and to stir up sentiment against it. Over 20,000 signatures (at the time of this writing) have been gathered in opposition to the new translation on a blog called *What If We Just Said Wait?*[1]

It seemed advisable once again to produce a new edition of *Mass Confusion* that reflects not only the new translation but also the changes that have taken place in liturgical law in the dozen years since the first volume appeared. So I set to work

---

[1] *http://whatifwejustsaidwait.org.*

on this volume. It has been retitled *Mass Revision* because it focuses more on the new translation of the *Roman Missal* than on the subject of liturgical abuses (though those are also dealt with extensively).

The Church's liturgical law is extensive and complex, and a book of this size cannot hope to deal with it comprehensively. It can't even cover all the variations in the celebration of the Mass. It was thus necessary to select with care what subjects the book would cover. Like its predecessor, *Mass Revision* primarily deals with the ordinary type of Mass one encounters in a typical parish. This means that it does not deal extensively with (1) Masses celebrated by a bishop, (2) Masses without a congregation in attendance, (3) Masses celebrated for young children, (4) Masses concelebrated by several priests, (5) communion services performed in the absence of a priest, and (6) Masses celebrated according to the "extraordinary form" (1962 *Missal*) of the Roman rite. It touches on some of these types of Mass briefly, but it does not go into substantial detail.

Despite its orientation toward the ordinary Masses that most people experience, it was impossible to ignore the best-known liturgical event of recent years, the 2007 release of Pope Benedict XVI's *motu proprio* on the extraordinary form of the Mass, *Summorum Pontificum*. The buildup to its release, the release itself, and the ensuing controversy made this the most discussed liturgical event since the 1970s. In the popular press it overshadowed the initial release of the new *Roman Missal*, and for a time technical ecclesiastical terms like *motu proprio* (see Glossary) were found in the pages of mainstream newspapers. Because of this issue's prominence, we have reproduced the document and Pope Benedict's accompanying letter in the Bonus Materials section of the book.

Mass Revision covers the state of liturgical affairs at the time of its publication. The regulations recorded here are those currently in force. Changes in the Church's liturgical law will be reflected in future editions.

I also should point out that the intention of this book is to describe what the liturgical law of the Church is, not my opinions on what I think it should be.

I am not a professional liturgist. However, the liturgy is not the exclusive domain of liturgical experts. It belongs to the whole people of God. Even the most humble person has the right to study and inform himself of what constitutes authentic Catholic liturgy and to compare it with the liturgies he experiences.

Let us pray that the situation with the liturgy continues to improve and show forth the glory of Christ and the unity he wills for his people.

> Jimmy Akin
> August 6, 2010
> *Feast of the Transfiguration of Our Lord*

1. The Changing Liturgy

We are living in a time of liturgical change. The last fifty years have seen almost constant change in the liturgy, including the introduction of a new order of Mass in the 1970s and the celebration of the Mass in English. Today we are experiencing the most dramatic change since that time. Another version of the Mass is being implemented, and with it comes a new, improved translation into English.

This time will not be easy. The previous version and translation of the Mass was in use for almost forty years. Its prayers have become familiar, ingrained in memory by years of use. Some Catholics today have never known any other form of Mass than the one introduced in the 1970s. And yet the Church deems it necessary to change the Mass again.

Why?

Part of the reason is that we live in a world of change. Times change; customs change; languages change. The reason that the Mass used to be said in Latin was because that is what people in many areas used to speak. But Latin fell out of popular use, and the local, vernacular languages arose. Eventually the Church decided it was prudent to allow Mass to be celebrated in the newer languages, such as English.

That was a momentous transformation, but there is always a certain amount of minor adjustment going on in the liturgy. In fact, there has never been a time when the liturgy was absolutely static. The Church is always making small modifications as it seeks to adapt the liturgy to the conditions of the day. Most popes, and certainly all the recent popes, have left their mark on the liturgy in different ways. In other words, change in the liturgy is not unexpected.

But there is another reason the new version of Mass is being introduced, and it has to do with the magnitude of the change that happened in the 1970s. The Second Vatican Council, which had met in the previous decade, released a document on the liturgy known as *Sacrosanctum Concilium*. It called for modest reform of the liturgy, proposing that certain rites in the Mass be simplified, that certain rites that had fallen out of use be restored, that texts be clarified so that the faithful might understand them more easily, and that the vernacular languages play a greater but still limited role in the Mass.

Over the next few years a group known as the Concilium worked on this project and, in consultation with various bishops' conferences, proposed changes that went much further than those the Council had indicated. They included the use of English and other modern languages for the entire Mass, not just parts of it. Eventually, Pope Paul VI approved the proposals.

When the then-new version of Mass was implemented in the 1970s, it represented two huge changes: a major revision of the rites of the Mass itself and the translation of those rites into the vernacular. Either one of these would have been a huge change on its own. The two put together were even more massive. And that leads to the second reason significant changes are again being made in the liturgy.

Any time one makes a big change, it can have unforeseen consequences, and not all of them good. That's why newly built boats have shakedown voyages, newly designed computer programs have bug releases, and so forth. It takes a while for a new or changed system to show how it works in practice, and often a little experience with it shows that some tweaking is necessary.

That is essentially what has happened with the liturgy. A big change was made in the 1970s, and from the decades of pastoral experience that followed, Pope John Paul II became convinced that the liturgy could be improved. Thus in the early 2000s he issued a new edition of the *Missale Romanum*, which is the book containing the rites and prayers of the Mass in Latin. The changes made to this version were not large—certainly nowhere near as large as those that Paul VI had approved—just minor modifications. Many of them were implemented without much fuss in 2003.

What had to wait was the new translation of the *Missale Romanum*. The translation that had been prepared in the 1970s was put together somewhat hastily, and it used a trendy philosophy of translation known as "dynamic equivalence." In this method, a translator tries to take the thoughts expressed in one language (in this case Latin) and bring them into another language without carefully mirroring the vocabulary, word order, or style of the original. One way to think of dynamic equivalence is as a thought-for-thought translation rather than a word-for-word translation.

For example, in Matthew 16:18, Jesus tells Peter that he will build his Church and that "the gates of *hades*" will not prevail against it. This is a literal translation of what he says, but it could be confusing to some English-speakers, because in our language *hades* is often thought of as the same thing as hell—the place of the damned. In Greek, that's not the case. *Hades* is the place of the dead—both good and bad. To avoid potential confusion, one might translate what Jesus said more freely ("dynamically") and try to get at the same thought without following his exact words. Thus the translators of the Revised Standard Version of the Bible avoided the phrase "the gates of *hades*" and used "the powers of death" instead.

Although dynamic translations have some advantages, they

also have drawbacks. One potential one is the "dumbing down" or "flattening out" of language that is meant to be noble and elevating. That is one of the concerns about the translation of the *Missal* that was produced in the 1970s. It uses casual, everyday language that does not reflect the sense of the sacred in the original. All languages have a dignified, formal way of speaking that is used in worship. Formality underscores the sacredness of the experience and helps us recognize the glory and majesty of God.

John Paul II thus ordered that when the new edition of the *Missale Romanum* was translated into English, it be rendered more literally, with greater faithfulness to what is in the Latin. This meant that the new translation would have that more formal, elevated tone in which English speakers have traditionally addressed the Lord. It took several years to prepare the new translation, and John Paul II's successor, Pope Benedict XVI, continued to oversee the process and introduced a few changes of his own. In 2010 approval was given for the new English version of the *Missale Romanum*, or *Roman Missal*.

Thus several factors led to the current change in the liturgy, but the overarching one was the desire of the Church to shape the liturgy in a way that provides Catholics with the best possible experience of the Mass so their devotion to God will grow deeper, their experience of our Lord in the Eucharist will be more profound, and they will grow in the love of the Holy Spirit.

The transition will not be easy. In a speech to some of the advisors who helped with the translation, Pope Benedict XVI stated:

> Many will find it hard to adjust to unfamiliar texts after nearly forty years of continuous use of the previous translation. The change will need to be introduced with due sensitivity, and the opportunity for catechesis that it will present will need to be

firmly grasped. I pray that in this way any risk of confusion or bewilderment will be averted, and the change will serve instead as a springboard for a renewal and a deepening of eucharistic devotion all over the English-speaking world.[1]

This book was written to help achieve that goal. In the coming chapters we will go into detail about the history of the Mass, the Church's liturgical documents, and many other issues, but for now let us look at some of the basic facts regarding the current change in the liturgy.

How We Got Here

This change, as we have seen, is based on a new translation of the *Missale Romanum*, which is one of the Church's liturgical books. It contains the prayers the priest says during Mass, as well as the instructions (rubrics) for what he is to do at Mass. The previous English version of this work is called the *Sacramentary*, but it was decided that the new version would be referred to by a literal translation of its official name: the *Roman Missal*. It is called that because it is the book for celebrating Mass, or Missal, that is used by the Church in Rome and in countries around the world.

In 1969, Pope Paul VI released a version of the *Roman Missal* as part of the liturgical reform that followed the Second Vatican Council. In 1975 he released another, which contained slight modifications. In 2000, Pope John Paul II announced a third edition that would contain updated instructions for the celebration of Mass, prayers for Masses for recently canonized

---

[1] "Address to the *Vox Clara* Committee," April 28, 2010, printed in the U.S. Committee on Divine Worship *Newsletter*, May–June 2010, p. 18.

saints, new Masses for various needs and intentions, and additional prefaces for the Eucharistic Prayers. It is this edition that has been newly translated.

Because the *Roman Missal* contains only the prayers for the Mass, the changes will not affect the other sacraments. However, they may be translated in the future. For example, the Holy See revised the rite of matrimony in 1990, but that revised version has not yet been rendered in English, so it's due for a new translation.

The new translation will not have an immediate effect the hymns we sing at Mass, most of which were originally written in English and therefore are not translated at all. The change will have an impact on the music we hear at Mass, though, because there will be new musical settings for the parts of the Mass that are or can be sung, such as the *Gloria* ("Glory to God in the Highest") and the *Sanctus* ("Holy, Holy, Holy"). In these cases adaptations of familiar melodies may be available or new melodies may be composed.

The initial work on the new translation was done by the International Commission on English in the Liturgy (ICEL), a body that serves the bishops' conferences of the countries that use English in the liturgy. These countries include not only those in which English is the main language—such as England, the United States, Canada, Australia, and Ireland—but also those in which English has a prominent liturgical role—such as India, Pakistan, the Philippines, Kenya, and Bangladesh.

The commission produced initial translations of different parts of the *Roman Missal*. The versions they first issued were called "green books," for the color of their covers, and they were circulated to the different English-speaking bishops' conferences for comment. Based on the feedback they got, new versions of the translations were then produced. These were called "grey books," and they were again submitted to the bishops' conferences for review and approval. When the bishops voted on and approved these versions, they were forwarded to Rome for approval.

The department (or "dicastery") at Rome tasked with reviewing the translations was the Congregation for Divine Worship and the Discipline of the Sacraments (a prodigiously long name!). This congregation was assisted by an advisory group of English-speaking bishops known as the *Vox Clara* (Latin, "Clear Voice") Committee. When it was satisfied, the Congregation for Divine Worship then gave its approval—known as its *recognitio* ("recognition")—to the different parts of the *Roman Missal*. These final versions were known as "white books." By 2010 the process of translating and approving the whole *Missal* was complete.

How the New Translation Is Different

Earlier we noted that the translation produced in the 1970s was based on a translation philosophy called "dynamic equivalence." The main alternative to this philosophy is called "formal equivalence" or "literal translation." In this method, a translator tries to bring the thoughts expressed in one language into another language in a way that closely reflects the vocabulary, word order, and style of the original.

Formal equivalence strives to be a word-for-word translation to the extent it is possible.

For example, translators using formal equivalence would be inclined to render Jesus' phrase from Matthew 16:18 as "the gates of *hades*" or something close. Thus the translators of the *New American Bible* (which tends to use dynamic equivalence but not in this case) rendered this phrase "the gates of the netherworld."

Whether formal or dynamic equivalence is better depends on the purpose of the translation. In fact, virtually all translations use a mix of the two methods. Even very literal translations include some dynamic elements, because for a large text it is never possible to represent in one language exactly what is said in another. There will always be places where the words in the original language have a different sense than their equivalents in the translation's language, places where there is no expression equivalent to that in the original, or places where a literal translation would be misleading.

Translations exist on a spectrum between dynamic and formal equivalence. Those toward the dynamic end tend to be easier to understand since they don't try to capture as many elements of the original. This makes them better for people who do not have a firm grasp of English. Translations toward the formal end of the spectrum are a bit harder to understand but capture more of the nuances of the original text. This makes them better for serious study, where details are more important.

The new translation of the Mass seeks to lift the mind and heart to God by drawing more upon English's historic vocabulary for worship than on everyday forms of speech. The more word-for-word translation also allows the richness of the Latin rite of the liturgy to shine through into English. Experience has shown that trying to make the Mass sound contemporary makes liturgists want to continually tinker with the texts. This is partly because everyday language changes rapidly in comparison with the elevated language traditionally used to speak to God.

Specific Examples of Changes

"And with Your Spirit"

One well-known change between the previous and the new translation is the response the congregation makes when the priest says, "The Lord be with you." Previously the congregation responded, "And also with you." The new translation renders this "And with your spirit." That is what the Latin original literally says ("*et cum spiritu tuo*")—as do translations of the Mass in other languages. English has been the exception.

"Through My Fault . . ."

Another change is the restoration of the line *mea culpa, mea culpa, mea maxima culpa* ("through my fault, through my fault, through my most grievous fault"), which was drastically shortened in the previous translation of the Penitential Rite.

Previous Translation	*New Translation*
I confess to almighty God,	I confess to almighty God,
and to you, my brothers and sisters,	and to you, my brothers and sisters,
that *I have sinned*	that *I have greatly sinned*
through my own fault,	in my thoughts and in my words,
in my thoughts and in my words,	in what I have done,
in what I have done,	and in what I have failed to do,
and in what I have failed to do;	*through my fault, through my fault,*
and I ask blessed Mary, ever virgin,	*through my most grievous fault;*
all the angels and saints,	*therefore* I ask blessed Mary,
and you, my brothers and sisters,	ever-Virgin,
to pray for me to the Lord,	all the angels and saints,
our God.	and you, my brothers and sisters,
	to pray for me to the Lord
	our God.

The Nicene Creed

The Nicene Creed has also been changed to reflect more accurately what is in the Latin original. Among the changes are these:

- The Creed now uses the singular pronoun *I* ("I believe") instead of the plural pronoun *we* ("We believe"). This change highlights the personal nature of faith. The articles of the Creed are not things that the Church believes in only in a collective, corporate sense. They are things that each Catholic personally believes.

- The Father is now described as the Creator of "all things visible and invisible" rather than "all that is seen and unseen." Many things in the material world are unseen because no one is looking at them, but the new literal translation makes it clear that God also created things that are invisible, that cannot be seen because they do not have a visible form (e.g., angels).

- Christ is now referred to as God's "only begotten Son" instead of as his "only Son." This underscores the uniqueness of Christ's sonship. All Christians belong to God's family by adoption, but Christ has a unique, eternal form of sonship, which the Creed will now reflect.

- The Holy Spirit is now said to be "adored and glorified" rather than "worshipped and glorified." This clarifies the specific kind of worship owed to the Holy Spirit: the adoration proper to God rather than the mere veneration proper to the saints.

"For You and for Many"

There will be changes, mostly minor, to the parts of the Mass that the priest says, but one of the best-known changes occurs in the words of consecration for the precious blood. Previously the translation said that Christ's blood was shed "for all," which is theologically true. Christ did die for all mankind. Thus Scripture states that Christ "is expiation for our sins, and not for our sins only but for those of the whole world" (1 John 2:2, NAB).

But when Jesus instituted the Eucharist, he didn't express himself exactly that way. He said, "This is my blood of the covenant, which will be shed on behalf *of many* for the forgiveness of sins" (Matt. 26:28, NAB) and "This is my blood of the covenant, which will be shed *for many*" (Mark 14:24, NAB). By using the word *many* in the words of consecration, the new translation more accurately reflects the words that our Lord used when he instituted the sacrament.[2]

Previous Translation	*New Translation*
Take this, all of you, and drink from it: this is the *cup* of my blood, the blood of the new and *everlasting* covenant. *It* will be *shed* for you and *for all so that sins may be forgiven.* Do this in memory of me.	Take this, all of you, and drink from it: for this is the *chalice* of my blood, the blood of the new and *eternal* covenant; *which* will be *poured out* for you and *for many for the forgiveness of sins.* Do this in memory of me.

Many of these changes may seem small and technical, but they are important and make for a more theologically precise presentation of the faith. As we've seen, saying that Christ is God's "only Son" can be misleading since all Christians are children of God by adoption (Eph. 1:5, Rom. 8:14–21). Saying that Christ is the "only begotten Son of God" points out the unique sonship of Christ (John 1:18) while leaving room for the rest of us to be sons and daughters of God.

This is a good example of how the new translation will help people who may need an explanation in order to understand what is meant by saying that Christ is the "only begotten" Son —that is, that he is the only Son who is not adopted but "born of the Father before all ages." Clearing up things like this is the purpose of catechesis, the homily, and religious education

---

[2] For more information on this, see Chapter 8.

in general. The new translation allows each of these to play its role in helping people learn their faith more deeply. You may have been saying something in the Mass all your life without thinking about its meaning. Saying the same thing in a new way will prompt thought and questions and ultimately deeper knowledge. Once you have learned the meaning of new terms such as "only begotten," you will be in a position to appreciate the riches in the liturgy that you may not have noticed before.

2. An Overview of the Mass

The Mass is the most important form of Christian worship. All worship is meant to draw us closer to God, but the Mass is special, not only because we approach God in it but because he also approaches us. In the Mass, Jesus Christ comes to meet us through the Eucharist.

The Mass is an act of worship, and the form of worship that we give to God is also called adoration. The *Catechism of the Catholic Church* gives an excellent explanation:

> Adoration is the first act of the virtue of religion. To adore God is to acknowledge him as God, as the Creator and Savior, the Lord and Master of everything that exists, as infinite and merciful Love. "You shall worship the Lord your God, and him only shall you serve," says Jesus [Luke 4:8], citing Deuteronomy [6:13].
>
> To adore God is to acknowledge, in respect and absolute submission, the "nothingness of the creature" who would not exist but for God. To adore God is to praise and exalt him and to humble oneself, as Mary did in the *Magnificat*, confessing with gratitude that he has done great things and holy is his name [see also Luke 1:46–49]. The worship of the one God sets man free from turning in on himself, from the slavery of sin and the idolatry of the world.[1]

The official worship of the Church is called "liturgy." Originally, liturgy meant a "public work." "In Christian tradition

---

[1] CCC 2096–2097.

it means the participation of people of God in 'the work of God.'"[2] Whenever the seven sacraments are celebrated, a liturgy is being performed. Each involves the worship of God for the benefit of the people.

The two largest and most important parts of the Mass are the Liturgy of the Word (the part of the service in which God's word is read and preached) and the Liturgy of the Eucharist (in which the Eucharist is consecrated and Communion is distributed). They form the core of the Mass. There are also brief Introductory Rites before the Liturgy of the Word and brief Concluding Rites after the Liturgy of the Eucharist. Thus the Mass has a four-part structure:

    I. Introductory Rites
   II. The Liturgy of the Word
  III. The Liturgy of the Eucharist
  IV. Concluding Rites

Though the details of various parts of the Mass have changed over the centuries, its basic structure has been the same since the very dawn of Christian history. Around A.D. 155, St. Justin Martyr wrote about how Mass was celebrated in his day:

> All [Christians] who dwell in the city or country gather in the same place.
>
> The memoirs of the apostles and the writings of the prophets are read, as much as time permits.
>
> When the reader has finished, he who presides over those gathered admonishes and challenges them to imitate these beautiful things.
>
> Then we all rise together and offer prayers* for ourselves . . . and for all others, wherever they may be, so that we may

---

[2] CCC 1069.

be found righteous by our life and actions, and faithful to the commandments, so as to obtain eternal salvation.

When the prayers are concluded we exchange the kiss [of peace].

Then someone brings bread and a cup of water and wine mixed together to him who presides over the brethren.

He takes them and offers praise and glory to the Father of the universe, through the name of the Son and of the Holy Spirit and for a considerable time he gives thanks [Greek, *eucharistian*] that we have been judged worthy of these gifts.

When he has concluded the prayers and thanksgivings, all present give voice to an acclamation by saying, "Amen."

When he who presides has given thanks and the people have responded, those whom we call deacons give to those present the "eucharisted" bread, wine and water and take them to those who are absent.[3]

This same fundamental structure is preserved in the Mass of today: All gather; Scripture is read; preaching is done on the readings; prayers are offered; a sign of peace is exchanged among the faithful (in St. Justin Martyr's day this was a kiss, as in the New Testament, see Rom. 16:16; 1 Cor. 16:20; 1 Pet. 5:14); the elements to be consecrated are brought and the priest consecrates them in prayer; the faithful respond, "Amen"; and Communion is distributed. It is impressive that the fundamental structure of Christian worship has not changed in two millennia.

We will now look briefly at the individual parts of the Mass in more detail.

---

[3] CCC 1345, quoting St. Justin Martyr, *First Apology*, 65–67; the text before the asterisk (*) is from chapter 67.

I. Introductory Rites

The purpose of the Introductory Rites is to prepare for the celebration of the Liturgy of the Word and the Liturgy of the Eucharist. They express several things: that the parish is coming together for worship, that we need to be purified for worship by remembering our sins and asking for God's mercy, and that we wish to give glory to God and ask him to bless our worship.

A. ENTRANCE (Latin, *Introit*, "He enters"). Mass begins when the priest who will celebrate Mass enters the church and approaches the altar. He is often accompanied by others who will serve with him (such as a deacon, lector, and altar servers). In Masses with music, the choir or the congregation will usually sing at the entrance.

B. VENERATION OF THE ALTAR. As the priest arrives at the altar, he venerates it, kissing it as a sign of reverence for the place where Jesus Christ will become present in the Eucharist. At some Masses, the priest incenses the altar as a symbol of reverence and prayer.

C. GREETING. The priest and the people make the sign of the cross as the priest calls upon God with the words "In the name of the Father and of the Son and of the Holy Spirit," to which we respond, "Amen." This reminder of baptism consecrates our actions to God. Afterward the priest greets the people by wishing them God's grace or by saying, "The Lord be with you," to which the people respond, "And with your spirit."

D. ACT OF PENITENCE. The priest then exhorts the people to prepare to worship God by recalling their sins, repenting of them, and asking for God's mercy. During a moment of silence, the people think about their sins and then pray together using various prayers from the missal or missalette. One of the most common is the *Confiteor*, which begins with the words "I confess to almighty God, and to you, my brothers and sisters, that I have greatly sinned through my own fault." Its name is its first words—"I confess"—in Latin.

E. *KYRIE* (Greek, "O Lord"). The acknowledgment of our sins concludes by asking God for forgiveness. At this point the people pray to the Lord Jesus, "Lord, have mercy. Christ, have mercy. Lord, have mercy." Sometimes this is sung, and sometimes it is said in Greek: "*Kyrie, eleison. Christe, eleison. Kyrie, eleison.*" Greek was the language most often used for celebrating Mass in the Church's earliest centuries, before Latin became more common.

F. BLESSING AND SPRINKLING (Latin, *Asperges*, "You will sprinkle"). This rite takes the place of the Act of Penitence and the *Kyrie* at some Masses.

The priest asks God to bless some water, thus making holy water, then he sprinkles the congregation with it. This action recalls our baptism, through which we were cleansed from sin (Acts 2:38; 22:16), and various biblical passages, such as when the Psalmist prays, "Wash me thoroughly from my iniquity, and cleanse me from my sin!" (Ps. 51:2; see also Ezek. 36:25–27).

G. *GLORIA* (Latin, "glory"). After purifying our hearts by recalling our sins and asking God's mercy, it is appropriate that there be a moment for praise, and so in many Masses a prayer called the *Gloria* (its first word in Latin) is said. It begins "Glory to God in the highest, and peace to his people on earth."

H. COLLECT (from the Latin, *oratio ad collectam*, "prayer over the assembly"). The priest then brings the Introductory Rites to a close by saying to the people, "Let us pray." He then says the opening prayer or collect, which differs for different Masses and days of the year. Collects thank God, ask his blessing, and frequently introduce the themes that will be part of the day's Mass. Afterward, all respond, "Amen."

Following the Introductory Rites, the Liturgy of the Word begins.

II. Liturgy of the Word

A. SCRIPTURE READINGS. Since this part of the Mass is focused on hearing God's word, it begins with a series of Scripture readings. There are always at least two, but on Sundays and certain holy days there are three, including the Gospel reading. The first is drawn from the Old Testament (except during the Easter season). Afterward the lector says, "The word of the Lord," and all reply, "Thanks be to God."

After the first reading, one of the Old Testament psalms or another biblical prayer is said or sung in a responsorial style—that is, the people singing it alternate, one group responding to what has just been sung by the other. Typically, the cantor sings a part of the psalm and the people give the response. This alternating style in worship goes back to before the time of Christ, when it was used in the Jerusalem temple (for example, with Psalm 136, whose refrain is "His mercy endures forever").

The second reading at a Sunday Mass is drawn from the New Testament. It can come from any of the New Testament books except the Gospels. Afterward, the lector again says, "The word of the Lord," and all reply, "Thanks be to God."

Then comes the reading of the Gospel. Because the Gospels contain the actual story of the life of Christ, this reading is especially solemn. This is reflected in a number of ways. During most of the year, an *Alleluia* (Hebrew, *Hallelujah,* "Praise the Lord") is said or sung before the reading. The reading may be done only by a bishop, priest, or deacon; and during the reading all stand as a sign of respect for Christ. Afterward the reader says, "The Gospel of the Lord," and all respond, "Praise to you, Lord Jesus Christ."

B. HOMILY. Once the readings are completed, a homily may be given. A homily is preached to help the people understand the readings and their application to our lives. Homilies are always given on Sundays and certain other days and are recommended at ordinary weekday Masses as well. A bishop, priest, or deacon gives the homily.

C. PROFESSION OF FAITH (CREED). The purpose of reading from and preaching about Scripture is to help the faithful grow in the faith. After these two tasks are done, it is natural to express one's faith. This is done on Sundays and certain other days in a formal Profession of Faith, in which either the Nicene Creed or the Apostles' Creed is recited by all.

D. PRAYER OF THE FAITHFUL (UNIVERSAL PRAYER OR BIDDING PRAYERS). The faith is not only something to be believed; it is also something to be lived, such as by helping others—both fellow Christians and non-Christians. One way of doing this is to pray for them. That is why the Liturgy of the Word concludes with the Prayer of the Faithful, in which the whole assembly prays for various people and their needs.

III. Liturgy of the Eucharist

A. PREPARATION OF THE OFFERINGS. In the first part of the Liturgy of the Eucharist, the gifts of the faithful are prepared. The collection, if there is one, is taken up at this juncture as one of the people's gifts to God. Even more important, this is when the bread and wine are brought forward to be used by God in the Eucharist.

B. PRAYER OVER THE OFFERINGS. After the gifts have been received, the priest prays over them, asking God to bless them. In particular, he asks God to bless the bread and the wine that will be used in the Eucharist.

During this time the priest also pours a little water into the wine in the chalice. The water, representing humanity, is united to the wine, representing Christ's divinity, together symbolizing the Incarnation of Christ. The priest also quietly prays at this point. He asks that just as Christ became like us in his humanity, we might be made divine—in the sense that God lets us share certain of his attributes, such as righteousness and holiness (see 2 Pet. 1:4).

Afterward the priest washes his hands in water. This rite is known as the *Lavabo* (Latin, "I will wash"). Its meaning is brought out by the prayer he quietly says: "Wash me, O Lord, from my iniquity, and cleanse me from my sin."

The priest also asks the people to pray that God will receive the sacrifice with favor, to which all reply, "May the Lord accept the sacrifice at your hands, for the praise and glory of his name, for our good, and the good of all his holy Church." We say this prayer because although Jesus Christ's gift of himself to the Father is always acceptable to God, our own limitations and weaknesses may prevent our actions from being pleasing to God. Thus we ask God to look favorably on our worship in spite of our weakness and sin.

C. EUCHARISTIC PRAYER. The priest then begins the Eucharistic Prayer. This is the most solemn part of the Mass. There are several Eucharistic Prayers that the Church uses. All of them follow the same basic structure.

1. Thanksgiving. The Eucharistic Prayer begins with a thanksgiving offered to God. Indeed, it is thanksgiving that gives the Eucharist its name (Greek, *eucharistia*, "thanks"). It begins with a short dialogue between the priest and the people:

PRIEST: The Lord be with you.
PEOPLE: And with your spirit.
PRIEST: Lift up your hearts [i.e., in prayer].
PEOPLE: We lift them up to the Lord.
PRIEST: Let us give thanks to the Lord, our God.
PEOPLE: It is right and just.

After this dialogue, the priest gives thanks to God for his saving acts by saying the Preface of the Eucharistic Prayer, which varies from Mass to Mass.

2. Acclamation (more commonly called the *Sanctus*, after the first word of the prayer). Following the thanksgiving, all present sing or say the *Sanctus* (Latin, "holy"):

Holy, holy, holy, Lord God of hosts.
Heaven and earth are full of your glory.
   Hosanna in the highest!
Blessed is he who comes in the name of the Lord.
   Hosanna in the highest!

This joins the prayer of the congregation to the prayer of the angels in heaven, whom the Bible represents as singing of God's supreme holiness with the prayer "Holy, holy, holy" (Is. 6:3; Rev. 4:8).

Hosanna is a Hebrew term that originally meant "O, save [us]!" but came to be used as a shout of joy. The second part of this prayer recalls the words the people cried out at Jesus' triumphal entry into Jerusalem (Matt. 21:9; Mark 11:9; John 12:13). Jesus also linked these words with his Second Coming (Matt. 23:39; Luke 13:35). By praying them now, we praise Jesus upon his eucharistic entry into the Mass and pray for his Second Coming.

3. Epiclesis. Afterward, all kneel as a sign of reverence for Christ, and the priest calls upon God to send his Spirit upon the bread and wine so that they may become the body and blood of Jesus Christ. This part of the Mass is called the *Epiclesis*, from a Greek word meaning "calling down upon" or "inviting upon." Often a bell is rung to signal that the most important part of the Mass is beginning.

4. *Institution Narrative and Consecration.* Next the priest recalls the very first Mass, which was part of the Last Supper on the night that Jesus was betrayed. The priest repeats what Jesus himself said on that night: "This is my body," and "This is the chalice of my blood." As he says these words, God performs a miracle that transforms the substances of bread and wine into the body and blood of Jesus Christ, together with his soul and his divinity.

After Christ has become present in the hosts and in the chalice, the priest holds them up so that the people may see them and worship Jesus. Frequently a bell is rung.

5. *Memorial Acclamation.* Because of this great mystery, the priest or deacon then says, "Let us proclaim the mystery of faith." The people then repeat one of several prayers commemorating what Christ has done for us—for example, the prayer, "When we eat this bread and drink this cup, we proclaim your death, O Lord, until you come again" (see 1 Cor. 11:26).

6. Anamnesis (Greek, "remembrance"). Jesus told the apostles, his first priests, to celebrate the Eucharist "in remembrance of me" (Luke 22:19; 1 Cor. 11:24–25). The priest now recites a part of the Eucharistic Prayer that commemorates God's saving actions in history, especially the life, death, and resurrection of Christ.

7. *Offering.* Because the Eucharist is a sacrifice, it involves a gift, or offering, that is given to God: Jesus Christ, who through the Eucharist continually offers himself to the Father in heaven. We also offer ourselves to God in union with Jesus. The priest asks God to accept and bless our offering of ourselves together with Christ, fulfilling Paul's exhortation in Romans 12:1 that we Christians are to "present [our] bodies as a living sacrifice, holy and acceptable to God, which is [our] spiritual worship."

8. *Intercessions.* The priest then asks the Father to bless the whole Christian family—living and dead—to give us his mercy, and to bring us to the fullness of salvation in heaven.

9. *Final Doxology.* The Eucharistic Prayer comes to a close when the priest gives the final doxology and the people or choir respond, "Amen."

A doxology is a prayer that praises God's glory (Greek, *doxa*, "glory" + *logion*, "a speech"). In the final doxology, the priest summarizes all that has come before by giving glory to God through Christ, saying, "Through him, and with him, and in him, to you, O God, almighty Father, in the unity of the Holy Spirit, all glory and honor is yours, for ever and ever." The people respond by saying or singing, "Amen," and stand.

Amen is a Hebrew word used to signify agreement with a prayer and confidence that God will hear and respond to it. It is sometimes translated into English as "So be it" or "May it be so." This Amen is the most important part of the people's role in the Eucharistic Prayer, since they give their assent to what the priest has just prayed on their behalf. Because of its importance, this Amen, which is often sung, is also called "the Great Amen."

D. COMMUNION RITE. The congregation now prepares for and receives Jesus Christ in Holy Communion.

1. The Lord's Prayer (the Our Father). The Communion Rite begins with the praying of the Lord's Prayer, or Our Father, the model of all Christian prayer (Matt. 6:9–13). It asks for "our daily bread," the food that sustains our physical lives and, in a spiritual sense, for Christ himself, the "Bread from Heaven" (John 6:32, 41) that sustains our spiritual lives (John 6:51). The Lord's Prayer also petitions for forgiveness of our sins. We must have this forgiveness if we are to receive Jesus in Communion (1 Cor. 11:27–28).

After the conclusion of the Lord's Prayer, the priest briefly prays for God to deliver all of us from every evil. The people then say to God, "For the kingdom, the power, and the glory are yours, now and forever." These words were not originally part of the Lord's Prayer; they do not appear in the earliest Scripture manuscripts. There are, however, early Christian writings (such as the first-century document known as the *Didachē*) showing that such words were used in the liturgy in the early Church.

2. The Rite of Peace. The priest then prays that Christ will "look not on our sins but on the faith of your Church, and grant us the peace and unity of your kingdom." In many parishes the priest or deacon invites the congregation to exchange "a sign of peace" (for example, a handshake) with those around them as a symbol of their peace and unity with each other in Christ. The apostles regularly exhorted their congregations to be at peace and of one mind (1 Cor. 1:10; Phil. 1:27; 2:2), and

Jesus himself warned us to be reconciled with our brethren prior to coming before God (Matt. 5:23–24), making the Rite of Peace a fitting preparation for Communion.

3. The Fraction. Reflecting Jesus' actions at the Last Supper (Luke 22:19), the priest then breaks the consecrated host (this is why it is called the "Fraction"). He drops a small part of the host into the chalice, symbolizing the Resurrection of Christ (reuniting body and blood as a living whole). Because all of the living Jesus is present under the appearances of both bread and wine, the priest's action does not actually separate and reunite Jesus' body and blood; it does so symbolically.

4. Communion. The priest then offers a prayer and holds up the Eucharist to the faithful, proclaiming, "Behold the Lamb of God, behold him who takes away the sins of the world. Blessed are those who are called to the supper of the Lamb." Then, echoing the words of the Roman centurion in Matthew 8:8, all pray, "Lord, I am not worthy that you should enter under my roof, but only say the word and my soul shall be healed." In many dioceses, people kneel during this exchange as a sign of their reverence for Christ.

The priest then receives Communion and, often with the assistance of other ministers (such as the deacon), he begins to distribute Communion to the faithful.

Each communicant is shown the host before receiving it, as the words "The body of Christ" are intoned. The reply, "Amen," is a confession of faith in the Real Presence of Christ. When Communion is also being offered from the chalice, the words intoned are "The blood of Christ." The reply of faith in the Real Presence is again "Amen."

In many parishes a hymn is sung during the distribution of Communion.

5. Prayer after Communion. After the faithful have received Communion they return to their places to pray and give thanks to God for the gift of receiving his Son in such a miraculous and intimate manner. Afterward, the priest offers a concluding prayer.

IV. Concluding Rites

Following the Liturgy of the Eucharist are the Concluding Rites. As they are less important than what has come before, they tend to be brief.

A. ANNOUNCEMENTS. Announcements of parish news that need to be made—for example, of upcoming parish events—may be made at this time.

B. GREETING. The priest then greets the people with customary words, such as "The Lord be with you," to which everyone responds, "And with your spirit."

C. BLESSING. The priest then gives a blessing to the people. This may be done in a simple or a solemn manner. When it is done solemnly, the priest or deacon begins by instructing the people, "Bow your heads and pray for God's blessing," after which a more elaborate blessing is said over them. Whether the blessing is done simply or solemnly, however, the priest always concludes by making the sign of the cross over the people, saying, "May almighty God bless you, the Father, the Son, and the Holy Spirit." All respond, "Amen."

D. DISMISSAL. After the blessing, the people are dismissed to go out and do good works in their lives, based on the grace and empowerment they have received at Mass. The priest or deacon dismisses them with a formula such as "Go forth, the Mass is ended," to which all respond, "Thanks be to God."

E. VENERATION OF THE ALTAR. Before departing, the priest again shows his reverence to God by honoring the place where Christ comes to us in the Eucharist by kissing the altar and making the customary act of veneration with the other ministers. Often the choir or congregation sings a concluding hymn while this is happening.

F. *EXEUNT* (Latin, "they exit"). Finally, the worship service concludes when the priest and other ministers exit.

3. Ministers at Mass

A Diversity of Roles

In the liturgy, not all people fulfill the same roles. There are a variety of ministers who celebrate and serve at Mass, and all have their own proper functions. In this chapter, we will look at some of the most important ones.

The *General Instruction of the Roman Missal* states:

> The eucharistic celebration is an action of Christ and the Church, namely, the holy people united and ordered under the bishop. It therefore pertains to the whole body of the Church, manifests it, and has its effect upon it. It also affects the individual members of the Church in different ways, according to their different orders, offices, and actual participation. In this way, the Christian people, "a chosen race, a royal priesthood, a holy nation, God's own people," expresses its cohesion and its hierarchical ordering. All, therefore, whether they are ordained ministers or lay Christian faithful, in fulfilling their office or their duty should carry out solely but completely that which pertains to them.[1]

Despite the many roles people may play at Mass, it is not necessary that a large number of ministers participate:

> If only one minister is present at a Mass with a congregation, that minister may exercise several different duties.[2]

---

[1] GIRM 91.
[2] GIRM 110.

Nevertheless, there is a minimum number of ministers that is preferable:

> If a deacon is present at any celebration of Mass, he should exercise his office. Furthermore, it is desirable that, as a rule, an acolyte, a lector, and a cantor should be there to assist the priest celebrant. In fact, the rite to be described below foresees a greater number of ministers.[3]

About the Term Minister

In recent years there has been growing concern over the use of the term *minister* in the Church. In the fullest sense, the term refers to the ordained—to bishops, priests, and deacons. The concern is that its overuse can lead to an erosion of people's understanding of the nature of ordained ministry.[4] However, the *Code of Canon Law* and the Church's liturgical documents apply the term *minister* in a restricted way to members of the laity who hold certain offices and fulfill certain duties in the liturgy. *Ecclesia de Mysterio* states:

> The non-ordained faithful may be generically designated "extraordinary ministers" when deputed by competent authority to discharge, solely by way of supply, those offices mentioned in canon 230 §3 and in canons 943 and 1112. Naturally, the concrete term [*minister*] may be applied to those to whom functions are canonically entrusted, e.g., catechists, acolytes, lectors, etc.[5]

Canon 230 §3 refers to those who, because of a lack of ministers such as lectors and acolytes, have been deputed to ex-

---

[3] GIRM 116.
[4] EM, Practical Provisions 1 §2.
[5] EM, Practical Provisions 1 §3.

ercise the ministry of the word regularly, preside over liturgical prayers, confer baptism, and distribute Holy Communion. Canon 943 refers to laity who, in accordance with the requirements of the law, have been deputed to expose and repose the Holy Eucharist regularly. Canon 1112 refers to laity who have been delegated by proper authority to assist at weddings where priests and deacons are lacking.

In all these things, the term *extraordinary minister* may be applied to those who have been deputed to supply these functions regularly. The document states:

> Temporary deputation for liturgical purposes . . . does not confer any special or permanent title on the non-ordained faithful.[6]

It also adds:

> It is unlawful for the non-ordained faithful to assume titles such as "pastor," "chaplain," "coordinator," "moderator" or other such similar titles which can confuse their role and that of the pastor, who is always a bishop or priest.[7]

With that said, let us look at some of the more important ministerial roles at Mass.

The Role of the Ordained

The sacrament of the Holy Eucharist depends in a special way on the sacrament of holy orders. In order for Mass to be celebrated at all, a bishop or a priest is needed, since only they can consecrate the elements. Deacons also play an important role in the liturgy, although their presence is not necessary.

---

[6] Ibid.
[7] Ibid.

The Role of Bishops

Because bishops are central to the life of the Church, liturgical celebrations are specially adapted when they are present. These adaptations are significant enough that there is a special Church document dealing with liturgical celebrations at which bishops are present. It is known as the *Ceremonial of Bishops*, and it was published by the Congregation for Divine Worship after Pope John Paul II approved it in 1984. Although we will have occasion to quote it because it sheds light on the celebration of Mass in general, we will not focus on the parts that deal particularly with bishops. Bishops do not directly participate in most Masses that people attend, and it is the ordinary parish Mass that is our focus.

Even when the bishop is not present, the legitimacy of the Mass depends on it being celebrated under his authority:

> Every legitimate celebration of the Eucharist is directed by the bishop, either in person or through priests who are his helpers.[8]

Celebrations of the Eucharist by priests who do not have proper authorization are therefore illegitimate.

The Role of Priests

Priests are the principal ministers at Mass. It cannot be celebrated without them, since only they are capable of consecrating the Eucharist. The common or universal priesthood shared by all the Christian faithful is not capable of consecrating the Eucharist.

One of the most important duties of a priest at Mass is the saying of the Presidential Prayers:

---

[8] GIRM 92.

Among the parts assigned to the priest, the foremost is the Eucharistic Prayer, which is the high point of the entire celebration. Next are the orations: that is to say, the collect, the prayer over the offerings, and the prayer after Communion. These prayers are addressed to God in the name of the entire holy people and all present, by the priest who presides over the assembly in the person of Christ. It is with good reason, therefore, that they are called the Presidential Prayers.[9]

It is not appropriate for others to share in these prayers, except as allowed by the liturgical texts that have been approved by the Holy See.

The *Code of Canon Law* states:

In the eucharistic celebration deacons and lay persons are not permitted to offer prayers, especially the Eucharistic Prayer, or to perform actions which are proper to the celebrating priest [CIC 907].

This point was forcefully reiterated in *Ecclesia de Mysterio*:

To promote the proper identity (of various roles) in this area, those abuses which are contrary to the provisions of Canon 907 are to be eradicated. In eucharistic celebrations deacons and non-ordained members of the faithful may not pronounce prayers—e.g. especially the Eucharistic Prayer, with its concluding doxology—or any other parts of the liturgy reserved to the celebrant priest. Neither may deacons or non-ordained members of the faithful use gestures or actions which are proper to the same priest celebrant. It is a grave abuse for any member of the non-ordained faithful to "quasi-preside" at the Mass while leaving only that minimal participation to the priest which is necessary to secure validity.[10]

---

[9] GIRM 30.
[10] EM, Practical Provisions 6 § 1.

The above refers to the participation of non-priests in the duties reserved to priests. It is possible, however, for multiple priests to take part in the celebration of the Eucharist. There are special adaptations for priests saying Mass together, a practice known as concelebration. However, since most Masses that people attend are not concelebrated, we will not focus on these adaptations.

According to the *General Instruction*:

> The nature of the "presidential" texts demands that they be spoken in a loud and clear voice and that everyone listen with attention. Thus, while the priest is speaking these texts, there should be no other prayers or singing, and the organ or other musical instruments should be silent.
>
> The priest, in fact, as the one who presides, prays in the name of the Church and of the assembled community; but at times he prays only in his own name, asking that he may exercise his ministry with greater attention and devotion. Prayers of this kind— which occur before the reading of the Gospel, at the Preparation of the Gifts, and also before and after the Communion of the priest—are said quietly.[11]

The Role of Deacons

In addition to bishops and priests, deacons also share in the sacrament of holy orders, and they correspondingly have a unique place in the liturgy:

> After the priest, the deacon, in virtue of the sacred ordination he has received, holds first place among those who minister in the eucharistic celebration. For the sacred order of the diaconate has been held in high honor in the Church even from the time of the apostles. At Mass the deacon has his own part in proclaim-

----

[11] GIRM 32-33.

ing the Gospel, in preaching God's word from time to time, in announcing the intentions of the Prayer of the Faithful, in ministering to the priest, in preparing the altar and serving the celebration of the sacrifice, in distributing the Eucharist to the faithful, especially under the species of wine, and sometimes in giving directions regarding the people's gestures and posture.[12]

In general, the deacon:

a. Assists the priest and remains at his side.

b. Ministers at the altar, with the chalice as well as the book.

c. Proclaims the Gospel and, at the direction of the priest celebrant, may preach the homily.

d. Guides the faithful by appropriate introductions and explanations, and announces the intentions of the Prayer of the Faithful.

e. Assists the priest celebrant in distributing Communion, and purifies and arranges the sacred vessels.

f. As needed, fulfills the duties of other ministers himself if none of them is present.[13]

The *Ceremonial of Bishops* also stresses the importance of deacons in the eucharistic celebration:

Deacons hold the highest place among ministers [below the rank of priest] and from the Church's earliest age the diaconate has been held in great honor. As men of good repute and full of wisdom, they should act in such a way that, with the help of God, all may know them to be true disciples of One who came not to be served but to serve, and who was among his disciples as one who serves.

Strengthened by the gifts of the Holy Spirit, the deacons assist the bishop and his presbyters in the ministry of the word, the altar, and of charity. As ministers of the altar they proclaim

---

[12] GIRM 94.
[13] GIRM 171.

the Gospel reading, help at the celebration of the sacrifice, and serve as eucharistic ministers.

Deacons should therefore look on the bishop as a father and assist him as they would the Lord Jesus Christ himself, who is the eternal high priest, present in the midst of his people.[14]

Deacons are permitted to do many things in the liturgy. They will be discussed further in the chapters on the Liturgy of the Word and the Liturgy of the Eucharist.

The Roles Open to Lay Men and Women

There are a number of roles non-ordained people can play in the liturgy. In fact, the non-ordained may perform any function below those reserved to the deacon.

The Holy See has been concerned by a trend in recent years to multiply the number of lay ministers at Mass beyond the number actually needed. In some cases it seemed that this was a deliberate effort to minimize the role of ordained ministers and to blur the line between clergy and laity, which was one of the concerns dealt with in *Ecclesiae de Mysterio*. *Redemptionis Sacramentum* also dealt with the matter, stating:

> To be avoided is the danger of obscuring the complementary relationship between the action of clerics and that of lay persons, in such a way that the ministry of lay persons undergoes what might be called a certain "clericalization," while the sacred ministers inappropriately assume those things that are proper to the life and activity of the lay faithful.[15]

In other cases the push to create large numbers of lay ministers stems from a misunderstanding of Vatican II's call for

[14] CB 23–24.
[15] RS 45.

the "active participation" of the laity in the liturgy.[16] In this view, to ensure the laity's active participation, as many people as possible should be given tasks in the liturgy. To correct this misunderstanding, the Holy See has repeatedly explained what the Council meant by "active participation." Rather than meaning having a specific task, it meant consciously following the Mass, saying the responses, singing the hymns, etc., rather than tuning the Mass out and engaging in a private devotion, for example. Thus *Redemptionis Sacramentum* explains:

> For promoting and elucidating active participation, the recent renewal of the liturgical books according to the mind of the Council fostered acclamations of the people, responses, psalmody, antiphons, and canticles, as well as actions or movements and gestures, and called for sacred silence to be maintained at the proper times, while providing rubrics for the parts of the faithful as well. In addition, ample flexibility is given for appropriate creativity aimed at allowing each celebration to be adapted to the needs of the participants, to their comprehension, their interior preparation and their gifts, according to the established liturgical norms. . . .
>
> Nevertheless, from the fact that the liturgical celebration obviously entails activity, it does not follow that everyone must necessarily have something concrete to do beyond the actions and gestures, as if a certain specific liturgical ministry must necessarily be given to the individuals to be carried out by them. Instead, catechetical instruction should strive diligently to correct those widespread superficial notions and practices often seen in recent years in this regard.[17]

When laity are used to supply special functions in the liturgy and in parish life, a careful selection and training process must be used:

---

[16] SC 14.
[17] RS 39–40.

Should it become necessary to provide for "supplementary" assistance [by laity as extraordinary ministers of various kinds], the competent authority is bound to select lay faithful of sound doctrine and exemplary moral life. Catholics who do not live worthy lives or who do not enjoy good reputations or whose family situations do not conform to the teaching of the Church may not be admitted to the exercise of such functions. In addition, those chosen should possess that level of formation necessary for the discharge of the responsibilities entrusted to them. . . . Great care must be exercised so that these courses conform absolutely to the teaching of the ecclesiastical magisterium and they must be imbued with a true spirituality.[18]

Lector and acolyte are two historically important offices. They were formerly ranked as "minor orders" and were typically reserved for those in preparation for the reception of sacred orders.[19]

That changed in 1972, when Pope Paul VI issued a *motu proprio* titled *Ministeria Quaedam* on first tonsure, minor orders, and the subdiaconate.[20] This document simplified the ministries below that of deacon and, among other things, mandated the following:

I. First tonsure is no longer conferred; entrance into the clerical state is joined to the diaconate.

II. What up to now were called minor orders are henceforth to be called ministries.

III. Ministries may be assigned to lay Christians; hence they are no longer to be considered as reserved to candidates for the sacrament of orders.

IV. Two ministries, adapted to present-day needs, are to be preserved in the whole Latin church, namely, those of reader

---

[18] EM, Practical Provisions 13.
[19] DOL 2922.
[20] DOL 2922–38.

[i.e., lector] and acolyte. The functions heretofore assigned to the subdeacon are entrusted to the reader and the acolyte; consequently, the major order of subdiaconate no longer exists in the Latin church. There is, however, no reason why the acolyte cannot be called a subdeacon in some places, at the discretion of the conference of bishops.

V. In accordance with the ancient tradition of the Church, institution to the ministries of reader and acolyte is reserved to men.[21]

The continuing nature of the roles of lector and acolyte are also stressed in the *Ceremonial of Bishops*:

The ministries of reader and acolyte are to be preserved in the Latin Church. These ministries may be assigned to the lay Christians and are no longer to be considered as reserved to candidates for the sacrament of orders.

Unless they have already done so, candidates for ordination as deacons and presbyters are to receive these ministries and are to exercise them for a suitable time in order to be better disposed for the future service of the word and of the altar.[22]

The requirement that only men serve as formally instituted lectors and acolytes is preserved in the current (1983) *Code of Canon Law*:

§1. Lay men [Latin, *viri laici*] who possess the age and qualifications established by decree of the conference of bishops can be admitted on a stable basis through the prescribed liturgical rite to the ministries of lector and acolyte [CIC 230 §1].[23]

---

[21] DOL 2926–29, 2932.

[22] CB 790.

[23] It is possible that this canon will be changed. At the time of this writing, the Holy See is considering a request made by the 2008 Synod of Bishops on the Word of God. One of the propositions authored by the synod fathers stated: "It is hoped that the ministry of lector be opened also to women, so that in the Christian community their role in the proclamation

In the United States, the following complementary norm (dated July 10, 2000) specifies the requirements for these roles:

> The National Conference of Catholic Bishops, in accord with the prescriptions of canon 230 §1, hereby decrees that a layman who is to be installed in the ministries of lector or acolyte on a stable basis must have completed his twenty-first (21) year of age [that is, he must be 21; the first year of legal age begins at birth]. The candidate must also possess the skills necessary for an effective proclamation of the Word or service at the altar, be a fully initiated member of the Catholic Church, be free of any canonical penalty, and live a life which befits the ministry to be undertaken.[24]

This does not mean that only formally instituted lectors and acolytes may fulfill these functions:

> The liturgical duties that are not proper to the priest or the deacon and are listed above . . . may also be entrusted by a liturgical blessing or a temporary deputation to suitable lay persons chosen by the pastor or rector of the church. All should observe the norms established by the bishop for his diocese regarding the office of those who serve the priest at the altar.[25]

Women in the Liturgy

The requirement that only men may serve as instituted lectors and acolytes does not mean that women cannot fulfill these functions by temporary deputation. The *Code* goes on to state:

---

of the Word of God is recognized" (Proposition 17). Further information on this may be available upon the release of Pope Benedict XVI's expected post-synodal apostolic exhortation, which will constitute his response to the propositions submitted to him by the synod fathers.

[24] Posted among the complementary norms on the U.S. bishops' Web site at *www.usccb.org/norms*.

[25] GIRM 107.

§2. Lay persons [Latin, *laici*[26]] can fulfill the function of lector in liturgical actions by temporary designation. All lay persons can also perform the functions of commentator or cantor, or other functions, according to the norm of law [CIC 230 §2].

In exceptional circumstances, the laity can play still further roles in the liturgy. The *Code* states:

When the need of the church warrants it and ministers are lacking, lay persons, even if they are not lectors or acolytes, can also supply certain of their duties, namely, to exercise the ministry of the Word, to preside over liturgical prayers, to confer baptism, and to distribute Holy Communion, according to the prescripts of the law [CIC 230 §3].

In 1971, the Sacred Congregation for Divine Worship issued the following directive concerning the role of women in the liturgy:

According to the norms established for these matters . . . women are allowed to:

a. Proclaim the readings, except the Gospel. . . . The conferences of bishops are to give specific directions on the place best suited for women to read the word of God in the liturgical assembly.

b. Announce the intentions in the general intercessions.

c. Lead the liturgical assembly in singing and play the organ or other instruments.

d. Read the commentary assisting the people toward a better understanding of the rite.

---

[26] Section 1 of the Canon, quoted above, referred to *viri laici*, which literally means "lay men" (*viri* is Latin for "men"). This section of the canon drops *viri*, leaving *laici* ("laity," "lay persons"). It thus broadens the scope of eligible candidates to include women.

e. Attend to other functions, customarily filled by women in other settings, as a service to the congregation, for example, ushering, organizing processions, taking up the collection.[27]

Prior to the new edition of the *Roman Missal* in 2000, a document known as the American *Appendix to the General Instruction* dealt with the adaptations of the liturgy approved for use in the United States. Though this document no longer has legal force, it provides a helpful summary of the actions the U.S. bishops had taken in previous years regarding the roles of women in the liturgy:

The Conference of Bishops has given permission for women to serve as readers in accord with no. 66 of the *General Instruction* (November 1969).

In February 1971, the Bishops' Committee on the Liturgy prepared a commentary on the liturgical ministry of women:

a. With the exception of service at the altar itself, women may be admitted to the exercise of other liturgical ministries. In particular the designation of women to serve in such ministries as reader, cantor, leader of singing, commentator, director of liturgical participation, etc., is left to the judgment of the pastor or the priest who presides over the celebration, in the light of the culture and mentality of the congregation.

b. Worthiness of life and character and other qualifications are required in women who exercise liturgical ministries in the same way as for men who exercise the same ministries.

c. Women who read one or other biblical readings during the Liturgy of the Word (other than the Gospel, which is reserved to a deacon or priest) should do so from the lectern or ambo where the other readings are proclaimed: the reservation of a single place for all the biblical readings is more significant

---

[27] *Notitiae* 7 (1971) 10–26, section 7; DOL 525.

than the person of the reader, whether ordained or lay, whether woman or man.

d. Other ministries performed by women, such as leading the singing or otherwise directing the congregation, should be done either within or outside the sanctuary area, depending on the circumstances or convenience.[28]

Foot Washing on Holy Thursday

Today virtually the only role women technically cannot play in the liturgy, even on the basis of temporary deputation, is found in the symbolic washing of feet on Holy Thursday, which reenacts Christ's washing of the apostles' feet (John 13:3-20). By Christ's intention, the apostolic college was composed of men, so this role is limited to men in the rubrics for the Mass of Holy Thursday, which state:

> Depending on pastoral circumstances, the washing of feet follows the homily. The men [*viri*] who have been chosen are led by the ministers to chairs prepared in a suitable place. Then the priest (removing his chasuble if necessary) goes to each man. With the help of the ministers, he pours water over each one's feet and dries them.[29]

The Latin word *viri* indicates males only. When this word appears in Church documents, it indicates that males are required for whatever function the text refers to. If a text intends either a male *or* a female, it uses a different Latin word, such as *homo*, which is not gender specific.

Paschalis Solemnitatis, the 1988 document that governs the celebration of Holy Week, also indicates that the role is reserved to men:

---

[28] AGI 66.

[29] This is from the previous translation. The current translation was not available at the time of this writing.

The washing of the feet of chosen men [*viri*] which, according to tradition, is performed on this day, represents the service and charity of Christ, who came "not to be served, but to serve" [Matt. 20:28]. This tradition should be maintained, and its proper significance explained.[30]

Although the Church's official texts use language that indicates only men can have their feet washed on Holy Thursday, the situation today is more complex. In 2004, the new archbishop of Boston, Seán O'Malley, was criticized for varying from the practice of his predecessor, Cardinal Bernard Law, and washing only the feet of men. He explained that this was what the law required but said that he would query the Holy See about the matter. In 2005 the *Boston Globe* reported,

O'Malley promised to consult with Rome, and yesterday his spokeswoman said the Congregation for Divine Worship, which oversees liturgical practices, had suggested the archbishop make whatever decision he thought was best for Boston.

"The Congregation [for Divine Worship] affirmed the liturgical requirement that only the feet of men be washed at the Holy Thursday ritual." However, the Congregation did "provide for the archbishop to make a pastoral decision."[31]

Cardinal O'Malley then included women in the foot-washing rite. This sequence of events created a situation that was significantly muddier than existed before. If the archbishop of Boston was allowed to make pastoral exceptions to the rule, it would be difficult to argue that other bishops could not do the same in their dioceses. This had the effect of creating a doubt as to what the law requires. According to the *Code of Canon*

---

[30] PS 51.

[31] Michael Paulson, "O'Malley to Wash Women's Feet in Rite," *Boston Globe*, March 19, 2005, *www.boston.com*.

Law, "Laws, even invalidating and incapacitating ones, do not oblige when there is a doubt of law."[32]

Until such time as the Holy See clarifies the matter, it appears that the law provides that only men are to have their feet washed in the ceremony but that the local bishop can choose to include women in his diocese if he deems it the best decision pastorally.

It also should be noted that the washing of feet is not mandatory but optional, depending on pastoral circumstances.

Lectors

The role of lector, referred to in some translations as "reader," is an ancient one in the Church. The public reading of Scripture has been part of Christian worship since apostolic times (see also Col. 4:16; 1 Thess. 5:27; 1 Tim. 4:13). The *Ceremonial of Bishops* remarks:

> The office of reader was historically the first of the lesser ministries to emerge. This office exists in all churches and has never disappeared. Readers receive institution for an office proper to them: to proclaim the word of God in liturgical assembly. Hence at Mass and in other rites of the liturgy readers proclaim the readings other than the Gospel reading. When there is no cantor of the psalm present, the leader also leads the assembly in the responsorial psalm; when no deacon is present, the reader announces the intentions of the general intercessions.
>
> Whenever necessary, the reader should see to the preparation of any members of the faithful who may be appointed to proclaim the readings from the Sacred Scripture in liturgical celebrations. But in celebrations presided over by the bishop, it is fitting that the readers formally instituted proclaim the readings

---

[32] CIC 14.

and, if several readers are present, they should divide the readings accordingly.[33]

Though lacking the historical introduction and the adaptation for Masses with bishops, the *General Instruction* describes the basic function of the lector in this way:

The lector is instituted to proclaim the readings from Sacred Scripture, with the exception of the Gospel. He may also announce the intentions for the Prayer of the Faithful and, in the absence of a psalmist, proclaim the psalm between the readings.

In the eucharistic celebration, the lector has his own proper office . . . which he must exercise personally.[34]

The *Ceremonial of Bishops* also mentions another function of lectors:

In addition, the reader is entrusted with the special office of instructing children and adults in the faith and of preparing them to receive the sacraments worthily.[35]

Lectors are expected to take their duties seriously:

Conscious of the dignity of God's word and the importance of their office, readers should be eager to learn how best to speak and proclaim, in order that those who listen may clearly hear and understand the word of God.

In proclaiming the word of God to others, readers should themselves receive it with docility and meditate on it with devotion so that they may bear witness to the word in their daily lives.[36]

---

[33] CB 31.
[34] GIRM 99.
[35] CB 794.
[36] CB 32.

Because of their special role at Mass, lectors have a place in the Entrance procession at the beginning of the liturgy:

> In coming to the altar, when no deacon is present, the lector, wearing approved attire, may carry the Book of the Gospels, which is to be slightly elevated. In that case, the lector walks in front of the priest but otherwise along with the other ministers.
>
> Upon reaching the altar, the lector makes a profound bow with the others. If he is carrying the Book of the Gospels, he approaches the altar and places the Book of the Gospels upon it. Then the lector takes his own place in the sanctuary with the other ministers.[37]

When the time comes to give the Scripture readings, the lector goes to the appointed place:

> The lector reads from the ambo the readings that precede the Gospel. If there is no psalmist, the lector may also proclaim the responsorial psalm after the first reading.[38]

The lector may also play a special role during the Prayer of the Faithful:

> When no deacon is present, the lector, after the introduction by the priest, may announce from the ambo the intentions of the Prayer of the Faithful.[39]

The lector may play additional roles depending on whether music is used at the Mass:

> If there is no singing at the Entrance or at Communion and the antiphons in the missal are not recited by the faithful, the lector may read them at the appropriate time.[40]

---

[37] GIRM 194–95.

[38] GIRM 150.

[39] GIRM 197.

[40] GIRM 198.

Cantors

The responsorial psalm comes between the first and second
readings at Sunday Mass. It may be sung or chanted by a cantor (singer), who in this case functions as psalmist or "cantor
of the Psalm":[41]

> The psalmist's role is to sing the psalm or other biblical can-
> ticle that comes between the readings. To fulfill this function
> correctly, it is necessary that the psalmist have the ability for
> singing and a facility in correct pronunciation and diction.[42]

The presence of a properly trained cantor is especially desired at Masses at which a bishop presides:

> The chants between the readings are very important liturgically
> and pastorally. It is therefore desirable in celebrations presided
> over by the bishop, especially in the cathedral church, that there
> be a psalmist or cantor who has the necessary musical ability and
> devotion to the liturgy. The cantor of the psalm is responsible
> for singing, either responsorially or directly, the chants between
> the readings—the psalm or other biblical canticle, the gradual
> and *Alleluia*, or other chant—in such a way as to reflect on the
> meaning of the texts.[43]

Commentators

In many Masses, the celebrating priest will introduce or explain the readings with brief comments. It is permissible, however, for another person—known as a commentator—to do
this also:

---

[41] See GIRM 61.
[42] GIRM 67.
[43] CB 33.

The commentator, who provides the faithful, when appropriate, with brief explanations and commentaries with the purpose of introducing them to the celebration and preparing them to understand it better. The commentator's remarks must be meticulously prepared and clear though brief. In performing this function the commentator stands in an appropriate place facing the faithful, but not at the ambo.[44]

Although it is not a liturgical abuse for a person other than the priest to introduce the Scripture readings, it is a liturgical abuse for a commentator to give a homily (see Chapter 5) or to use a commentator but omit the homily on days when a homily is mandated, such as on Sundays.

Acolytes

Like the office of lector, the role of acolyte is ancient.

The acolyte is instituted to serve at the altar and to assist the priest and deacon. In particular, it is his responsibility to prepare the altar and the sacred vessels and, if it is necessary, as an extraordinary minister, to distribute the Eucharist to the faithful.

In the ministry of the altar, the acolyte has his own functions . . . which he must perform personally.[45]

The *Ceremonial of Bishops* also adds two other functions for acolytes—providing necessary instruction for certain other ministers in the liturgy and, in extraordinary cases, exposing the Blessed Sacrament:

When necessary, acolytes should instruct those who serve as ministers in liturgical rites by carrying the book, the cross, candles, or the censer by performing other similar duties. But in

---

[44] GIRM 105b.
[45] GIRM 98.

celebrations presided over by the bishop it is fitting that all such ministerial functions be carried out by formally instituted acolytes, and if a number are present, they should divide up the ministry accordingly.[46]

In extraordinary circumstances an acolyte may be entrusted with publicly exposing the Blessed Sacrament for adoration by the faithful and afterward replacing it, but not blessing the people with the Blessed Sacrament.[47]

An acolyte has a distinct role in the liturgy and should not have this role supplanted by other ministers:

In the ministry of the altar acolytes have their own proper functions and should exercise these even though ministers of a higher rank may be present.[48]

As one of the ministers at Mass, the acolyte has a place in the Entrance procession at the beginning of the liturgy:

In the procession to the altar, the acolyte may carry the cross, walking between two ministers with lighted candles. Upon reaching the altar, the acolyte places the cross upright near the altar so that it may serve as the altar cross; otherwise, he puts it in a worthy place. Then he takes his place in the sanctuary.[49]

During the liturgy the acolyte assists the priest and deacon:

Through the entire celebration, the acolyte is to approach the priest or the deacon, whenever necessary, in order to present the book to them and to assist them in any other way required. Thus it is appropriate, insofar as possible, that the acolyte occupy a place from which he can conveniently carry out his ministry either at the chair or at the altar.[50]

---

[46] CB 28.
[47] CB 808.
[48] CB 27.
[49] GIRM 188.
[50] GIRM 189.

The acolyte also assists in preparing the altar at the beginning of the Liturgy of the Eucharist:

> If no deacon is present, after the Prayer of the Faithful is concluded and while the priest remains at the chair, the acolyte places the corporal, the purificator, the chalice, the pall, and the Missal on the altar. Then, if necessary, the acolyte assists the priest in receiving the gifts of the people and, if appropriate, brings the bread and wine to the altar and hands them to the priest. If incense is used, the acolyte presents the thurible to the priest and assists him while he incenses the gifts, the cross, and the altar. Then the acolyte incenses the priest and the people.[51]

Acolytes may also serve as extraordinary ministers of Holy Communion:

> A duly instituted acolyte, as an extraordinary minister, may, if necessary, assist the priest in giving Communion to the people. If Communion is given under both kinds, when no deacon is present, the acolyte administers the chalice to the communicants or holds the chalice if Communion is given by intinction.[52]

The acolyte may also play a role in purifying the vessels after Communion (see the section on the purification of the vessels in Chapter 8 for more information):

> Likewise, when the distribution of Communion is completed, a duly instituted acolyte helps the priest or deacon to purify and arrange the sacred vessels. When no deacon is present, a duly instituted acolyte carries the sacred vessels to the credence table and there purifies, wipes, and arranges them in the usual way.[53]

---

[51] GIRM 190.
[52] GIRM 191.
[53] GIRM 192.

Extraordinary Ministers of Holy Communion

The ordinary ministers of Communion are priests and deacons. Instituted acolytes are *de iure* (by law) extraordinary ministers of the Eucharist. Other lay persons are authorized to act as extraordinary ministers of Holy Communion by the Holy See's 1973 instruction *Immensae Caritatis*:

> I. Local Ordinaries [normally the bishop] possess the faculty enabling them to permit fit persons, each chosen by name as [an extraordinary[54]] minister, in a given instance or for a set period or even permanently, to give Communion to themselves and others of the faithful and to carry it to the sick residing at home:
> a. Whenever no priest, deacon, or acolyte is available.
> b. Whenever the same ministers are impeded from administering Communion because of another pastoral ministry, ill health, or old age.
> c. Whenever the number of faithful wishing to receive Communion is so great that the celebration of Mass or the giving of Communion outside Mass would take too long.
>
> II. The same local Ordinaries possess the faculty of granting individual priests in the course of their ministry the power to appoint, for a given occasion, a fit person to distribute Communion in cases of genuine necessity. . . .

---

[54] The English language collection *Documents on the Liturgy* (DOL) misleadingly translates the phrase "extraordinary ministers of Holy Communion" and its variants. In an attempt to deprive the position of its extraordinary character, the translators have systematically mistranslated the term "extraordinary" (*extraordinarius*) as "special" (which, in Latin, would be *peculiaris*). Here and in the other citations from DOL, we have restored the correct term in square brackets. The problem also appears in some other works, and we have followed the same procedure for restoring the correct term.

Because these faculties have been granted exclusively in favor of the spiritual good of the faithful and for cases of genuine
need, let priests remember that such faculties do not release
them from the obligation of giving the Eucharist to the faithful
who lawfully request it and especially of bringing and administering it to the sick.

The faithful who are [extraordinary] ministers of Communion must be persons whose good qualities of Christian life,
faith, and morals recommend them. Let them strive to be worthy of this great office, foster their own devotion to the Eucharist, and show an example to the rest of the faithful by their
own devotion and reverence toward the most august sacrament
of the altar. No one is to be chosen whose appointment the
faithful might find disquieting.[55]

Though the use of extraordinary ministers of Holy Communion was authorized by the Holy See, there have been persis-
tent problems with their overuse in various areas. As a result,
the Holy See has issued multiple warnings against their inappropriate use. For example, the 1980 instruction *Inaestimabile
Donum* stated:

> The faithful, whether religious or lay, who are authorized as
> extraordinary ministers of the Eucharist can distribute Com-
> munion only when there is no priest, deacon, or acolyte, when
> the priest is impeded by illness or advanced age, or when the
> number of the faithful going to Communion is so large as to
> make the celebration of Mass excessively long. Accordingly, a
> reprehensible attitude is shown by those priests who, though
> present at the celebration, refrain from distributing Commu-
> nion and leave this task to the laity.[56]

Special attention has also been paid to the overuse of extraordinary ministers in the United States. In 1987, after receiving

---

[55] IC 1; DOL 2075–2076, 2081.
[56] ID 10.

numerous complaints about the too-frequent use of extraordinary ministers, the Congregation of Sacraments sent a *dubium* to the Pontifical Commission for the Authentic Interpretation of the *Code of Canon Law* asking the following:

> Whether the extraordinary minister of Holy Communion, appointed according to [CIC] 910, §2, and 230, §3, may exercise his supplementary task when there are present in the church, even if they are not participating in the celebration of the Eucharist, unimpeded ordinary ministers.[57]

In a plenary session on February 20, 1987, the Pontifical Commission replied: "In the Negative."[58] Cardinal Augustin Mayer, prefect of the Congregation of the Sacraments, then communicated this decision in a circular letter to the various papal representatives. In response, the apostolic pro-nuncio to the United States sent a letter to the president of the U.S. National Conference of Catholic Bishops, in which he explained:

> Such abuses have led to situations where the extraordinary character of this ministry has been lost. At times, it also appears as though the designation of extraordinary ministers becomes a kind of reward to repay those who have worked for the Church (ibid.).

Cardinal Mayer notes that the abuses he speaks of happen if:

> The extraordinary ministers of the Eucharist *ordinarily* distribute Holy Communion together with the celebrant, both when the number of communicants would not require their assistance, and when there are other concelebrants or other ordinary ministers available, though not celebrating;
>
> the extraordinary ministers distribute Holy Communion to themselves and to the faithful while the celebrant and concelebrants, if there are any, remain inactive. . . .

---

[57] *Roman Replies and CLSA Advisory Opinions* 1988:4.
[58] Ibid., 5.

The reply of the Pontifical Commission clearly indicates that, when ordinary ministers (bishop, priest, deacon) are present at the Eucharist, whether they are celebrating or not, and are in sufficient number and not prevented from doing so by other ministries, the extraordinary ministers of the Eucharist are not allowed to distribute Communion either to themselves or to the faithful.[59]

The 1997 document *Ecclesia de Mysterio* also addressed the overuse of extraordinary ministers of Holy Communion:

A non-ordained member of the faithful, in cases of true necessity, may be deputed by the diocesan bishop, using the appropriate form of blessing for these situations, to act as an extraordinary minister to distribute Holy Communion outside of liturgical celebrations *ad actum vel ad tempus* ["for a particular occasion or for a time"] or for a more stable period. In exceptional cases or in unforeseen circumstances, the priest presiding at the liturgy may authorize such *ad actum* ["for a particular occasion"].[60]

The role of extraordinary ministers inside Mass is also addressed:

Extraordinary ministers may distribute Holy Communion at eucharistic celebrations only when there are no ordained ministers present or when those ordained ministers present at a liturgical celebration are truly unable to distribute Holy Communion. They may also exercise this function at eucharistic celebrations where there are particularly large numbers of the faithful and which would be excessively prolonged because of an insufficient number of ordained ministers to distribute Holy Communion. . . .

To avoid creating confusion, certain practices are to be avoided and eliminated where such have emerged in particu-

---

[59] Ibid., 6–7.
[60] EM, Practical Provisions 8 §1.

lar Churches [including] . . . the habitual use of extraordinary ministers of Holy Communion at Mass thus arbitrarily extending the concept of "a great number of the faithful."[61]

To help promote the correct use of extraordinary ministers, the document suggests that the local bishop draft norms—in accordance with the universal law of the Church—to help explain how extraordinary ministers of Holy Communion are to be used and how they are to perform their role:

> This function is supplementary and extraordinary and must be exercised in accordance with the norm of law. It is thus useful for the diocesan bishop to issue particular norms concerning extraordinary ministers of Holy Communion which, in complete harmony with the universal law of the Church, should regulate the exercise of this function in his diocese. Such norms should provide, amongst other things, for matters such as the instruction in eucharistic doctrine of those chosen to be extraordinary ministers of Holy Communion, the meaning of the service they provide, the rubrics to be observed, the reverence to be shown for such an august Sacrament and instruction concerning the discipline on admission to Holy Communion.[62]

The 2004 instruction *Redemptionis Sacramentum* continued to stress this issue:

> If there is usually present a sufficient number of sacred ministers for the distribution of Holy Communion, extraordinary ministers of Holy Communion may not be appointed. Indeed, in such circumstances, those who may have already been appointed to this ministry should not exercise it. The practice of those Priests is reprobated who, even though present at the celebration, abstain from distributing Communion and hand this function over to lay persons.

---

[61] Ibid., 8 §2.
[62] Ibid.

Indeed, the extraordinary minister of Holy Communion may administer Communion only when the priest and deacon are lacking, when the Priest is prevented by weakness or advanced age or some other genuine reason, or when the number of faithful coming to Communion is so great that the very celebration of Mass would be unduly prolonged. This, however, is to be understood in such a way that a brief prolongation, considering the circumstances and culture of the place, is not at all a sufficient reason.

Let the diocesan bishop give renewed consideration to the practice in recent years regarding this matter, and if circumstances call for it, let him correct it or define it more precisely. Where such extraordinary ministers are appointed in a widespread manner out of true necessity, the diocesan bishop should issue special norms by which he determines the manner in which this function is to be carried out in accordance with the law, bearing in mind the tradition of the Church.[63]

Redemptionis Sacramentum also rejected the mistranslation or alteration of the name of this role:

"[T]he only minister who can confect the sacrament of the Eucharist *in persona Christi* is a validly ordained priest" [CIC 900 §1]. Hence the name "minister of the Eucharist" belongs properly to the priest alone. . . .[64]

This function is to be understood strictly according to the name by which it is known, that is to say, that of extraordinary minister of Holy Communion, and not "special minister of Holy Communion" nor "extraordinary minister of the Eucharist" nor "special minister of the Eucharist," by which names the meaning of this function is unnecessarily and improperly broadened.[65]

---

[63] RS 157, 158, 160.

[64] This would also eliminate the title "eucharistic minister" except in the case of priests.

[65] RS 154, 156. See footnote 54, above, p. 65.

Finally, *Redemptionis Sacramentum* rejected an abuse that had not previously been commented on in a document of this nature:

> It is never allowed for the extraordinary minister of Holy Communion to delegate anyone else to administer the Eucharist, as for example a parent or spouse or child of the sick person who is the communicant.[66]

Lay women were permitted in 1969 to be extraordinary ministers of Holy Communion. The Holy See ruled:

> A lay Christian who is to be chosen as [an extraordinary] minister of Communion should be outstanding in Christian life, in faith, and in morals, and one whose mature age warrants the choice and who is properly trained to carry out so exalted a function. A woman of outstanding piety may be chosen in cases of necessity, that is, whenever another fit person cannot be found.[67]

This role has been expanded to be as open for women as for men. The Holy See's 1973 instruction *Immensae Caritatis* made no differentiation between men and women as extraordinary ministers of Holy Communion:

> [Extraordinary ministers of Holy Communion] will be designated according to the order of this listing (which may be changed at the prudent discretion of the local ordinary): reader, major seminarian, man religious, woman religious, catechist, one of the faithful—a man or a woman.[68]

All the same rules regarding male extraordinary ministers of Holy Communion also apply to women (e.g., the rules regarding the occasions on which extraordinary ministers may be used and what they may wear).

---

[66] RS 159.

[67] FC 5; DOL 2048.

[68] IC 1:iv; DOL 2078.

Altar Servers

The Church created the position of altar server centuries ago to allow boys to serve in the place of acolytes at the altar. However, altar servers do not perform all the functions of acolytes —distributing Communion, for example—which they do not do unless they are also extraordinary ministers of Holy Communion.

More recently there was a significant controversy surrounding the question of whether there can be female altar servers (in particular, those young enough to be altar girls, parallel to altar boys). Canon 230 §2 in the 1983 *Code of Canon Law* states:

> Lay persons [*laici*] can fulfill the function of lector during liturgical actions by temporary deputation; likewise all lay persons can fulfill the functions of commentator or cantor or other functions, in accord with the norm of law.

Because this section of the canon speaks only of "lay persons" (*laici*) rather than "lay men" (*viri laici*), women were implicitly allowed to fulfill the same liturgical roles that are open to lay men unless there is an express statement to the contrary (as with instituted lectors and acolytes). The law did not contain an express prohibition for females serving at the altar, and in many places female altar servers began to be used, resulting in significant controversy.

This was settled in 1994, when the Holy See allowed national conferences of bishops to decide whether to permit female altar servers in their jurisdiction. In an audience granted on July 11, 1992, Pope John Paul II approved a response that the Pontifical Council for the Interpretation of Legal Texts had given to an inquiry on this question:

> *Dubium*: Whether, among the liturgical functions lay persons, whether men or women, are able to perform according to CIC

can. 230 §2, may also be included service at the altar (*servitium ad altare*).

Responsum: Affirmative, and in accordance with instructions to be given by the Apostolic See.

This decision was published in the journal of the Congregation for Divine Worship and the Discipline of the Sacraments.[69] Along with this was published a clarification by Cardinal Javierre Ortas.[70] The same two pieces were also published in the June 6, 1994, issue of *Acta Apostolicae Sedis*.[71]

For a time, some tried to argue against the legality of female altar servers by claiming that the documents were not properly signed, properly approved by the pope, or published in the proper journals. None of these things were true. The pope did approve the response given on canon 230 §2. The documents were signed both by the prefects and the secretaries of the relevant bodies, and they were published in *Notitiae*, the record of the congregation that has oversight of the sacraments, and in *Acta Apostolicae Sedis*, the official record in which the Holy See publishes the laws, decrees, and acts of congregations and tribunals in the Roman Curia. There is no doubt concerning the legality of female altar servers, whatever one may feel about the appropriateness or prudence of their use.

The two pieces were summarized and communicated to the presidents of the bishops' conferences by Cardinal Ortas:

Rome, 15 March 1994

Excellence,

It is my duty to communicate to the presidents of the episcopal conferences that an authentic interpretation of canon 230

---

[69] *Notitiae*, June–July 1994, 346–47.

[70] Ibid., 347–348.

[71] AAS 86:6:541–42.

§2 of the *Code of Canon Law* will soon be published in *Acta Apostolicae Sedis*.

As you know, canon 230 §2 lays down that:

> *"Laici ex temporanea deputatione in actionibus liturgicis munus lectoris implere possunt; item omnes laici muneribus commentatoris, cantoris aliisve ad normam iuris fungi possunt."*[72]

The Pontifical Council for the Interpretation of Legislative Texts was recently asked if the liturgical functions which, according to the above canon, can be entrusted to the lay faithful, may be carried out equally by men and women, and if serving at the altar may be included among those functions, on a par with the others indicated by the canon.

At its meeting of 30 June 1992, the members of the Pontifical Council for the Interpretation of Legislative Texts examined the following *dubium* which had been proposed to them:

> *"Utrum inter munera liturgica quibus laici, sive viri sive mulieres, iuxta CIC can. 230 §2, fungi possunt, adnumerari etiam possit servitium ad altare."*

The following response was given: "Affirmative et iuxta instructiones a Sede Apostolica dandas."[73]

Subsequently, at an audience granted on 11 July 1992 to the Most Reverend Vincenzo Fagiolo, Archbishop Emeritus of Chieti-Vasto and President of the Pontifical Council for the Interpretation of Legislative Texts, Pope John Paul II confirmed the decision and ordered its promulgation. This will be done in the near future.

In communicating the above information to your episcopal conference, I feel obliged to clarify certain aspects of canon 230 §2 and of its authentic interpretation:

1) Canon 230 §2 has a permissive and not a preceptive character: "*Laici . . . possunt.*" Hence the permission given in this regard by some bishops can in no way be considered as binding

---

[72] Quoted above in English, p. 72.

[73] Both parts of the *dubium* quoted above in English, pp. 72–73.

on other bishops. In fact, it is the competence of each bishop, in his diocese, after hearing the opinion of the episcopal conference, to make a prudential judgment on what to do, with a view to the ordered development of liturgical life in his own diocese.

2) The Holy See respects the decision adopted by certain bishops for specific local reasons on the basis of the provisions of canon 230 §2. At the same time, however, the Holy See wishes to recall that it will always be very appropriate to follow the noble tradition of having boys serve at the altar. As is well known, this has led to a reassuring development of priestly vocations. Thus the obligation to support such groups of altar boys will always continue.

3) If in some diocese, on the basis of canon 230 §2, the bishop permits that, for particular reasons, women may also serve at the altar, this decision must be clearly explained to the faithful, in the light of the above-mentioned norm. It shall also be made clear that the norm is already being widely applied, by the fact that women frequently serve as lectors in the liturgy and can also be called upon to distribute Holy Communion as extraordinary ministers of the Eucharist and to carry out other functions, according to the provisions of the same canon 230 §3.

4) It must also be clearly understood that the liturgical services mentioned above are carried out by lay people "*ex temporanea deputatione*," according to the judgment of the bishop, without lay people, be they men or women, having any right to exercise them.

In communicating the above, the Congregation for Divine Worship and the Discipline of the Sacraments has sought to carry out the mandate received from the Supreme Pontiff to provide directives to illustrate what is laid down in canon 230 §2 of the *Code of Canon Law* and its authentic interpretation, which will shortly be published.

In this way the bishops will be better able to carry out their mission to be moderators and promoters of liturgical life in their own dioceses, within the framework of the norms in force of the Universal Church.

In deep communion with all the members of your Episcopal Conference. I remain,

Yours sincerely in Christ,

> Antonio Maria Javierre Ortas
> Prefect
> Sacred Congregation for Divine Worship
> and the Discipline of the Sacraments

While altar girls are now permitted, there is also still a need for altar boys. *Redemptionis Sacramentum* states:

> It is altogether laudable to maintain the noble custom by which boys or youths, customarily termed servers, provide service of the altar after the manner of acolytes, and receive catechesis regarding their function in accordance with their power of comprehension. Nor should it be forgotten that a great number of sacred ministers over the course of the centuries have come from among boys such as these. Associations for them, including also the participation and assistance of their parents, should be established or promoted, and in such a way greater pastoral care will be provided for the ministers. Whenever such associations are international in nature, it pertains to the competence of the Congregation for Divine Worship and the Discipline of the Sacraments to establish them or to approve and revise their statutes. Girls or women may also be admitted to this service of the altar, at the discretion of the diocesan Bishop and in observance of the established norms.[74]

The Role of Children

Particular norms governing Masses in which a large number of children participate are set down in a 1973 document put

---

[74] RS 47.

out by the Holy See's then Congregation for Divine Worship. The document, titled *Directory for Masses with Children*, authorizes special adaptations for Masses involving children. They vary depending on the number of adults at Mass. Concerning Masses where adults predominate, the *Directory* states:

> In many places parish Masses are celebrated, especially on Sundays and holy days, at which a good many children take part along with the large number of adults. On such occasions the witness of adult believers can have a great effect upon the children. Adults can in turn benefit spiritually from experiencing the part that the children have within the Christian community. The Christian spirit of the family is greatly fostered when children take part in these Masses together with their parents and other family members.[75]

While it is desirable that children take part in the entire Mass along with their parents, other arrangements are possible. The *Directory* goes on to state:

> Infants who as yet are unable or unwilling to take part in the Mass may be brought in at the end of Mass to be blessed together with the rest of the community. This may be done, for example, if parish helpers have been taking care of them in a separate area.[76]

It is also important to make children feel at home in Masses at which adults predominate:

> [I]n Masses of this kind it is necessary to take great care that the children present do not feel neglected because of their inability to participate or to understand what happens and what is proclaimed in the celebration. Some account should be taken of their presence: for example, by speaking to them directly in

---

[75] DMC 16.
[76] Ibid.

the introductory comments (as at the beginning and the end of Mass) and at some point in the homily.[77]

Parishes are also authorized, in appropriate circumstances, to have separate celebrations of the Liturgy of the Word for children:

> Sometimes, moreover, if the place itself and the nature of the community permit, it will be appropriate to celebrate the liturgy of the word, including a homily, with the children in a separate, but not too distant room. Then, before the eucharistic liturgy begins, the children are led to the place where the adults have meanwhile celebrated their own Liturgy of the Word.[78]

It is also permissible for children to perform certain roles at Masses at which adults participate:

> It may also be very helpful to give some tasks to the children. They may, for example, bring forward the gifts or perform one or other of the songs of the Mass.[79]

There are even cases when the degree of adaptation approaches that given to Masses at which children predominate:

> If the number of children is large, it may at times be suitable to plan the Mass so that it corresponds more closely to the needs of the children. In this case the homily should be directed to them but in such a way that the adults may also benefit from it. Where the bishop permits, in addition to the adaptations already provided in the Order of Mass, one or other of the particular adaptations described later in the Directory may be employed in a Mass celebrated with adults in which children also participate.[80]

---

[77] DMC 17.

[78] DMC 17.

[79] DMC 18.

[80] DMC 19.

These circumstances, however, are uncommon at Sunday Masses. It is more common for there to be a Mass with a large number of children and only a few adults present at a Catholic school during the week. For such cases, the *Directory for Masses with Children* has a different set of adaptations. It recommends the use of the special adaptations for these Masses, but it also cautions against too many modifications:

> In addition to the Masses in which children take part with their parents and other family members (which are not always possible everywhere), Masses with children in which only a few adults take part are recommended, especially during the week. . . .
>
> It is always necessary to keep in mind that these eucharistic celebrations must lead children toward the celebration of Mass with adults, especially the Masses at which the Christian community must come together on Sundays. Thus, apart from adaptations that are necessary because of the children's age, the result should not be entirely special rites, markedly different from the Order of Mass celebrated with a congregation. The purpose of the various elements should always correspond with what is said in the *General Instruction of the Roman Missal* on individual points, even if at times for pastoral reasons an absolute *identity* cannot be insisted upon.[81]

Because these Masses are not ones that adults commonly experience, we will not go into detail concerning the adaptations, though they include more roles for the children, such as allowing them to give the Scripture readings (except, of course, for the Gospel, which is still reserved to a priest or deacon).

For those who wish to read more concerning Masses with children in which only a few adults participate, a copy of the *Directory for Masses with Children* should be available at any local parish—and especially parishes that operate Catholic schools.

It should be noted that the *Directory for Masses with Children*

---

[81] DMC 20-21.

applies only to children below a certain age. It does not, for example, apply to teenagers. It states:

> The Directory is concerned with children who have *not yet entered the period of preadolescence*. It does not speak directly of children who are physically or mentally handicapped, because a broader adaptation is sometimes necessary for them. Nevertheless, the following norms may also be applied to the handicapped, with the necessary changes.[82]

The period of preadolescence is commonly understood to begin around age ten for both boys and girls and ending with the onset of puberty two or three years later.

Also, it should be noted that the Eucharistic Prayers for Masses with Children—should they be reauthorized for use in the United States—are restricted only to Masses with children below the age of preadolescence:

> Use of a Eucharistic Prayer for Masses with Children is restricted to Masses that are celebrated with children alone or Masses at which the majority of the participants are children.
>
> A community of children means one so considered by the *Directory for Masses with Children*, that is, one consisting of children who have not yet reached the age referred to as preadolescence.[83]

---

[82] DMC 6, emphasis added.

[83] Sacred Congregation for Divine Worship, *Postquam de Precibus* 4 (November 1, 1974); DOL 1998.

4. Preparation for Mass

Before Mass begins, it is necessary to prepare the altar and the various articles that will be used. Maintaining the church's cleanliness ensures that it is a beautiful and dignified place for celebrating Mass. The *Ceremonial of Bishops* states:

> The first of all the elements belonging to the beauty of the place where the liturgy is celebrated is the spotless cleanliness of the floor and walls and of all the images and articles that will be used during a service. In all the liturgical appurtenances both ostentation and shabbiness are to be avoided; instead the norms of noble simplicity, refinement, gracefulness, and artistic excellence are to be respected. The culture of the people and the local tradition should guide the choice of objects and their arrangement, "on condition that they serve the places of worship and sacred rites with the reverence and honor due them."
>
> The adornment and décor of a church should always be such as to make the church a visible sign of love and reverence toward God of the real meaning of the feasts celebrated there and to inspire in them a sense of joy and devotion.[1]

For additional information concerning liturgical furnishings, see Chapter 12.

Preparation of General Liturgical Furnishings

When preparations are being made for a normal celebration of Mass, the following is directed:

---

[1] CB 38.

The altar is to be covered with at least one white cloth. In addition, on or next to the altar are to be placed candlesticks with lighted candles: at least two in any celebration, or even four or six, especially for a Sunday Mass or a holy day of obligation. If the diocesan bishop celebrates, then seven candles should be used. Also on or close to the altar, there is to be a cross with a figure of Christ crucified. The candles and the cross adorned with a figure of Christ crucified may also be carried in the Entrance procession. On the altar itself may be placed the Book of the Gospels, distinct from the book of other readings, unless it is carried in the Entrance procession.

The following are also to be prepared:

a. Next to the priest's chair: the *Missal* and, as needed, a hymnal.

b. At the ambo: the *Lectionary*.

c. On the credence table: the chalice, a corporal, a purificator, and, if appropriate, the pall; the paten and, if needed, ciboria; bread for the Communion of the priest who presides, the deacon, the ministers, and the people; cruets containing the wine and the water, unless all of these are presented by the faithful in procession at the Offertory; the vessel of water to be blessed, if the asperges occurs; the Communion-plate for the Communion of the faithful; and whatever is needed for the washing of hands.

It is a praiseworthy practice to cover the chalice with a veil, which may be either the color of the day or white.[2]

Special preparations are made at certain times of the liturgical year—for example, during penitential seasons:

During Lent the altar is not to be decorated with flowers and the use of musical instruments is allowed only to support singing. The fourth Sunday of Lent, called *Laetare* Sunday, solemnities

---

[2] GIRM 117–118.

and feasts are exceptions to this rule. On *Laetare* Sunday rose vestments may be used.[3]

It is a custom in some countries to veil the crosses in a church on the Saturday before the fifth Sunday of Lent:

The practice of covering the crosses and images in the church may be observed if the episcopal conference should so decide. The crosses are to be covered until the end of the celebration of the Lord's Passion on Good Friday. Images are to remain covered until the beginning of the Easter Vigil.[4]

For many years the U.S. bishops had not authorized this, but in 2001 they did. The Bishops' Committee on Liturgy's newsletter stated:

On June 14, 2001, the Latin Church members of the USCCB approved an adaptation to number 318 of the *General Instruction of the Roman Missal* which would allow for the veiling of crosses and images in this manner. On April 17, 2002, Cardinal Jorge Medina Estevez, Prefect of the Congregation for Divine Worship and the Discipline of the Sacraments, wrote to Bishop Wilton D. Gregory, USCCB president (Prot. no. 1381/01/L), noting that this matter belonged more properly to the rubrics of the fifth Sunday of Lent. While the decision of the USCCB will be included with this rubric when the *Roman Missal* is eventually published, the veiling of crosses and images may now take place at the discretion of the local pastor.[5]

The final version of the *Roman Missal* that was confirmed in August 2010 states:

In the dioceses of the United States, the practice of covering crosses and images throughout the Church from [the fifth

---

[3] CB 252.
[4] PS 26.
[5] BCL *Newsletter*, March 2006, p. 12.

Sunday of Lent] may be observed. Crosses remain covered until the end of the celebration of the Lord's Passion on Good Friday, but images remain covered until the beginning of the Easter Vigil.[6]

If the pastor decides not to veil the images on the fifth Sunday of Lent, they are still usually veiled following the Mass of the Lord's Supper on Holy Thursday, when the altar is stripped:

After Mass the altar should be stripped. It is fitting that any crosses in the church be covered with a red or purple veil, unless they have already been veiled on the Saturday before the fifth Sunday of Lent. Lamps should not be lit before the images of saints.[7]

The altar is still bare when the Good Friday liturgy is begun, and following the liturgy it is again stripped:

After the celebration, the altar is stripped; the cross remains, however, with four candles. An appropriate place (for example, the chapel of repose used for reservation of the Eucharist on Maundy Thursday) can be prepared within the church, and there the Lord's cross is placed so that the faithful may venerate and kiss it, and spend some time in meditation.[8]

The altar is left bare on Holy Saturday. The rubrics for Holy Saturday in the *Roman Missal* state:

On Holy Saturday the Church waits at the Lord's tomb, meditating on his suffering and death. The altar is left bare, and the sacrifice of the Mass is not celebrated. Only after the solemn vigil during the night, held in anticipation of the resurrection, does the Easter celebration begin, with a spirit of joy that overflows into the following period of fifty days.

---

[6] *BCDW Newsletter*, Aug.-Sept. 2010, p. 33.

[7] PS 57.

[8] PS 71.

On this day Holy Communion may be given only as *viaticum*.[9]

Though not stripped on All Souls' Day, the altar's adornments are similarly diminished:

On All Souls' there are no flowers on the altar, and the use of the organ and other instruments is permitted only to sustain the singing.[10]

For further information on the proper preparations for Mass on specific days of the liturgical year, see the rubrics of the *Roman Missal*.

Preparation of Incense

If incense is to be used at Mass, it also will need to be prepared. The purpose of using incense in Mass is explained in the *Ceremonial of Bishops*:

The rite of incensation or thurification is a sign of reverence and of prayer, as is clear from Psalm 141(140):2 and Revelation 8:3.[11]

Though not as common as it was, incense is permitted at any Mass. The *General Instruction* states:

Thurification or incensation is an expression of reverence and of prayer, as is signified in Sacred Scripture (see also Ps. 141 [140]:2; Rev. 8:3).

Incense may be used if desired in any form of Mass:

a. During the Entrance procession.

---

[9] This is the previous translation. The current translation not available at the time of this writing.

[10] CB 397.

[11] CB 84.

b. At the beginning of Mass, to incense the cross and the altar.

c. At the Gospel procession and the proclamation of the Gospel itself.

d. After the bread and the chalice have been placed upon the altar, to incense the offerings, the cross, and the altar, as well as the priest and the people.

e. At the showing of the host and the chalice after the Consecration.[12]

The use of incense is recommended on a number of occasions:

In addition, incense should be used as a rule during the procession for the feast of the Presentation of the Lord, Passion Sunday (Palm Sunday), the Mass of the Lord's Supper, the Easter Vigil, the solemnity of the body and blood of Christ (Corpus Christi), and the solemn translation of relics, and in general, in any procession of some solemnity.[13]

Concerning the type of incense that is to be used, the *Ceremonial of Bishops* states:

The substance placed in the censer should be pure sweet-scented incense alone or at least in larger portion than any additive mixed with the incense.[14]

Regarding the method of using incense, the *General Instruction* states:

The priest, having put incense into the thurible, blesses it with the sign of the cross, without saying anything.

Before and after an incensation, a profound bow is made to the person or object that is incensed, except for the incensation of the altar and the offerings for the sacrifice of the Mass.

---

[12] GIRM 276.

[13] CB 88.

[14] CB 85.

The following are incensed with three swings of the thurible: the Most Blessed Sacrament, a relic of the Holy Cross and images of the Lord exposed for public veneration, the offerings for the sacrifice of the Mass, the altar cross, the Book of the Gospels, the Paschal Candle, the priest, and the people.

The following are incensed with two swings of the thurible: relics and images of the Saints exposed for public veneration. This should be done, however, only at the beginning of the celebration, after the incensation of the altar.

The altar is incensed with single swings of the thurible in this way:

a. If the altar is freestanding with respect to the wall, the priest incenses walking around it.

b. If the altar is not freestanding, the priest incenses it while walking first to the righthand side, then to the left.

The cross, if situated on or near the altar, is incensed by the priest before he incenses the altar; otherwise, he incenses it when he passes in front of it.

The priest incenses the offerings with three swings of the thurible or by making the sign of the cross over the offerings with the thurible, then going on to incense the cross and the altar.[15]

If a deacon is present, he has a role helping the priest with the incense, most notably at the reading of the Gospel:

If incense is used, the deacon assists the priest when he puts incense in the thurible during the singing of the *Alleluia* or other chant. Then he makes a profound bow before the priest and asks for the blessing, saying in a low voice, *Iube, domine, benedicere* ("Father, give me your blessing"). The priest blesses him, saying, *Dominus sit in corde tuo* ("The Lord be in your heart"). The deacon signs himself with the sign of the cross and responds, "Amen." Having bowed to the altar, he then takes up

---

[15] GIRM 277.

the Book of the Gospels, which was placed upon it. He proceeds to the ambo, carrying the book slightly elevated. He is preceded by a thurifer, carrying a thurible with smoking incense, and by servers with lighted candles. There the deacon, with hands joined, greets the people, saying, *Dominus vobiscum* ("The Lord be with you"). Then, at the words *Lectio sancti Evangelii* ("A reading from the holy Gospel"), he signs the book with his thumb and, afterward, himself on his forehead, mouth, and breast. He incenses the book and proclaims the Gospel reading. When the reading is concluded, he says the acclamation *Verbum Domini* ("The Gospel of the Lord"), and all respond, *Laus tibi, Christe* ("Praise to you, Lord Jesus Christ"). He then venerates the book with a kiss, saying privately, *Per evangelica dicta* ("May the words of the Gospel"), and returns to the priest's side.

When the deacon is assisting the Bishop, he carries the book to him to be kissed, or else kisses it himself, saying quietly, *Per evangelica dicta* ("May the words of the Gospel"). In more solemn celebrations, as the occasion suggests, a Bishop may impart a blessing to the people with the Book of the Gospels.

Lastly, the deacon may carry the Book of the Gospels to the credence table or to another appropriate and dignified place.[16]

The deacon also plays a role in the use of incense at other times, as do other ministers, especially if a deacon is not present. For more information, consult the rubrics in the *Roman Missal*.

Preparation of the Hosts to Be Consecrated

The elements that will be consecrated during Mass should be prepared beforehand. In order to have a licit and valid celebration of the Eucharist, very specific kinds of elements must be used. The *Code of Canon Law* states:

---

[16] GIRM 175.

The most holy eucharistic sacrifice must be offered with bread and with wine in which a little water must be mixed [CIC 924 §1].

Any celebration of the Eucharist that does not use bread and wine of the type described in the *Code of Canon Law* (see below) is illicit, meaning it is not permitted. If the deviation from the requisite type of bread and wine is substantial enough, the celebration of the sacrament will be invalid, meaning that the elements do not become the body and blood of Christ when the priest says the words of Consecration.

Ingredients of the Host

Concerning the kind of bread that is to be used, the *Code of Canon Law* states:

> The bread must be only wheat and recently made so that there is no danger of spoiling [CIC 924 §2].

In many Eastern rite Catholic churches, leavened bread is mandated. This is a legitimate difference between the Eastern and Western parts of the Catholic Church. However, leavened bread is not permitted in Latin rite Catholic churches, which are the most common ones in Europe and the Americas. In Latin rite churches:

> The bread for celebrating the Eucharist must be made only from wheat, must be recently baked, and, according to the ancient tradition of the Latin Church, must be unleavened.[17]

This is also specifically mandated by the *Code of Canon Law:*

> According to the ancient tradition of the Latin Church, the priest is to use unleavened bread in the eucharistic celebration whenever he offers it [CIC 926].

---

[17] GIRM 320.

The nature of the bread to be consecrated is further elaborated in *Inaestimabile Donum*:

> The bread for the celebration of the Eucharist, in accordance with the tradition of the whole Church, must be made solely of wheat, and, in accordance with the tradition proper to the Latin Church, it must be unleavened. By reason of the sign, the matter of the eucharistic celebration "should appear as actual food." This is to be understood as linked to the consistency of the bread, and not to its form, which remains the traditional one [i.e., a wafer]. No other ingredients are to be added to the wheaten flour and water. The preparation of the bread requires attentive care to ensure that the product does not detract from the dignity due to the eucharistic bread, can be broken in a dignified way, does not give rise to excessive fragments, and does not offend the sensibilities of the faithful when they eat it.[18]

Redemptionis Sacramentum notes that since eucharistic bread must be made from wheat alone:

> It follows therefore that bread made from another substance, even if it is grain, or if it is mixed with another substance different from wheat to such an extent that it would not commonly be considered wheat bread, does not constitute valid matter for confecting the sacrifice and the eucharistic sacrament. It is a grave abuse to introduce other substances, such as fruit or sugar or honey, into the bread for confecting the Eucharist.[19]

The late Fr. Nicholas Halligan, a leading sacramental theologian, described what may be considered invalid matter:

> The bread must be made from wheat, mixed with natural water, baked by the application of fire heat (including electric cooking) and substantially uncorrupted. The variety of the wheat or the region of its origin does not affect its validity, but bread made

---

[18] ID 8.
[19] RS 48.

from any other grain is invalid matter. Bread made with milk, wine, oil, etc., either entirely or in a notable part, is invalid material. Any natural water suffices for validity, e.g., even mineral water or sea water. The addition of a condiment, such as salt or sugar, is unlawful but valid, unless added in a notable quantity. Unbaked dough or dough fried in butter or cooked in water is invalid matter; likewise bread which is corrupted substantially, but not if it has merely begun to corrupt. Therefore, the valid material of this sacrament must be in the common estimation of reasonable men bread made from wheat and not mixed notably with something else so that it is no longer wheat. Those who make altar breads must be satisfied that they have purchased genuine and pure wheat flour. . . . It is gravely unlawful to consecrate with doubtful matter.[20]

Low-Gluten Hosts

In recent years, the question has arisen as to what provision can be made for sufferers of celiac sprue disease, which causes the gluten found in regular wheat to irritate the intestinal lining of the sufferers.

One solution has been to offer celiac individuals Communion under the species of wine only, even if Communion from the chalice is not being offered to the rest of the faithful.[21] This allows the communicant to receive the whole Christ, who is present body, blood, soul, and divinity under both the form of bread and the form of wine.

Another solution involves the use of low-gluten altar breads. The current regulations concerning this are found in a letter

---

[20] Fr. Nicholas Halligan, *The Sacraments and Their Celebration* (Eugene, Ore.: Wipf and Stock, 2004), 65–66.

[21] When this is done, it may be necessary to have a separate chalice for the celiac individual. This is because the priest drops part of the host into his own chalice at the Fraction.

issued by the Congregation for the Doctrine of the Faith on July 24, 2003. The full text of this letter is found in "Low-Gluten Hosts and Mustum" in the Bonus Materials. For here it should be noted that:

- Hosts that are completely gluten-free are invalid matter for the celebration of the Eucharist; and

- Low-gluten hosts (partially gluten-free) are valid matter, provided they contain a sufficient amount of gluten to obtain the confection of bread without the addition of foreign materials and without the use of procedures that would alter the nature of bread.[22]

Shape of the Host

Regarding the shape of the bread to be consecrated, the *General Instruction* states:

> The meaning of the sign demands that the material for the eucharistic celebration truly have the appearance of food. It is therefore expedient that the eucharistic bread, even though unleavened and baked in the traditional shape, be made in such a way that the priest at Mass with a congregation is able in practice to break it into parts for distribution to at least some of the faithful. Small hosts are, however, in no way ruled out when the number of those receiving Holy Communion or other pastoral needs require it. The action of the fraction or breaking of bread, which gave its name to the Eucharist in apostolic times, will bring out more clearly the force and importance of the sign of unity of all in the one bread, and of the sign of charity by the fact that the one bread is distributed among the brothers and sisters.[23]

Because of confusion over this passage, which led to some priests abandoning the use of standard, wafer-like hosts for the

---

[22] CDF letter of July 24, 2003, section A 1-2.
[23] GIRM 321.

Eucharist (or at least for the priest's host), the Holy See issued a clarification of this passage (which was numbered 283 in the previous edition of the GIRM):

> *Dubium*: In the GIRM no. 283, what does eucharistic bread mean?

> *Responsum*: The term means the same thing as the "host" hitherto in use, except that the bread is larger in size. The term "eucharistic bread" in line 2 is explained by the words of line 4: "The priest is able actually to break the host into parts." Thus line 2 is about this eucharistic element as to its kind and line 4 as to its shape. Therefore it was incorrect to interpret "eucharistic bread" in line 2 as a reference to its shape as though the term implies that bread in the shape designed for its everyday use may be substituted for the host in its traditional shape [i.e., a wafer]. The GIRM in no way intended to change the shape of the large and small hosts, but only to provide an option regarding size, thickness, and color in order that the host may really have the appearance of bread that is shared by many people.[24]

That the hosts normally have the traditional wafer shape was also stressed in *Inaestimabile Donum* (see quotation above).

Preparation of Wine to Be Consecrated

General Type of Wine

Just as the kind of hosts that are to be used at Mass are carefully stipulated, so is the kind of wine. The *Code of Canon Law* states:

> The wine must be natural from the fruit of the vine and not spoiled [CIC 924 §3].

---

[24] *Notitiae* 6 (1970) 37, no. 24.

This is further elaborated in *Inaestimabile Donum*:

Faithful to Christ's example, the Church has constantly used
bread and wine mixed with water to celebrate the Lord's Supper. . . . The wine for the eucharistic celebration must be of
"the fruit of the vine" (Luke 22:18) and be natural and genuine,
that is to say, not mixed with other substances.[25]

Redemptionis Sacramentum adds:

It is altogether forbidden to use wine of doubtful authenticity
or provenance, for the Church requires certainty regarding the
conditions necessary for the validity of the sacraments. Nor are
other drinks of any kind to be admitted for any reason, as they
do not constitute valid matter.[26]

In discussing what may be considered invalid matter for the
wine, Fr. Halligan wrote:

To be valid material, wine must be made from ripe grapes of
the vine and not substantially corrupted; it cannot come from
any other fruits or from unripe grapes or from the stems and
skins of the grapes after all the juice has been pressed out. In
regions where fresh grapes cannot be obtained, it is lawful to
use raisin wine, i.e., wine made by adding water to raisins. Wine
from which all alcohol has been removed or which on the other
hand has more than twenty percent alcohol or to which foreign
ingredients (e.g., water) have been added in equal or greater
quantities is invalid material. Wine is likewise invalid which
has turned to acid or which is not natural but was manufactured
by some chemical process, i.e., by mixing the constituents found
in wine so that the product resembles wine. Wine must also be
in a potable [i.e., drinkable] state, and thus if it is congealed
(although most probably valid), it must be melted. The color,
strength, or origin of wine does not affect its validity.

---

[25] ID 8.
[26] RS 50.

It is gravely unlawful to use doubtful material, and thus it is unlawful to consecrate wine which is just beginning to turn sour or to corrupt. Wine must be naturally fermented and the use of "must" (unfermented grape juice) is gravely unlawful. To be lawful, wine must be pure, free from the lees, diseases, and foreign ingredients. Lawful wine may not contain more than eighteen percent alcohol (obtained from the grape); wines which would not ordinarily ferment beyond twelve percent alcohol cannot be fortified beyond this limit. The Holy See has been insistent that the sacramental or Mass wine come from sources beyond suspicion, since there are many ways in which wine can be vitiated or adulterated, many methods which are actually used in this country to preserve, age, ameliorate wines. Wines should be purchased regularly only from reputable vendors of Mass wine or only when otherwise guaranteed to be pure and unadulterated.[27]

Non-Alcoholic Wine

In recent years, attention has been paid to the possible sacramental use of unfermented or partially fermented grape juice (called "must" or "mustum") by priests and others who suffer from alcoholism. The current regulations are expressed in the same letter from the Congregation for the Doctrine of the Faith issued July 24, 2003. The full text of this letter is found in "Low-Gluten Hosts and Mustum" in the Bonus Materials. For here it should be noted that:

> Mustum, which is grape juice that is either fresh or preserved by methods that suspend its fermentation without altering its nature (for example, freezing), is valid matter for the celebration of the Eucharist.[28]

---

[27] Halligan, *The Sacraments and Their Celebration*, 66–67.
[28] CDF, letter of July 24, 2003, section A 3.

5. Introductory Rites

Entrance Procession

The *General Instruction* specifies that for the basic form of the celebration of Mass, the Introductory Rites begin in this way:

Once the people have gathered, the priest and ministers, clad in the sacred vestments, go in procession to the altar in this order:

a. The thurifer carrying a thurible with burning incense, if incense is used.

b. The ministers who carry lighted candles, and between them an acolyte or other minister with the cross.

c. The acolytes and the other ministers.

d. A lector, who may carry the Book of the Gospels (though not the *Lectionary*), which should be slightly elevated.

e. The priest who is to celebrate the Mass.

If incense is used, before the procession begins, the priest puts some in the thurible and blesses it with the sign of the cross without saying anything.

During the procession to the altar, the Entrance chant takes place.[1]

If a deacon is present, he also takes part in the Entrance procession:

Carrying the Book of the Gospels slightly elevated, the deacon precedes the priest as he approaches the altar or else walks at the priest's side.[2]

---

[1] GIRM 120–21.
[2] GIRM 172.

The *General Instruction* also clarifies the purpose of the Entrance chant and how it is to be performed:

> After the people have gathered, the Entrance chant begins as the priest enters with the deacon and ministers. The purpose of this chant is to open the celebration, foster the unity of those who have been gathered, introduce their thoughts to the mystery of the liturgical season or festivity, and accompany the procession of the priest and ministers.
>
> The singing at this time is done either alternately by the choir and the people or in a similar way by the cantor and the people, or entirely by the people, or by the choir alone. In the dioceses of the United States of America there are four options for the Entrance chant: (1) the antiphon from the *Roman Missal* or the Psalm from the Roman Gradual as set to music there or in another musical setting; (2) the seasonal antiphon and Psalm of the Simple Gradual; (3) a song from another collection of psalms and antiphons, approved by the Conference of Bishops or the diocesan Bishop, including psalms arranged in responsorial or metrical forms; (4) a suitable liturgical song similarly approved by the Conference of Bishops or the Diocesan Bishop.
>
> If there is no singing at the entrance, the antiphon in the *Missal* is recited either by the faithful, or by some of them, or by a lector; otherwise, it is recited by the priest himself, who may even adapt it as an introductory explanation.[3]

Veneration of the Altar

In most countries the priest and ministers venerate the Book of the Gospels (as the word of God, containing the story of Christ) and the altar (as the place where the eucharistic sacrifice occurs) with a kiss:

> According to traditional practice, the altar and the Book of the Gospels are venerated by means of a kiss. Where, however, a

---

[3] GIRM 47–48.

sign of this kind is not in harmony with the traditions or the culture of some region, it is for the Conference of Bishops to establish some other sign in its place, with the consent of the Apostolic See.[4]

This veneration is to be performed at the end of the Entrance procession:

On reaching the altar, the priest and ministers make a profound bow.

The cross adorned with a figure of Christ crucified and perhaps carried in procession may be placed next to the altar to serve as the altar cross, in which case it ought to be the only cross used; otherwise it is put away in a dignified place. In addition, the candlesticks are placed on the altar or near it. It is a praiseworthy practice that the Book of the Gospels be placed upon the altar.

The priest goes up to the altar and venerates it with a kiss. Then, as the occasion suggests, he incenses the cross and the altar, walking around the latter.[5]

If a deacon is present, he also venerates the altar:

When he reaches the altar, if he is carrying the Book of the Gospels, he omits the sign of reverence and goes up to the altar. It is particularly appropriate that he should place the Book of the Gospels on the altar, after which, together with the priest, he venerates the altar with a kiss.

If, however, he is not carrying the Book of the Gospels, he makes a profound bow to the altar with the priest in the customary way and with him venerates the altar with a kiss.

Lastly, if incense is used, he assists the priest in putting some into the thurible and in incensing the cross and the altar.[6]

---

[4] GIRM 273.
[5] GIRM 122–23.
[6] GIRM 173.

Greeting the Congregation

The priest then greets the congregation, and all bless themselves with the sign of the cross:

> After doing these things, the priest goes to the chair. Once the Entrance chant is concluded, the priest and faithful, all standing, make the sign of the cross. The priest says, *In nomine Patris et Filii et Spiritus Sancti* ("In the name of the Father, and of the Son, and of the Holy Spirit"). The people answer, "Amen."
>
> Then, facing the people and extending his hands, the priest greets the people, using one of the formulas indicated. The priest himself or some other minister may also very briefly introduce the faithful to the Mass of the day.[7]

During the course of the Mass, the priest may make various explanations of specific parts of the Mass at the points indicated in the rubrics:

> It is also up to the priest, in the exercise of his office of presiding over the gathered assembly, to offer certain explanations that are foreseen in the rite itself. Where it is indicated in the rubrics, the celebrant is permitted to adapt them somewhat in order that they respond to the understanding of those participating. However, he should always take care to keep to the sense of the text given in the *Missal* and to express them succinctly. The presiding priest is also to direct the word of God and to impart the final blessing. In addition, he may give the faithful a very brief introduction to the Mass of the day (after the initial Greeting and before the Act of Penitence), to the Liturgy of the Word (before the readings), and to the Eucharistic Prayer (before the Preface), though never during the Eucharistic Prayer itself; he may also make concluding comments to the entire sacred action before the dismissal.[8]

---

[7] GIRM 124.
[8] GIRM 31.

Penitential Rite

The congregants then reflect on their sins and ask God to forgive them so that they may be spiritually purified for the celebration of the liturgy:

> Then the priest invites those present to take part in the Act of Penitence, which, after a brief pause for silence, the entire community carries out through a formula of general confession. The rite concludes with the priest's absolution, which, however, lacks the efficacy of the sacrament of penance.
>
> On Sundays, especially in the season of Easter, in place of the customary Act of Penitence, from time to time the blessing and sprinkling of water to recall baptism may take place.[9]

It is important to note that the absolution referred to in this passage is not a sacramental absolution and does not replace going to the sacrament of confession. One who has an unconfessed mortal sin may not receive Communion on the basis of the penitential rite.

The *Code of Canon Law* states:

> Individual and integral confession and absolution constitute the only ordinary means by which a member of the faithful conscious of grave sin is reconciled with God and the Church. Only physical or moral impossibility excuses from confession of this type; in such a case reconciliation can be obtained by other means [CIC 960].

The Holy See has been very concerned that in some parishes priests have actually given a general sacramental absolution at the end of the penitential rite. This is strictly prohibited. A general sacramental absolution can be given only in highly

---

[9] GIRM 51.

exceptional circumstances. The *Code of Canon Law* goes on to state:

> Absolution cannot be imparted in a general manner to many penitents at once without previous individual confession unless:
>
> 1° Danger of death is imminent and there is insufficient time for the priest or priests to hear the confessions of the individual penitents.
>
> 2° There is grave necessity, that is, when in view of the number of penitents, there are not enough confessors available to hear the confessions of individuals properly within a suitable period of time in such a way that the penitents are forced to be deprived for a long while of sacramental grace or Holy Communion through no fault of their own. Sufficient necessity is not considered to exist when confessors cannot be present due only to the large number of penitents such as can occur on some great feast or pilgrimage [CIC 961 §1].

An example of the kind of situation mentioned in number 1 would be a platoon of soldiers about to rush into battle or passengers in a crashing airplane. An example of the kind of situation mentioned in number 2 would be a large group of people on an island or in a remote area who have access to a priest every few months for only long enough to have him say Mass before he has to leave.

In the latter kind of case, however, there is no imminent danger, and an individual priest is not authorized to judge that such a situation exists. Instead, the diocesan bishop must make this determination:

> It belongs to the diocesan bishop to judge whether the conditions required according to the norm of §1, n. 2 are present. He can determine the cases of such necessity, attentive to the criteria agreed upon with the other members of the conference of bishops [CIC 961 §2].

If a priest were to make an illicit but otherwise valid sacramental absolution, it would have its intended effect so long as the penitent has the required dispositions and intentions:

§1. For a member of the Christian faithful validly to receive sacramental absolution given to many at one time, it is required not only that the person is properly disposed but also at the same time intends to confess within a suitable period of time each grave sin which at the present time cannot be so confessed.

§2. Insofar as it can be done even on the occasion of the reception of general absolution, the Christian faithful are to be instructed about the requirements of the norm of §1. An exhortation that each person take care to make an act of contrition is to precede general absolution even in the case of danger of death, if there is time [CIC 962].

A person who receives a general absolution must then go to regular confession within a reasonable period of time. General absolution is not a substitute for individual confession:

Without prejudice to the obligation mentioned in can. 989, a person whose grave sins are remitted by general absolution is to approach individual confession as soon as possible, given the opportunity, before receiving another general absolution, unless a just cause intervenes [CIC 963].

Sometimes people ask about the omission of the Penitential Act at the beginning of a Sunday Mass and whether this is permitted. The answer is that it is *supposed* to be omitted in some cases. Concerning the Rite of Blessing and Sprinkling, the rubrics state that:

From time to time on Sundays, especially during Easter time, *instead of the customary Penitential Act*, the blessing and sprinkling of water may take place . . . as a reminder of baptism.[10]

---

[10] Emphasis added.

On the other hand, the penitential rite is not an optional part of Mass that can be omitted for no cause.

Kyrie Eleison and Gloria

If it has not already been sung or recited, the *Kyrie Eleison* ("Lord, have mercy") is then sung:

> After the Act of Penitence, the *Kyrie* is always begun, unless it has already been included as part of the Act of Penitence. Since it is a chant by which the faithful acclaim the Lord and implore his mercy, it is ordinarily done by all, that is, by the people and with the choir or cantor having a part in it.
>
> As a rule, each acclamation is sung or said twice, though it may be repeated several times, by reason of the character of the various languages, as well as of the artistry of the music or of other circumstances. When the *Kyrie* is sung as a part of the Act of Penitence, a trope may precede each acclamation.[11]

In current liturgical law, a trope phrase or sentence may be injected into the *Kyrie* before each petition. For example, "You were sent to heal the contrite of heart," "You came to call sinners," and "You are seated at the right hand of the Father to intercede for us" are tropes that the priest may say before "Lord, have mercy."

On most Sundays, this is followed by the *Gloria* ("Glory to God in the highest, and peace to his people on earth"):

> The *Gloria* is a very ancient and venerable hymn in which the Church, gathered together in the Holy Spirit, glorifies and entreats God the Father and the Lamb. The text of this hymn may not be replaced by any other text. The *Gloria* is intoned by the priest or, if appropriate, by a cantor or by the choir; but it is

---

[11] GIRM 52.

sung either by everyone together, or by the people alternately with the choir, or by the choir alone. If not sung, it is to be recited either by all together or by two parts of the congregation responding one to the other.

It is sung or said on Sundays outside the seasons of Advent and Lent, on solemnities and feasts, and at special celebrations of a more solemn character.[12]

The Collect

The Introductory Rites come to a conclusion with the Collect (formerly called the Opening Prayer):

Next the priest invites the people to pray. All, together with the priest, observe a brief silence so that they may be conscious of the fact that they are in God's presence and may formulate their petitions mentally. Then the priest says the prayer which is customarily known as the Collect and through which the character of the celebration is expressed. In accordance with the ancient tradition of the Church, the collect prayer is usually addressed to God the Father, through Christ, in the Holy Spirit, and is concluded with a trinitarian, that is to say the longer ending. . . .

The people, uniting themselves to this entreaty, make the prayer their own with the acclamation, "Amen."

There is always only one Collect used in a Mass.[13]

With the introductory rites accomplished, the Liturgy of the Word begins.

---

[12] GIRM 53.
[13] GIRM 54.

6. Liturgy of the Word

The *General Instruction* describes the Liturgy of the Word and its parts in this way:

> The main part of the Liturgy of the Word is made up of the readings from Sacred Scripture together with the chants occurring between them. The homily, Profession of Faith, and Prayer of the Faithful, however, develop and conclude this part of the Mass. For in the readings, as explained by the homily, God speaks to his people, opening up to them the mystery of redemption and salvation and offering them spiritual nourishment; and Christ himself is present in the midst of the faithful through his word. By their silence and singing the people make God's word their own, and they also affirm their adherence to it by means of the Profession of Faith. Finally, having been nourished by it, they pour out their petitions in the Prayer of the Faithful for the needs of the entire Church and for the salvation of the whole world.[1]

Scripture Readings

Who May Do the Readings

The *General Instruction of the Roman Missal* states:

> By tradition, the function of proclaiming the readings is ministerial, not presidential. The readings, therefore, should be proclaimed by a lector, and the Gospel by a deacon or, in his ab-

---

[1] GIRM 55.

sence, a priest other than the celebrant. If, however, a deacon or another priest is not present, the priest celebrant himself should read the Gospel. Further, if another suitable lector is also not present, then the priest celebrant should also proclaim the other readings.

The *General Instruction* further discusses the role of the lector and who can substitute for him as follows:

> The lector is instituted to proclaim the readings from Sacred Scripture, with the exception of the Gospel. He may also announce the intentions for the Prayer of the Faithful and, in the absence of a psalmist, proclaim the psalm between the readings.
>
> In the eucharistic celebration, the lector has his own proper office . . . which he must exercise personally.
>
> In the absence of an instituted lector, other lay persons may be commissioned to proclaim the readings from Sacred Scripture. They should be truly suited to perform this function and should receive careful preparation, so that the faithful by listening to the readings from the sacred texts may develop in their hearts a warm and living love for Sacred Scripture.[2]

Concerning the reading of the Gospel, it states:

> The reading of the Gospel is the high point of the Liturgy of the Word. The liturgy itself teaches that great reverence is to be shown to it by setting it off from the other readings with special marks of honor: whether the minister appointed to proclaim it prepares himself by a blessing or prayer; or the faithful, standing as they listen to it being read, through their acclamations acknowledge and confess Christ present and speaking to them; or the very marks of reverence are given to the Book of the Gospels.[3]

---

[2] GIRM 99, 101.
[3] GIRM 60.

Regarding the manner in which the Gospel reading is to be done, the *General Instruction* states:

> At the ambo, the Priest opens the book and, with hands joined, says, *The Lord be with you*, to which the people reply, *And with your spirit*. Then he says, *A reading from the holy Gospel*, making the Sign of the Cross with his thumb on the book and on his forehead, mouth, and breast, which everyone else does as well. The people acclaim, *Glory to you, O Lord*. The Priest incenses the book, if incense is being used (cf. nos. 276–77). Then he proclaims the Gospel and at the end pronounces the acclamation *The Gospel of the Lord*, to which all reply, *Praise to you, Lord Jesus Christ*. The Priest kisses the book, saying quietly the formula *Per evangelica dicta* (*Through the words of the Gospel*).[4]

As a result of frequent violations in some areas of the rule of reserving the Gospel reading to the ordained, *Redemptionis Sacramentum* was especially firm on the Gospel's reading being reserved to a deacon or priest:

> Within the celebration of the sacred liturgy, the reading of the Gospel, which is the high point of the Liturgy of the Word, is reserved by the Church's tradition to an ordained minister. Thus it is not permitted for a lay person, even a religious, to proclaim the Gospel reading in the celebration of Holy Mass, nor in other cases in which the norms do not explicitly permit it.[5]

The only exceptions to this are on two Sundays of the year. On Palm Sunday (Passion Sunday) the Gospel is read as a dialogue with a priest always taking the part of Christ:

> The passion narrative occupies a special place [in the liturgy of Palm Sunday]. It should be sung or read in the traditional way, that is, by three persons who take the parts of Christ, the

---

[4] GIRM 134.

[5] RS 63.

narrator, and the people. The passion is proclaimed by deacons or priests, or by lay readers. In the latter case, the part of Christ should be reserved to the priest. . . . For the spiritual good of the faithful, the passion should be proclaimed in its entirety, and the readings which precede it should not be omitted.[6]

The same is true of the Gospel on Good Friday.[7]

Which Translations May Be Used

Since the Holy See has reserved to itself the approval of translations of Scripture readings used at Mass,[8] only lectionaries approved by the Holy See may be used for the Scripture readings.

At the time of this writing, there is only one English-language lectionary approved for use at normal Masses in the United States. Known as the *Lectionary for Mass*, it is based on the *New American Bible*, with some modifications. Its use has been mandatory since Pentecost of 2002. There is also an approved *Lectionary for Masses with Children*, but it is not used in ordinary Masses for adults.

On March 19, 2010, the Congregation for Divine Worship and the Discipline of the Sacraments approved the *Revised Grail Psalter by the Monks of Conception Abbey* for use in the United States. It became the official psalter for use in all liturgical books in the United States. However, the Bishops' Committee on Divine Worship's newsletter noted:

> While the *New American Bible* translation of the Psalms as contained in the *Lectionary* remains the official translation of the

---

[6] PS 33.

[7] See PS 66.

[8] CIC 838 §§2–3, quoted in Chapter 14 in the section on who can change the liturgy; see also CIC 826 §1.

Responsorial Psalms, the *Revised Grail Psalter* is now considered approved for use within the liturgy, and may be included in seasonal and annual hymnals and participation aids. Composers of liturgical music can use the text of the *Revised Grail Psalter* especially in preparing arrangements of Psalms for the *Lectionary* for use at Mass, even though it will be some time before new editions of affected texts are published.[9]

Because the Holy See has reserved to itself the approval of Scripture texts in lectionary form for Mass, it is not permissible for any individual to revise these texts, such as doing spontaneous gender revisions to the language of texts that one perceives as "sexist." Tampering with the text of the sacred page to fit a modern social-political agenda is a liturgical abuse.

Which Texts May Be Used

The *General Instruction of the Roman Missal* sets out the general guidelines for the number and kind of readings required on Sunday:

> For Sundays and solemnities, three readings are assigned: that is, from a prophet, an apostle, and a Gospel. By these the Christian people are brought to know the continuity of the work of salvation according to the God's wonderful plan. These readings should be followed strictly. During the Easter season, according to the tradition of the Church, instead of the reading from the Old Testament, the reading is taken from the Acts of the Apostles.
>
> For feasts, on the other hand, two readings are assigned. If, however, according to the norms a feast is raised to the rank of a solemnity, a third reading is added, taken from the Common.
>
> For memorials of saints, unless strictly proper readings are given, the readings assigned for the weekday are customarily

---

[9] BCDW *Newsletter*, April, 2010, 13.

used. In certain cases, readings are provided that highlight some particular aspect of the spiritual life or activity of the saint. The use of such readings is not to be insisted upon, unless a pastoral reason suggests it.[10]

The *General Instruction* also deals with the kind of readings used at daily Masses during the week:

> In the *Lectionary* for weekdays, readings are provided for each day of every week throughout the entire year; as a result, these readings are for the most part to be used on the days to which they are assigned, unless there occurs a solemnity, feast, or memorial that has its own proper New Testament readings, that is to say, readings in which mention is made of the saint being celebrated.
>
> If, however, the continuous reading during the week is interrupted by the occurrence of some solemnity or feast, or some particular celebration, then the priest, taking into consideration the entire week's scheme of readings, is allowed either to combine parts omitted with other readings or to decide which readings are to be preferred over others.
>
> In Masses with special groups, the priest is allowed to choose texts more suited to the particular celebration, provided they are taken from the texts of an approved *Lectionary*.[11]

Though a set program of readings is normally required, there are exceptions to this rule:

> In Masses with special groups, the priest may choose texts more suited to the particular celebration, provided they are taken from the texts of an approved *Lectionary*.[12]

Under no circumstances, however, can non-biblical readings be used:

---

[10] GIRM 357.
[11] GIRM 358.
[12] Ibid.

Moreover, it is unlawful to substitute other, non-biblical texts for the readings and Responsorial Psalm, which contain the word of God.[13]

Chants between the Readings

In addition to the reading of Scripture, chanting and singing have been important parts of Christian liturgy throughout history. They are today as well, especially with the psalms, which were originally sung in the Jewish liturgy before the time of Christ.

The *General Instruction* states:

> After the first reading comes the Responsorial Psalm, which is an integral part of the Liturgy of the Word and holds great liturgical and pastoral importance, because it fosters meditation on the word of God.
>
> The Responsorial Psalm should correspond to each reading and should, as a rule, be taken from the *Lectionary*.
>
> It is preferable that the Responsorial Psalm be sung, at least as far as the people's response is concerned. Hence, the psalmist, or the cantor of the psalm, sings the verses of the psalm from the ambo or another suitable place. The entire congregation remains seated and listens but, as a rule, takes part by singing the response, except when the psalm is sung straight through without a response. In order, however, that the people may be able to sing the psalm response more readily, texts of some responses and psalms have been chosen for the various seasons of the year or for the various categories of saints. These may be used in place of the text corresponding to the reading whenever the psalm is sung. If the psalm cannot be sung, then it should be recited in such a way that it is particularly suited to fostering meditation on the Word of God.

---

[13] GIRM 57.

In the dioceses of the United States of America, the following may also be sung in place of the psalm assigned in the *Lectionary for Mass*: either the proper or seasonal antiphon and psalm from the lectionary, as found either in the Roman Gradual or Simple Gradual or in another musical setting; or an antiphon and psalm from another collection of the psalms and antiphons, including psalms arranged in metrical form, providing that they have been approved by the United States Conference of Catholic Bishops or the diocesan Bishop. Songs or hymns may not be used in place of the Responsorial Psalm.[14]

Note the explicit prohibition on using songs or hymns in place of the Responsorial Psalm. The fact that the musicians or choir don't know a musical setting for an approved form does not allow such a substitution. A non-musical recitation of the psalm would be the logical course of action in that case, since singing the psalm is only a preference, not a requirement.

In most seasons of the liturgical year, an *Alleluia* is sung prior to the reading of the Gospel:

After the reading that immediately precedes the Gospel, the *Alleluia* or another chant indicated by the rubrics is sung, as required by the liturgical season. An acclamation of this kind constitutes a rite or act in itself, by which the assembly of the faithful welcomes and greets the Lord who is about to speak to them in the Gospel and professes their faith by means of the chant. It is sung by all while standing and is led by the choir or a cantor, being repeated if this is appropriate. The verse, however, is sung either by the choir or by the cantor.

a. The *Alleluia* is sung in every season other than Lent. The verses are taken from the *Lectionary* or the *Graduale*.

b. During Lent, in place of the *Alleluia*, the verse before the

---

[14] GIRM 61.

Gospel is sung, as indicated in the *Lectionary*. It is also permissible to sing another psalm or tract, as found in the *Graduale*.[15]

The above applies when there are two readings before the Gospel (as typical on Sundays and solemnities),[16] but when there is only one reading before the Gospel (as on normal weekdays), there are additional options:

When there is only one reading before the Gospel:

a. During a season when the *Alleluia* is to be said, either the *Alleluia* Psalm or the Responsorial Psalm followed by the *Alleluia* with its verse may be used;

b. During the season when the *Alleluia* is not to be said, either the psalm and the verse before the Gospel or the psalm alone may be used;

c. The *Alleluia* or verse before the Gospel may be omitted if they are not sung.[17]

Homily

The *General Instruction* states:

The homily is part of the liturgy and is strongly recommended, for it is necessary for the nurturing of the Christian life. It should be an exposition of some aspect of the readings from Sacred Scripture or of another text from the Ordinary or from the Proper of the Mass of the day and should take into account both the mystery being celebrated and the particular needs of the listeners.[18]

Inaestimabile Donum clarifies the homily's purpose:

---

[15] GIRM 62.
[16] The Responsorial Psalm does not count as a reading.
[17] GIRM 63.
[18] GIRM 65.

The purpose of the homily is to explain to the faithful the Word of God proclaimed in the readings and to apply its message to the present. Accordingly the homily is to be given by the priest or the deacon.[19]

Redemptionis Sacramentum also clarifies the purpose of the homily, as well as giving cautions regarding what is to be avoided in it:

Particular care is to be taken so that the homily is firmly based upon the mysteries of salvation, expounding the mysteries of the faith and the norms of Christian life from the biblical readings and liturgical texts throughout the course of the liturgical year and providing commentary on the texts of the Ordinary or the Proper of the Mass, or of some other rite of the Church. It is clear that all interpretations of Sacred Scripture are to be referred back to Christ himself as the one upon whom the entire economy of salvation hinges, though this should be done in light of the specific context of the liturgical celebration. In the homily to be given, care is to be taken so that the light of Christ may shine upon life's events. Even so, this is to be done so as not to obscure the true and unadulterated word of God: for instance, treating only of politics or profane subjects, or drawing upon notions derived from contemporary pseudoreligious currents as a source.[20]

Who May Give the Homily?

The *General Instruction* specifies that the homily at Mass is to be given only by a member of the clergy:

The Homily should ordinarily be given by the priest celebrant himself. He may entrust it to a concelebrating priest or occasionally, according to circumstances, to the deacon, but never to

---

[19] ID 3.
[20] RS 67.

a lay person. In particular cases and for a just cause, the homily may even be given by a bishop or a priest who is present at the celebration but cannot concelebrate.[21]

This requirement is also stressed in the *Code of Canon Law:*

§1. Among the forms of preaching, the homily, which is part of the liturgy itself and is reserved to a priest or deacon, is pre-eminent; in the homily the mysteries of faith and the norms of Christian life are to be explained from the sacred text during the course of the liturgical year [CIC 767].

In some areas there has been a problem with laity, including nuns, giving homilies—in part because the Holy See had previously allowed this on an experimental basis.[22] To make it clear that this is no longer permitted, *Redemptionis Sacramentum* stresses:

It should be borne in mind that any previous norm that may have admitted non-ordained faithful to give the homily during the eucharistic celebration is to be considered abrogated by the norm of canon 767 §1. This practice is reprobated, so that it cannot be permitted to attain the force of custom.[23]

---

[21] GIRM 66.

[22] See DOL 2953–63, which records a letter of November 20, 1973, from the Sacred Congregation for Clergy, in response to a request from the German Conference of Bishops, authorizing lay persons to give homilies in some circumstances.

[23] RS 65. The statement that the custom of lay persons giving homilies at Mass cannot attain the force of custom is intended to head off a particular argument to allow it. The *Code of Canon Law* makes provision for practices not provided for in the law to become lawful or even obligatory in certain circumstances (see canons 23–28). This is not possible, however, when the practice has been specifically reprobated (rejected) in the law itself (canon 24 §2). *Redemptionis Sacramentum* here points out that lay preaching of homilies has been so rejected and thus one cannot use an argument based on custom to allow it to continue.

The document goes on to anticipate potential "exceptions" that might be wrongly introduced:

> The prohibition of the admission of lay persons to preach within the Mass applies also to seminarians, students of theological disciplines, and those who have assumed the function of those known as "pastoral assistants"; nor is there to be any exception for any other kind of lay person, or group, or community, or association.[24]

There are limited cases in which a lay person can preach in a church or oratory,[25] but they may not preach the homily during Mass. The Holy See confirmed this in an authentic interpretation of canon 767:

> *Dubium*: Whether the diocesan bishop is able to dispense from the prescription of canon 767 §1, by which the homily is reserved to priests and deacons.
>
> *Responsum*: Negative.[26]

Ecclesia de Mysterio similarly stresses this point while also explaining the reason for it in more detail than other documents do:

> The homily, therefore, during the celebration of the Holy Eucharist, must be reserved to the sacred minister-priest or deacon —to the exclusion of the non-ordained faithful, even if these should have responsibilities as "pastoral assistants" or catechists in whatever type of community or group. This exclusion is not based on the preaching ability of sacred ministers nor their theological preparation, but on that function which is reserved to them in virtue of having received the sacrament of holy orders. For the same reason the diocesan Bishop cannot validly

---

[24] RS 66.

[25] CIC 766.

[26] AAS 79 (1987), 1249; see also DOL 1768.

dispense from the canonical norm. . . . For the same reason, the practice, on some occasions, of entrusting the preaching of the homily to seminarians or theology students who are not clerics is not permitted. Indeed, the homily should not be regarded as a training for some future ministry. . . .

In no instance may the homily be entrusted to priests or deacons who have lost the clerical state or who have abandoned the sacred ministry.[27]

The instruction also clarifies the non-homiletic role the laity can play during the Mass:

A form of instruction designed to promote a greater understanding of the liturgy, including personal testimonies, or the celebration of eucharistic liturgies on special occasions (e.g., day of the seminary, day of the sick, etc.) is lawful, if in harmony with liturgical norms, [and] should such be considered objectively opportune as a means of explicating the regular homily preached by the celebrant priest. Nonetheless, these testimonies or explanations may not be such so as to assume a character which could be confused with the homily.

As an expositional aide and providing it does not delegate the duty of preaching to others, the celebrant minister may make prudent use of "dialogue" in the homily, in accord with the liturgical norms.[28]

Despite this, the instruction alludes to circumstances in which the laity are able to preach homilies in non-eucharistic liturgies (i.e., liturgies that are not Masses or Communion services) under strict conditions:

Homilies in non-eucharistic liturgies may be preached by the non-ordained faithful only when expressly permitted by law and when its prescriptions for doing so are observed.[29]

---

[27] EM, Practical Provisions 3 § 1, 5.
[28] Ibid., 3 §§ 2, 3.
[29] Ibid. 3 § 4.

Redemptionis Sacramentum also notes:

If the need arises for the gathered faithful to be given instruction or testimony by a lay person in a church concerning the Christian life, it is altogether preferable that this be done outside Mass. Nevertheless, for serious reasons it is permissible that this type of instruction or testimony be given after the priest has proclaimed the prayer after Communion. This should not become a regular practice, however. Furthermore, these instructions and testimony should not be of such a nature that they could be confused with the homily, nor is it permissible to dispense with the homily on their account.[30]

And:

As regards other forms of preaching, if necessity demands it in particular circumstances, or if usefulness suggests it in special cases, lay members of Christ's faithful may be allowed to preach in a church or in an oratory outside Mass in accordance with the norm of law. This may be done only on account of a scarcity of sacred ministers in certain places, in order to meet the need, and it may not be transformed from an exceptional measure into an ordinary practice, nor may it be understood as an authentic form of the advancement of the laity. All must remember besides that the faculty for giving such permission belongs to the local Ordinary, and this as regards individual instances; this permission is not the competence of anyone else, even if they are priests or deacons.[31]

---

[30] RS 74.
[31] RS 161. Note that preaching is distinct from Bible study, religious education, catechetics, apologetics, etc.

When Are Homilies to Be Given?

Homilies are normally required on Sundays and holy days of obligation. They are also recommended but not required on other days. The *Code of Canon Law* states:

§2. A homily must be given at all Masses on Sundays and holy days of obligation which are celebrated with a congregation, and it cannot be omitted except for a grave cause.

§3. It is strongly recommended that if there is a sufficient congregation, a homily is to be given even at Masses celebrated during the week, especially during the time of Advent and Lent or on the occasion of some feast day or a sorrowful event.

§4. It is for the pastor or rector of a church to take care that these prescripts are observed conscientiously [CIC 767].

Place of the Homily

Concerning the location from which the homily is to be given, the *General Instruction* states:

The priest, standing at the chair or at the ambo itself or, when appropriate, in another suitable place, gives the homily. When the homily is completed, a period of silence may be observed.[32]

In Jesus' day, the customary position from which to teach was sitting (see John 8:2), but today the practice is to stand. The homily is normally given standing at the ambo, though the celebrant's chair is also expressly mentioned. Under the previous edition of the *General Instruction*, these were the only two places that were permitted, but the law has now changed so that the homily also can be given "when appropriate, in an-

---

[32] GIRM 136.

other suitable place." This basically allows the priest to give the homily anywhere he wants since, unless expressly contradicted by a higher authority (an unlikely event), he is the judge of when it is appropriate to give the homily in another place and of what other places are suitable. Hopefully this new liberty will not lead to priests walking up and down the aisle of the nave while giving the homily. This practice is distracting and irritating, and the people in the front rows may have trouble hearing the priest and be forced to turn around to look at him while he speaks.

Profession of Faith

After the homily, all profess their faith in God and the chief truths of Christianity by reciting the Profession of Faith:

> The purpose of the *Symbolum* or Profession of Faith, or Creed, is that the whole gathered people may respond to the word of God proclaimed in the readings taken from Sacred Scripture and explained in the homily and that they may also call to mind and confess the great mysteries of the faith by reciting the rule of faith in a formula approved for liturgical use, before these mysteries are celebrated in the Eucharist.[33]

Without special permission, it is not permitted for a pastor to omit the recitation of the creed on Sundays and solemnities:

> The Creed is to be sung or said by the priest together with the people on Sundays and Solemnities. It may be said also at particular celebrations of a more solemn character.
> If it is sung, it is begun by the priest or, if this is appropriate, by a cantor or by the choir. It is sung, however, either by all together or by the people alternating with the choir.

---

[33] GIRM 67.

If not sung, it is to be recited by all together or by two parts of the assembly responding one to the other.[34]

The creed that is most commonly used is the Nicene Creed (i.e., the Niceno-Constantinopolitan Creed), but in a notable change of law, the Apostles' Creed is now an option. Previously the Apostles' Creed was used only in special circumstances, such as Masses with children or Masses in which a baptism occurs. Now, however, the rubrics allow it to be used at the celebrant's discretion:

> Instead of the Niceno-Constantinopolitan Creed, especially during Lent and Easter time, the baptismal symbol [i.e., creed] of the Roman Church, known as the Apostles' Creed, may be used.

During the recitation of the Nicene Creed, all make the appropriate sign of reverence at the mention of our Lord's Incarnation:

> The Creed is sung or recited by the priest together with the people . . . with everyone standing. At the words *et incarnatus est* ("by the power of the Holy Spirit . . . became man") all make a profound bow; but on the Solemnities of the Annunciation and of the Nativity of the Lord, all genuflect.[35]

According to the rubrics, when the Nicene Creed is said or sung:

> *At the words that follow up to and including* and became man, *all bow:*
>
> And by the Holy Spirit was incarnate
> Of the Virgin Mary
> And became man.

When the Apostles' Creed is said or sung, the rubrics state:

---

[34] GIRM 68.
[35] GIRM 137.

At the words that follow, up to and including "the Virgin Mary," all bow:

> Who was conceived by the Holy Spirit
> Born of the Virgin Mary

Since the Holy See has reserved approval of all liturgical texts to itself,[36] it is not permissible to use alternative creeds, altered versions of the creeds, or unapproved translations of the creeds during Mass.[37] For example, it is not permissible to delete the word *men* from "for us men and for our salvation."

Prayer of the Faithful

The final stage of the Liturgy of the Word is the Prayer of the Faithful, also called the "universal prayer" or "bidding prayers" (and formerly called the "general intercessions"). The *General Instruction of the Roman Missal* explains the purpose of the Prayer of the Faithful:

> In the Prayer of the Faithful, the people respond in a certain way to the word of God which they have welcomed in faith and, exercising the office of their baptismal priesthood, offer prayers to God for the salvation of all. It is fitting that such a prayer be included, as a rule, in Masses celebrated with a congregation, so that petitions will be offered for the holy Church, for civil authorities, for those weighed down by various needs, for all men and women, and for the salvation of the whole world.[38]

The priestly function of the faithful is an exercise of the common or universal priesthood shared by all the baptized. St. Peter refers to this priesthood when he tells his readers: "Let

---

[36] CIC 838 §2, 846 §1.
[37] RS 69.
[38] GIRM 69.

yourselves be built into a spiritual house to be a holy priesthood to offer spiritual sacrifices acceptable to God through Jesus Christ. . . . [Y]ou are a chosen race, a royal priesthood, a holy nation" (1 Pet. 2:5b, 9). This priesthood is referred to elsewhere in Scripture (see also Rev. 1:6; cf. Rev. 5:9–10). It is distinct from the ministerial priesthood exercised by the ordained, and it does suffice for one to perform the eucharistic sacrifice. The *Catechism of the Catholic Church* states:

> The ministerial priesthood differs in essence from the common priesthood of the faithful because it confers a sacred power for the service of the faithful. The ordained ministers exercise their service for the people of God by teaching (*munus docendi*), divine worship (*munus liturgicum*), and pastoral governance (*munus regendi*).[39]

However, the universal priesthood of the faithful is sufficient for them to intercede with God in prayer, as expressed in the Prayer of the Faithful in Mass. In most cases there is to be a specific order for the intentions:

> As a rule, the series of intentions is to be:
>
> a. For the needs of the Church.
> b. For public authorities and the salvation of the whole world.
> c. For those burdened by any kind of difficulty.
> d. For the local community.
>
> Nevertheless, in a particular celebration, such as confirmation, marriage, or a funeral, the series of intentions may reflect more closely the particular occasion.[40]

Even in the exercise of the priesthood of the faithful in prayer, the laity are presided over by a ministerial priest, and it is preferred that a deacon announce the intentions:

---

[39] CCC 1592.
[40] GIRM 70.

It is for the priest celebrant to direct this prayer from the chair. He himself begins it with a brief introduction, by which he invites the faithful to pray, and likewise he concludes it with a prayer. The intentions announced should be sober, be composed freely but prudently, and be succinct, and they should express the prayer of the entire community.

The intentions are announced from the ambo or from another suitable place, by the deacon or by a cantor, a lector, or one of the lay faithful.

The people, however, stand and give expression to their prayer either by an invocation said together after each intention or by praying in silence.[41]

Note that the intentions are announced either from the ambo or "another suitable place" (that is, basically anywhere at the celebrant's discretion). Normally they are announced by the deacon if one is present:

After the introduction by the priest it is the deacon himself who normally announces the intentions of the Prayer of the Faithful, from the ambo.[42]

The Prayer of the Faithful concludes the Liturgy of the Word, and following it the Liturgy of the Eucharist begins.

---

[41] GIRM 71.
[42] GIRM 177.

7. Preparation of the Altar and the Gifts

The Liturgy of the Eucharist now begins. This part of the liturgy was directly instituted by Christ:

> At the Last Supper Christ instituted the paschal sacrifice and banquet by which the sacrifice of the cross is continuously made present in the Church whenever the priest, representing Christ the Lord, carries out what the Lord himself did and handed over to his disciples to be done in his memory.

> For Christ took the bread and the chalice and gave thanks; he broke the bread and gave it to his disciples, saying, "Take, eat, and drink: this is my Body; this is the cup of my blood. Do this in memory of me." Accordingly, the Church has arranged the entire celebration of the Liturgy of the Eucharist in parts corresponding to precisely these words and actions of Christ:

> 1. At the Preparation of the Gifts, the bread and the wine with water are brought to the altar, the same elements that Christ took into his hands.

> 2. In the Eucharistic Prayer, thanks is given to God for the whole work of salvation, and the offerings become the body and blood of Christ.

> 3. Through the Fraction and through Communion, the faithful, though they are many, receive from the one bread the Lord's body and from the one chalice the Lord's blood in the same way the apostles received them from Christ's own hands.[1]

The role of the deacon in preparing the altar and gifts is described as follows:

---

[1] GIRM 72.

After the Prayer of the Faithful, while the priest remains at the chair, the deacon prepares the altar, assisted by the acolyte, but it is the deacon's place to take care of the sacred vessels himself. He also assists the priest in receiving the people's gifts. Next, he hands the priest the paten with the bread to be consecrated, pours wine and a little water into the chalice, saying quietly, *Per huius aquae* ("By the mystery of this water"), and after this presents the chalice to the priest. He may also carry out the preparation of the chalice at the credence table. If incense is used, the deacon assists the priest during the incensation of the gifts, the cross, and the altar; afterwards, the deacon himself or the acolyte incenses the priest and the people.[2]

Preparation of the Altar

The Liturgy of the Eucharist typically begins with the Offertory chant, which is often a hymn, during which the articles needed for the celebration of the Eucharist are bought to the altar:

> When the Prayer of the Faithful is completed, all sit, and the Offertory chant begins. . . .
>
> An acolyte or other lay minister arranges the corporal, the purificator, the chalice, the pall, and the *Missal* upon the altar.[3]

The corporal is a square piece of linen. The chalice, paten, and host are placed on it during this part of the Mass. The purificator is a linen cloth used to dry the sacred vessels at the end of or after Mass, that is, when they are purified. The pall is a stiffened square of linen that is used to cover the chalice. The chalice is the vessel used to hold the wine that is consecrated to become the precious blood, while a *Missal*, formerly

---

[2] GIRM 178.
[3] GIRM 139.

called a *Sacramentary*, is the book from which the priest reads the prayers of the Mass.

The *General Instruction* notes that there is an exception to placing the chalice on the altar:

> At the beginning of the Liturgy of the Eucharist the gifts, which will become Christ's body and blood, are brought to the altar.
>
> First, the altar, the Lord's table, which is the center of the whole Liturgy of the Eucharist, is prepared by placing on it the corporal, purificator, *Missal*, and chalice (unless the chalice is prepared at the credence table).[4]

Thus it is not an abuse to prepare the chalice on a side table rather than on the altar.

Presentation of the Elements and Offerings

Also at this time, the elements—the bread and wine that will be consecrated—are presented:

> The offerings are then brought forward. It is praiseworthy for the bread and wine to be presented by the faithful. They are then accepted at an appropriate place by the priest or the deacon and carried to the altar. Even though the faithful no longer bring from their own possessions the bread and wine intended for the liturgy as in the past, nevertheless the rite of carrying up the offerings still retains its force and its spiritual significance.[5]

As before, the reference to "an appropriate place" means that the elements may be received anywhere, at the discretion of the celebrant.

For information on the kind of hosts and wine that are to be used, see Chapter 3.

---

[4] GIRM 73.
[5] GIRM 73.

At the same time that the elements to be consecrated are brought forward, it is also typical to receive other offerings. These are usually from a collection that has just been taken up:

It is well also that money or other gifts for the poor or for the Church, brought by the faithful or collected in the church, should be received. These are to be put in a suitable place but away from the eucharistic table.[6]

Note that the altar is not an acceptable location for the faithful's monetary offerings to be placed. It is not proper for a priest or minister to put a collection basket on or under the altar.

All of this activity occurs during the Offertory chant, which does not end until the gifts have been received and the elements placed on the altar:

The procession bringing the gifts is accompanied by the Offertory chant . . . which continues at least until the gifts have been placed on the altar. The norms on the manner of singing are the same as for the Entrance chant. . . . Singing may always accompany the rite at the Offertory, even when there is no procession with the gifts.[7]

Preparation of the Elements

Once the elements to be consecrated have been received, they may be incensed:

The bread and wine are placed on the altar by the priest to the accompaniment of the prescribed formulas. The priest may incense the gifts placed upon the altar and then incense the cross and the altar itself, so as to signify the Church's offering and

---

[6] GIRM 73.
[7] GIRM 74.

prayer rising like incense in the sight of God. Next, the priest, because of his sacred ministry, and the people, by reason of their baptismal dignity, may be incensed by the deacon or another minister.[8]

Even after the gifts are received, there are rites to be performed over the elements.

At the altar the priest accepts the paten with the bread. With both hands he holds it slightly raised above the altar and says quietly, *Benedictus es, Domine* ("Blessed are you, Lord"). Then he places the paten with the bread on the corporal.[9]

The rubrics in the *Roman Missal* reveal what the priest does at this point:

The priest, standing at the altar, takes the paten with the bread and, holding it slightly raised above the altar with both hands, saying in a low voice:

Blessed are you, Lord God of all creation,
for through your goodness we have received
the bread we offer you:
fruit of the earth and work of human hands,
it will become for us the bread of life.

Then he places the paten with the bread on the corporal.

If, however, the Offertory chant is not sung, the priest may speak these words aloud; at the end, the people may acclaim:

Blessed be God for ever.

There is significant flexibility in the above. If there is an Offertory chant being sung, the priest is supposed to say the prayer in a low voice (that is, quietly). However, if no song is sung, then he has the *option* of saying them aloud ("*may* speak

---

[8] GIRM 75.
[9] GIRM 141.

these words aloud"), in which case the people have the *option* of responding "Blessed be God for ever" ("the people *may* acclaim"). Thus it is not a liturgical abuse for the priest to say the words inaudibly even if there is no singing, nor is it an abuse for the people not to respond. If the priest is not saying the words in an audible voice, the people do not need to strain to hear when he finishes so that they can respond. In fact, the rubrics do not suggest that they respond if he says the prayer inaudibly.

The preparation of the chalice proceeds similarly to the preparation of the bread:

> After this, as the minister presents the cruets, the priest stands at the side of the altar and pours wine and a little water into the chalice, saying quietly, *Per huius aquae* ("By the mystery of this water"). He returns to the middle of the altar, takes the chalice with both hands, raises it a little, and says quietly, *Benedictus es, Domine* ("Blessed are you, Lord"). Then he places the chalice on the corporal and covers it with a pall, as appropriate.
>
> If, however, there is no Offertory chant and the organ is not played, in the presentation of the bread and wine the priest may say the formulas of blessing aloud, to which the people make the acclamation, *Benedictus Deus in saecula* ("Blessed be God for ever").[10]

Again, the rubrics provide more detail:

> *The deacon, or the priest, pours wine and a little water into the chalice, saying quietly:*
>
>> By the mystery of this water and wine
>> may we come to share in the divinity of Christ
>> who humbled himself to share in our humanity.

Concerning the amount of water to be mixed with the wine, the late sacramental theologian Fr. Nicholas Halligan wrote:

---

[10] GIRM 142.

It is a serious precept which requires that a very small portion of water be mixed with the wine when about to be used in the Holy Sacrifice. This is not necessary by reason of the sacrament but by ecclesiastical precept in order to signify that both water and blood issued from the side of the crucified Savior [John 19:34]. . . . The quantity to be added is usually three to ten drops. Priests should avoid too great concern over the exact number of drops. Even a single drop, so long as it is sensible, satisfies the precept; even one-fifth water (or one-fourth if the wine is stronger) is not unlawful, although an excess of one-third the amount of wine renders the latter invalid or truly doubtful. If the quantity of water added appears to be more than lawful, the minister should add more wine or take fresh wine and add the correct amount of water.[11]

Then the priest prays over the chalice. According to the rubrics:

The priest then takes the chalice, and holds it slightly raised above the altar with both hands, saying in a low voice:

Blessed are you, Lord God of all creation,
for through your goodness we have received
the wine we offer you:
fruit of the vine and work of human hands,
it will become our spiritual drink.

Then he places the chalice on the corporal.

If, however, the Offertory chant is not sung, the priest may speak these words aloud; at the end, the people may acclaim:

Blessed be God for ever.

This has the same flexibility concerning whether it is said audibly or inaudibly and whether the people respond as does the corresponding prayer over the bread. Also, like the corre-

---

[11] Halligan, *The Sacraments and Their Celebration*, 67.

sponding prayer, there is no set height to which the priest is supposed to elevate the chalice (or in the case of the preceding prayer, the paten). He is merely directed to raise it slightly above the corporal.

One way in which the prayers over the bread and the wine are not flexible concerns a practice reported in some areas of a priest holding *both* the paten and the chalice above the corporal and fusing the two prayers together, along these lines:

> Blessed are you, Lord, God of all creation. Through your goodness we have this bread and wine to offer . . .

This is contrary to the rubrics, which require that the prayers over the bread and wine be said separately. The rubrics also require that the priest hold the paten with both hands and the chalice with both hands, not one in each hand. Finally, this practice requires the priest to ad lib as he fuses the two prayers. None of this is allowed.

The rubrics then state:

> *After this, the priest, bowing profoundly, says quietly:*
>
> With humble spirit and contrite heart
> May we be accepted by you, O Lord,
> And may our sacrifice in your sight this day
> Be pleasing to you, Lord God.
>
> *If appropriate, he also incenses the offerings, the cross, and the altar. A deacon or other minister then incenses the priest and the people.*

Lavabo *or Rite of Hand Washing*

Afterward comes a rite known as the *lavabo:*

> The priest then washes his hands at the side of the altar, a rite that is an expression of his desire for interior purification.[12]

---

[12] GIRM 76.

He typically washes his hands while a minister pours water over them:

> After the prayer *In spiritu humilitatis* ("Lord God, we ask you to receive us") or after the incensation, the priest washes his hands standing at the side of the altar and, as the minister pours the water, says quietly, *Lava me, Domine* ("Lord, wash away my iniquity").[13]

The *Roman Missal* indicates that the prescribed prayer at this point is:

> Wash me, O Lord, from my iniquity
> And cleanse me from my sin.

The apparent discrepancy between the translations of this prayer offered by the *General Instruction* and the *Roman Missal* ("Lord, wash away my iniquity" versus "Wash me, O Lord, from my iniquity") results from the fact that the *General Instruction* was translated and released several years before the full translation of the *Roman Missal* was produced. The translation in the *Roman Missal* is to be used.

The Holy See has called particular attention to the fact that the *lavabo* is not optional for the priest:

> *Dubium*: May the rite of washing the hands be omitted from the celebration of Mass?
>
> *Responsum*: In no way.
>
> Both the GIRM (nos. 52, 106, 222) and the Order of Mass (with a congregation, no. 24; without a congregation, no. 18) show the *lavabo* to be one of the prescribed rites in the preparation of the gifts. A rite of major importance is clearly not at issue, but it is not to be dropped since its meaning is: "an expression of the (priest's) desire to be cleansed within" (GIRM 52).

---

[13] GIRM 145.

In the course of the Concilium's work on the Order of Mass, there were a number of debates on the value and the place to be assigned to the *lavabo*, e.g., whether it should be a rite in silence or have an accompanying text. There was, however, unanimity that it must be retained. Even though there has been no practical reason for the act of hand washing since the beginning of the Middle Ages, its symbolism is obvious and understood by all (see SC 34). The rite is used in all liturgies of the West.

The Constitution on the Liturgy (SC 37–40) envisions ritual adaptations to be suggested by the conferences of bishops and submitted to the Holy See. Such adaptations must be based on serious reasons—for example, the specific culture and viewpoint of a people, contrary and unchangeable usages, the practical impossibility of adapting a new rite that is foreign to the genius of a people, and so on.

Apart from the envisioned exemptions from rubrics and differing translations of texts (see *Concilium, Instr.* 25 January 1969), the Order of Mass is presented as a single unit whose general structure and individual components must be exactly respected. Arbitrary selectiveness on the part of an individual or a community would soon result in the ruin of a patiently and thoughtfully constructed work.[14]

Final Prayer over the Gifts

Following the *lavabo*, the priest directs the people to pray. The rubrics of the Mass state:

Standing at the middle of the altar, facing the people, extending and then joining his hands, he says:

Pray, brethren (brothers and sisters),
That my sacrifice and yours

---

[14] *Notitiae* 6 (1970) 38–39, no. 27; DOL 1442 n. R12.

May be acceptable to God,
The almighty Father.

The people rise and reply:

May the Lord accept the sacrifice at your hands
For the praise and glory of his name,
For our good
And the good of all his holy Church.

There is something interesting to note here, because the release of the full *Roman Missal* clarifies something from the *General Instruction* that proved to be misleading in practice. According to the *General Instruction*:

> The faithful should stand . . . from the invitation, *Orate, fratres* ("Pray, brethren"), before the prayer over the offerings until the end of Mass, except at the places indicated below.[15]

When the *General Introduction* was first released, people read this passage and assumed it meant that the congregation was to stand from the beginning of the invitation "Pray, brethren." Instead, as the rubrics of the *Roman Missal* (quoted above) make clear, they are to stand at the end of this invitation to pray. It is only after the priest has said "the almighty Father" that the people "rise and reply."

This sequence is also indicated later in the *General Instruction* itself:

> Upon returning to the middle of the altar, the priest, facing the people and extending and then joining his hands, invites the people to pray, saying, *Orate, fratres* ("Pray, brethren"). The people rise and make their response: *Suscipiat Dominus* ("May the Lord accept"). Then the priest, with hands extended, says

---

[15] GIRM 43.

the prayer over the offerings. At the end the people make the acclamation, "Amen."[16]

However, this passage was overlooked as people focused on the previous passage. Because the first passage is found in the section of the *General Instruction* dealing specifically with posture, it is understandable that people would focus on that one and miss the implication of the later one. Nevertheless, it caused substantial discomfort as the faithful tried to guess when the priest was about to start the invitation so they could stand immediately beforehand.

The priest then makes the prayer over the offerings, which concludes the preparation of the gifts:

> Once the offerings have been placed on the altar and the accompanying rites completed, the invitation to pray with the priest and the Prayer over the Offerings conclude the preparation of the gifts and prepare for the Eucharistic Prayer.
>
> In the Mass, only one Prayer over the Offerings is said, and it ends with the shorter conclusion: *Per Christum Dominum nostrum* ["Through Christ Our Lord"]. If, however, the Son is mentioned at the end of this prayer, the conclusion is, *Qui vivit et regnat in saecula saeculorum* ["Who lives and reigns forever and ever"].
>
> The people, uniting themselves to this entreaty, make the prayer their own with the acclamation, "Amen."[17]

---

[16] GIRM 146.
[17] GIRM 77.

8. Eucharistic Prayer

The focus of the Liturgy of the Eucharist, of course, is the Eucharist itself, in which Christ becomes really present under the appearances of bread and wine—a miracle that the Church refers to as transubstantiation. The *General Instruction of the Roman Missal* states:

> [T]he wondrous mystery of the Lord's Real Presence under the eucharistic species, reaffirmed by the Second Vatican Council and other documents of the Church's magisterium in the same sense and with the same words that the Council of Trent had proposed as a matter of faith, is proclaimed in the celebration of Mass not only by means of the very words of Consecration, by which Christ becomes present through transubstantiation, but also by that interior disposition and outward expression of supreme reverence and adoration in which the eucharistic liturgy is carried out.[1]

Transubstantiation and the eucharistic sacrifice are the reasons why the Mass is so important in the Christian life. This is stressed by the *Code of Canon Law:*

> The most august sacrament is the Most Holy Eucharist in which Christ the Lord himself is contained, offered, and received and by which the Church continually lives and grows. The eucharistic sacrifice, the memorial of the death and resurrection of the Lord, in which the sacrifice of the cross is perpetuated through the ages, is the summit and source of all worship and Christian life, which signifies and effects the unity of the people of God

---

[1] GIRM 3.

and brings about the building up of the body of Christ. Indeed, the other sacraments and all the ecclesiastical works of the apostolate are closely connected with the Most Holy Eucharist and ordered to it [CIC 897].

The Christian faithful are to hold the Most Holy Eucharist in highest honor, taking an active part in the celebration of the most august sacrifice, receiving this sacrament most devoutly and frequently, and worshipping it with the highest adoration. In explaining the doctrine about this sacrament, pastors of souls are to teach the faithful diligently about this obligation [CIC 898].

The transubstantiation of the elements and the eucharistic sacrifice are accomplished in the Eucharistic Prayer, which makes it the central point of the liturgy. The *General Instruction* states:

> Now the center and summit of the entire celebration begins: namely, the Eucharistic Prayer, that is, the prayer of thanksgiving and sanctification.[2]

Because of its importance, the Eucharistic Prayer must be recited with great care and only by those authorized to conduct it.

Who May Say the Eucharistic Prayer

The Eucharistic Prayer is reserved to the priest:

> It is reserved to the priest, by virtue of his ordination, to proclaim the Eucharistic Prayer, which of its nature is the high point of the whole celebration. It is therefore an abuse to have some parts of the Eucharistic Prayer said by the deacon, by a lower minister, or by the faithful.[3]

---

[2] GIRM 78.
[3] ID 4.

This does not mean that the faithful are merely spectators during the Eucharistic Prayer:

> On the other hand the assembly does not remain passive and inert; it unites itself to the priest in faith and silence and shows its concurrence by the various interventions provided for in the course of the Eucharistic Prayer: the responses to the Preface dialogue, the *Sanctus* ["Holy, Holy, Holy"], the acclamation after the Consecration [the Mystery of Faith], and the final Amen after the *Per Ipsum*. The *Per Ipsum* itself ["Through him, and with him, and in him"] is reserved to the priest. This Amen especially should be emphasized by being sung, since it is the most important in the whole Mass.[4]

The *General Instruction* also specifies the appropriate role of the faithful during the Eucharistic Prayer:

> The priest invites the people to lift up their hearts to the Lord in prayer and thanksgiving; he unites the congregation with himself in the prayer that he addresses in the name of the entire community to God the Father through Jesus Christ in the Holy Spirit. Furthermore, the meaning of the prayer is that the entire congregation of the faithful should join itself with Christ in confessing the great deeds of God and in the offering of Sacrifice. The Eucharistic Prayer demands that all listen to it with reverence and in silence.[5]

Redemptionis Sacramentum also notes:

> While the priest proclaims the Eucharistic Prayer "there should be no other prayers or singing, and the organ or other musical instruments should be silent" [GIRM 32], except for the people's acclamations that have been duly approved.[6]

---

[4] Ibid.
[5] GIRM 78.
[6] RS 53.

If a deacon is present, the *General Instruction* is specific about where he is to stand and what he is to do during the Eucharistic Prayer:

> During the Eucharistic Prayer, the deacon stands near the priest but slightly behind him, so that when needed he may assist the priest with the chalice or the *Missal.*
>
> From the *Epiclesis* until the priest shows the chalice, the deacon normally remains kneeling. If several deacons are present, one of them may place incense in the thurible for the Consecration and incense the host and the chalice as they are shown to the people.[7]

Which Eucharistic Prayers May Be Used

The Church is very strict about which Eucharistic Prayers may be used, because of the possibility of scandal being given if something erroneous or infelicitous were said during the Eucharistic Prayer. As a result:

> Only the Eucharistic Prayers included in the *Roman Missal* or those that the Apostolic See has by law admitted, in the manner and within the limits laid down by the Holy See, are to be used. To modify the Eucharistic Prayers approved by the Church or to adopt others privately composed is a most serious abuse.[8]

Currently, seven Eucharistic Prayers are approved for use in the United States:[9]

---

[7] GIRM 179.

[8] ID 5.

[9] Three additional Eucharistic Prayers—those for use in Masses with children—are under discussion. These prayers were formerly authorized for use in the United States, but at the time of this writing their use has not been reapproved. They were not included in the retranslation of the

a) The Eucharistic Prayers I (Roman Canon), II, III, IV.

b) The Eucharistic Prayers for Masses of Reconciliation I and II.

c) The Eucharistic Prayer for Masses for Various Needs and Occasions (also called the Swiss Synod Eucharistic Prayer).

The Swiss Synod Eucharistic Prayer was approved by the United States NCCB in 1994 and confirmed on May 9, 1995, in a letter to Cardinal William Keeler (then-president of the NCCB). The letter was sent by Cardinal Antonio Javierre Ortas (former prefect of the Sacred Congregation for Divine Worship and the Discipline of the Sacraments) and approved the prayer for temporary use in the United States. Copies of the Swiss Synod Eucharistic Prayer and the letters authorizing its use may be found in a booklet titled *Eucharistic Prayer for Masses for Various Needs and Occasions*. It should be noted that this prayer has four variants that appear in the intercessions following the *anamnesis*. This is not unique, as the traditional canon of the Latin rite—Eucharistic Prayer I, also known as the Roman Canon—also has variants for special occasions.

Eucharistic Prayers Approved for Use in the U.S.

To help you recognize the approved Eucharistic Prayers, here are the opening lines of each. They occur right after the *Sanctus* or "Holy, Holy, Holy" (see below):

Roman Missal because, as they were written for use with children under the age of ten, they were not originally composed in Latin and thus are not part of the *Missale Romanum*. It is possible that they will receive a retranslation and reauthorization in the future.

Standard Eucharistic Prayers

I. "To you, therefore, most merciful Father, we make humble prayer and petition through Jesus Christ, your Son, our Lord."

II. "You are indeed holy, O Lord, the fount of all holiness."

III. "You are indeed holy, O Lord, and all you have created rightly gives you praise . . ."

IV. "We give you praise, Father most holy, for you are great, and you have fashioned all your works in wisdom and love."

Prayers for Reconciliation Masses[10]

I. "Father, from the beginning of time you have always done what is good for man . . ."

II. "God of power and might, we praise you through your Son, Jesus Christ . . ."

Swiss Synod Eucharistic Prayer

"You are truly blessed, O God of holiness: You accompany us with love as we journey through life . . ."

---

[10] The opening lines of these Eucharistic Prayers and the Swiss Synod Eucharistic Prayer are given according to the previous translation. The new translation was not available at the time of this writing.

Order of the Eucharistic Prayer
and Accompanying Actions

Introductory Prayer

The Eucharistic Prayer opens with the priest appealing to the people to elevate their hearts to the worship of God:

> As he begins the Eucharistic Prayer, the Priest extends his hands and sings or says, *The Lord be with you*. The people reply, *And with your spirit*. As he continues, saying, *Lift up your hearts*, he raises his hands. The people reply, *We lift them up to the Lord*. Then the Priest, with hands extended, adds, *Let us give thanks to the Lord our God*, and the people reply, *It is right and just*. After this, the Priest, with hands extended, continues the Preface. At its conclusion, he joins his hands and, together with all those present, sings or says aloud the *Sanctus (Holy, Holy, Holy)*.[11]

Preface

The Preface that is used with the Eucharistic Prayer varies depending on the day and/or the Eucharistic Prayer that has been selected. See a copy of the *Roman Missal* for the text of the approved prefaces and the circumstances in which individual ones are to be used.

One of the key elements expressed in the Preface is thanksgiving, which the *General Instruction* notes is one of the chief elements of the Eucharistic Prayer:

> Thanksgiving (expressed especially in the Preface): In which the priest, in the name of the entire holy people, glorifies God the

---

[11] GIRM 148.

Father and gives thanks for the whole work of salvation or for some special aspect of it that corresponds to the day, festivity, or season.[12]

Acclamation or *Sanctus*

Following the preface, the priest and the people make the acclamation by singing or saying the *Sanctus* (also known as the *Trisagion* or "Holy, Holy, Holy"). This is considered a principal part of the Eucharistic Prayer:

> Acclamation: In which the whole congregation, joining with the heavenly powers, sings the *Sanctus*. This acclamation, which is part of the Eucharistic Prayer itself, is sung or said by all the people with the priest.[13]

Epiclesis

The *Epiclesis*, or invocation asking God to send the Holy Spirit to transform the elements into the body and blood of Christ, is also a key part of the Eucharistic Prayer:

> Epiclesis: In which, by means of particular invocations, the Church implores the power of the Holy Spirit that the gifts offered by human hands be consecrated, that is, become Christ's body and blood, and that the spotless victim to be received in Communion be for the salvation of those who will partake of it.[14]

---

[12] GIRM 79a.
[13] GIRM 79b.
[14] GIRM 79c.

Ringing a Bell

Many people ask whether the ringing of a bell during key portions of the Mass is still required. The *General Instruction* states the following:

> A little before the Consecration, when appropriate, a server rings a bell as a signal to the faithful. According to local custom, the server also rings the bell as the priest shows the host and then the chalice.[15]

The ringing of a bell is thus optional and governed in part by local custom. The appropriate circumstances for ringing a bell were further explained by the Holy See:

Dubium: Is a bell to be rung at Mass?

Responsum: It all depends on the different circumstances of places and people. . . . From a long and attentive catechesis and education in liturgy, a particular liturgical assembly may be able to take part in the Mass with such attention and awareness that it has no need of this signal at the central part of the Mass. This may easily be the case, for example, with religious communities or with particular or small groups. The opposite may be presumed in a parish or public church, where there is a different level of liturgical and religious education and where often people who are visitors or are not regular churchgoers take part. In these cases the bell as a signal is entirely appropriate and is sometimes necessary. To conclude: usually a signal with the bell should be given, at least at the two elevations, in order to elicit joy and attention.[16]

---

[15] GIRM 150.
[16] *Notitiae 8* (1972) 343, DOL 1499 n. R28.

This reply was given in 1972, when the liturgy had just undergone a major revision and had been translated into the vernacular for the first time. Many may have still been engaging in private devotions during Mass (e.g., the rosary) or otherwise not actively following along with the service. It may have been the case at that time that an ordinary parish congregation needed a bell to be rung in order to get their attention at the Consecration and eucharistic elevations. It is more questionable whether this presumption holds today, at least in the United States. Make no mistake: I do not wish to discourage bell ringing. Personally, I prefer a bell to be rung. But the logic that applied in 1972 may not apply as broadly today, in which case the ringing of a bell would be more of an option than a preference on the part of the Church—at least in parishes where the congregation pays reasonable attention and responds to the solemnity of the Consecration and the two elevations.

Institution Narrative and Consecration

Now comes the portion of the Eucharistic Prayer in which the elements are consecrated and transformed into the body and blood of Christ. The *General Instruction* describes this portion of the Mass as follows:

> Institution narrative and Consecration: In which, by means of words and actions of Christ, the Sacrifice is carried out which Christ himself instituted at the Last Supper, when he offered his body and blood under the species of bread and wine, gave them to his apostles to eat and drink, and left them the command to perpetuate this same mystery.[17]

---

[17] GIRM 79d.

Words of Consecration

It is gravely illicit to use any formula for Consecration other than one printed in a translation of the Mass that has been confirmed by the Holy See. If the degree of departure is substantial enough, the Consecration will be rendered invalid (meaning the elements will not become the body and blood of Christ).

Currently there is only one English translation of the words of Consecration over the host that has been confirmed by the Holy See:

> Take this, all of you, and eat of it,
> For this is my Body,
> Which will be given up for you.

Redemptionis Sacramentum notes:

> In some places there has existed an abuse by which the priest breaks the host at the time of the Consecration in the Holy Mass. This abuse is contrary to the tradition of the Church. It is reprobated and is to be corrected with haste.[18]

At the time of this writing, there are two approved English translations of the words of Consecration over the chalice that have been confirmed by the Holy See. The first one—which is used in all Eucharistic Prayers except for those for children —is this:

> Take this, all of you, and drink from it,
> For this is the chalice of my blood,
> The blood of the new and eternal covenant,
> Which will be poured out for you and for many
> For the forgiveness of sins.
> Do this in memory of me.

---

[18] RS 55.

The Eucharistic Prayers for Masses with children contained a slight variation on the words of Consecration for the wine. It used the same words that were used in the previous translation of the Mass but with the addition of the clarifying phrase—"Then he said to them." The prayer read:

> Take this, all of you, and drink from it:
> This is the cup of my blood,
> The blood of the new and everlasting covenant.
> It will be shed for you and for all
> So that sins may be forgiven.
> *Then he said to them:*
> Do this in memory of me.

This variation did nothing to affect the validity of the Consecration and was not a liturgical abuse.

The future of this formula is uncertain. The Eucharistic prayers for Masses with children were set aside during the process of translating the new *Roman Missal*, and they are not included in it. It is possible that at a future date they will be translated again and reauthorized for use. If so, the translation for these words will be conformed to the translation they have in Masses that aren't for children (above), and it is doubtful —given the Holy See's preference for more exact translations and for unity in the words of Consecration—that the phrase "Then he said to them" would still be considered an addition needed to help children understand.

It should be noted that throughout Christian history (and today in the Eastern rites of the Catholic Church), a number of formulas have been used and are used in the Consecration. Regarding the formulas and what is needed for validity, Fr. Halligan wrote:[19]

---

[19] Note that Fr. Halligan wrote before the new translation of the *Roman*

The [standard Roman Rite] formula of Consecration of the bread is: "This is my body which will be given up for you"; of the wine: "This is the cup of my blood, the blood of the new and everlasting Covenant. It will be shed for you and for all so that sins may be forgiven." The words which precede these formulas in no way pertain to the validity of the formula. It is commonly taught today that the essential words of the formula of the Eucharist—and their omission would invalidate the form—are: "This is my body," "This is the cup of my blood" (or "This is my blood"). In practice it is seriously prescribed to pronounce the entire formula; if any of the words from "the blood of the new . . ." on are omitted, the whole formula is to be repeated conditionally.[20]

Three further points should be made with regard to the words of Consecration, as they are often raised by certain traditionalists.

"For You and for Many"

Until the new translation of the *Roman Missal*, the English translation of the words of Consecration over the cup required the priest to say, "It will be shed for you and for all so that sins may be forgiven." This was sometimes faulted on the grounds that it is not a fully literal translation of the Latin. The phrase rendered "for all" (Latin, *pro multis*) would more literally be translated "for the multitudes" or "for many." Some traditionalists even went so far as to question the validity of the Consecration using this translation.

When questioned about the translation, the Holy See responded as follows:

Missal, so the translation of the words of Consecration is now slightly different. The theological point he makes about what is needed for validity, however, is not affected.

[20] Halligan, *The Sacraments and Their Celebration*, 67.

In certain vernacular versions of the text for consecrating the wine, the words *pro multis* are translated thus: English, *for all*; Spanish, *por todos*; Italian, *per tutti*.

Dubium:

a. Is there a sufficient reason for introducing this variant and if so, what is it?

b. Is the pertinent traditional teaching in the Catechism of the Council of Trent to be considered superseded?

c. Are all other versions of the biblical passage in question to be regarded as less accurate?

d. Did something inaccurate and needing correction or emendation in fact slip in when the approval was given for such a version?

Responsum: The variant involved is fully justified:

a. According to exegetes the Aramaic word translated in Latin by *pro multis* has as its meaning "for all": the many for whom Christ died is without limit; it is equivalent to saying "Christ has died for all." The words of Saint Augustine are apposite: "See what he gave and you will discover what he bought. The price is Christ's blood. What is it worth but the whole world? What, but all peoples? Those who say either that the price is so small that it has purchased only Africans are ungrateful for the price they cost; those who say that they are so important that it has been given for them alone are proud" [*Enarr. in Ps.* 95, 5].

b. The teaching of the Catechism is in no way superseded: the distinction that Christ's death is sufficient for all but efficacious for many remains valid.

c. In the approval of this vernacular variant in the liturgical text nothing inaccurate has slipped in that requires correction or emendation.[21]

---

[21] *Notitiae* 6 (1970) 39–40, no. 28; DOL 1445 n. R13.

The validity of the Consecration if the formula "for all" is used is not in question since it is theologically *true* that Christ shed his blood for all (1 Tim. 4:10; 1 John 2:2). The claim that he shed his blood only for the elect or only for the faithful was condemned during the Jansenist controversy.[22] Finally, in biblical idiom, the word *many* is often used as a synonym for *all*. For example, when Paul says that "by one man's [Adam's] disobedience *many* were made sinners" (Rom. 5:19), he means that *all* men were made sinners.

The liceity of the translation "for all" is not in question because it is part of a Church-approved text of the Mass.

Despite the fact that "for all" was a licit and valid translation, it still was not a literal one, and it remained a neuralgic point with the traditionalist movement. Early in his pontificate, Benedict XVI decided to change the translation, and in 2006 the Congregation for the Divine Worship and the Discipline of the Sacraments issued a letter requesting bishops' conferences to prepare for the introduction of "a precise vernacular translation of the formula *pro multis* (e.g., "for many," "*per molti*," etc.)." Here is the text of the letter:

CONGREGATIO DE CULTU DIVINO
ET DISCIPLINA SACRAMENTORUM

Rome, 17 October 2006
Prot. no. 467/05/L

Your Eminence/Your Excellency,

In July 2005 this Congregation for Divine Worship and the Discipline of the Sacraments, by agreement with the Congregation for the Doctrine of the Faith, wrote to all Presidents of Conferences of Bishops to ask their considered opinion regarding the translation into the various vernaculars of the ex-

---

[22] D 1096, 1294 [DS 2005, 2304]; see also CCC 605f.

pression *pro multis* in the formula for the Consecration of the precious blood during the celebration of Holy Mass (ref. Prot. n. 467/05/L of 9 July 2005).

The replies received from the Bishops' Conferences were studied by the two Congregations and a report was made to the Holy Father. At his direction, this Congregation now writes to Your Eminence/Your Excellency in the following terms:

1. A text corresponding to the words *pro multis*, handed down by the Church, constitutes the formula that has been in use in the Roman rite in Latin from the earliest centuries. In the past 30 years or so, some approved vernacular texts have carried the interpretative translation "for all," "*per tutti*," or equivalents.

2. There is no doubt whatsoever regarding the validity of Masses celebrated with the use of a duly approved formula containing a formula equivalent to "for all" as the Congregation for the Doctrine of the Faith has already declared (see also *Sacra Congregatio pro Doctrina Fidei, Declaratio de sensu tribuendo adprobationi versionum formularum sacramentalium*, 25 Ianuarii 1974, AAS 66 [1974], 661). Indeed, the formula "for all" would undoubtedly correspond to a correct interpretation of the Lord's intention expressed in the text. It is a dogma of faith that Christ died on the cross for all men and women (see also John 11:52; 2 Cor. 5:14–15; Titus 2:11; 1 John 2:2).

3. There are, however, many arguments in favor of a more precise rendering of the traditional formula *pro multis*:

a. The Synoptic Gospels (Matt. 26:28; Mark 14:24) make specific reference to "many" for whom the Lord is offering the sacrifice, and this wording has been emphasized by some biblical scholars in connection with the words of the prophet Isaiah (53:11–12). It would have been entirely possible in the Gospel texts to have said "for all" (for example, see Luke 12:41); instead, the formula given in the institution narrative is "for many," and the words have been faithfully translated thus in most modern biblical versions.

b. The Roman rite in Latin has always said *pro multis* and never *pro omnibus* in the Consecration of the chalice.

c. The anaphoras of the various Oriental rites, whether in Greek, Syriac, Armenian, the Slavic languages, etc., contain the verbal equivalent of the Latin *pro multis* in their respective languages.

d. "For many" is a faithful translation of *pro multis*, whereas "for all" is rather an explanation of the sort that belongs properly to catechesis.

e. The expression "for many," while remaining open to the inclusion of each human person, is reflective also of the fact that this salvation is not brought about in some mechanistic way, without one's own willing or participation; rather, the believer is invited to accept in faith the gift that is being offered and to receive the supernatural life that is given to those who participate in this mystery, living it out in their lives as well so as to be numbered among the "many" to whom the text refers.

f. In line with the Instruction *Liturgiam authenticam*, effort should be made to be more faithful to the Latin texts of the typical editions.

4. The Bishops' Conferences of those countries where the formula "for all" or its equivalent is currently in use are therefore requested to undertake the necessary catechesis of the faithful on this matter in the next one or two years to prepare them for the introduction of a precise vernacular translation of the formula *pro multis* (e.g., "for many," "*per molti*," etc.) in the next translation of the *Roman Missal* that the bishops and the Holy See will approve for use in their country.

With the expression of my high esteem and respect, I remain, Your Eminence/Your Excellency,

Devotedly yours in Christ,
+ Francis Cardinal Arinze, Prefect

Mysterium Fidei

Second, certain traditionalists are also troubled by the absence of the words *mysterium fidei* ("mystery of faith"), which used to be in the words of Consecration over the cup. However, Josef Jungmann, S.J., probably the definitive scholar of the history of the Mass, pointed out in his landmark work *The Mass of the Roman Rite* that the words *mysterium fidei* are an insertion into the words of Consecration that was not in the original version but was included at a later date.[23]

Not only are the words *mysterium fidei* not original in the Mass of the Roman rite, they have never been and are not now in the Eucharistic Prayers of the Eastern rites in union with the pope. Yet the Church has always recognized the validity of these Eucharistic Prayers, illustrating that the words *mysterium fidei* are not necessary for validity.

The fact is that, although in the Roman rite there is only one licit form of the words of Consecration that may be used, there is no single valid formula. The New Testament presents us with four different accounts (Matt. 26:26–28; Mark 14:22–24; Luke 22:19–20; and 1 Cor. 11:24–25), the Eastern rites of the Church have used and still use different formulas, and even the words in the Latin rite's version have changed over time.

Intention of the Priest

A third matter raised by some traditionalists is the intention of the minister in saying the words of Consecration. What if the priest did not have the intention for transubstantiation to occur? The answer is that it is not necessary for the priest to have the *specific* intention that transubstantiation take place, so long as he has the *general* intention to celebrate the sacrament of

---

[23] *The Mass of the Roman Rite* 2:199–201.

the Eucharist. Ludwig Ott, in *Fundamentals of Catholic Dogma*, states that regarding the sacraments:

> Objectively considered, the intention of doing what the Church does suffices. The minister, therefore, does not need to intend what the Church intends, namely to produce the effects of the sacraments, for example, the forgiveness of sins; neither does he need to intend to execute a specific Catholic rite. It suffices if he has the intention of performing the religious action as it is current among Christians.[24]

Eucharistic Sacrifice

A question that commonly arises, since the text of the Mass and the *General Instruction* put so much stress on the sacrificial aspect of the Eucharist, is when the sacrifice itself occurs.

The common teaching is that it is the transubstantiation of the two elements that accomplishes the eucharistic sacrifice.[25] The Consecration of the elements is twofold: First the bread is consecrated, then the wine. Even though Christ's body and blood (and soul and divinity) are present under both forms, the two forms depict his body and blood in a state of separation, as they were when sacrificed on the cross. Thus it is commonly taught:

> The external sacrifice consists in the sacramental (*mystica*) separation of the body and blood of Christ, which is consummated *via verborum* ["by force of words"] by the double Consecration and which is an objective representation (*repraesentatio*) of the historical, real separation consummated on the cross.[26]

---

[24] Ludwig Ott, *Fundamentals of Catholic Dogma* (Charlotte, N.C.: TAN Books and Publishers, 2009), 344.

[25] Ibid., 409.

[26] Ibid., 410.

This is also the teaching of Saint Thomas Aquinas, who states that "the opportunity of offering sacrifice is considered . . . chiefly with regard to God, to whom the sacrifice of this sacrament is offered *by consecrating*. . . . [T]his sacrament is performed in the Consecration of the Eucharist, *whereby a sacrifice is offered* to God."[27]

Elevation and Presentation of the Host to the People

There are two times when the host and chalice are raised in connection with the words of Consecration. The first is as the words of Consecration are being said, and the second is just afterward.

Just before the Consecration of the host, the rubrics provide that:

> *The priest takes the bread and, holding it slightly raised above the altar, continues. . . .*

Then, immediately after the words of Consecration of the host, the rubrics specify:

> *He shows the consecrated host to the people, places it again on the paten, and genuflects in adoration.*

As he is preparing to consecrate the chalice, the rubrics state:

> *He takes the chalice and, holding it slightly raised above the altar, continues . . .*

And immediately after the words of Consecration for the chalice, the rubrics specify:

> *The priest shows the chalice to the people, places it on the corporal, and genuflects in adoration.*

---

[27] *Summa Theologiae* III:82:10 (emphasis added).

Sometimes the faithful are puzzled when priests elevate the host or the chalice to different heights, some scarcely elevating them at all and others holding them almost as high as their arms can reach.

The rubrics indicate that, during the Consecration of the respective elements, they should be "slightly raised above the altar." The Church hasn't further indicated what this means, but presumably it would be a matter of inches rather than feet.

More liberty is allowed when the priest shows the host and the chalice to the faithful. No specific amount of elevation is mandated at this point. What is mandated is that the consecrated elements be shown to the faithful for their adoration. Failure to elevate them is not a liturgical abuse. The priest may even turn around to face the congregation and show the sacred species, if he is celebrating Mass facing away from the people.

Elevation of the sacred species is mandated, however, at the Final Doxology (see below).

Memorial Acclamation or Mystery of Faith

After the chalice has been shown to the people, the rubrics in the *Roman Missal* specify:

Then the priest says:

The mystery of faith.

And the people continue, acclaiming:

We proclaim your death, O Lord,
And profess your Resurrection
Until you come again

Or:

When we eat this Bread and drink this Cup,
We proclaim your death, O Lord,
Until you come again

Or:

> Save us, Savior of the world,
> For by your cross and Resurrection
> You have set us free.

Note that these options do not include the acclamation "Christ has died, Christ is risen, Christ will come again." That is because this acclamation is not part of the *Roman Missal* but something introduced in America. When the final version of the new *Roman Missal* was approved in August 2010, this acclamation was not included. The *BCDW Newsletter* explained:

> One prominent adaptation not accepted was the Memorial Acclamation "Christ has died, Christ is risen, Christ will come again." In explaining its decision, the CDWDS wrote, "The proposed addition to the Memorial Acclamations, though part of the vernacular ICEL text for some time, introduces an acclamation not foreseen by the *editio typica*, which is to be avoided. As is also clear, the text is not consistent with the style and signification of the other Memorial Acclamations. Its origins are also obscure. For these reasons, the proposal cannot be accepted."[28]

In some places deacons rather than priests have invited the faithful to make the memorial acclamation, but this is not allowed. On January 14, 1983, the Sacred Congregation for the Sacraments and Divine Worship[29] issued a reply to the question of whether deacons could perform this function:

> The Vicar General of the Diocese of Green Bay (Wisconsin, U.S.A.) asked the Sacred Congregation for the Sacraments and Divine Worship if deacons may announce the "Mystery of Faith" at Mass, which seems to be a custom in [the] U.S.A.

---

[28] *BCDW Newsletter*, August–September 2010, p. 34.
[29] Later renamed the Congregation for Divine Worship and the Discipline of the Sacraments.

Reply. I am writing with reference to your letter of the 29 September, 1982, concerning the acclamation "mysterium fidei" and the possibility of allocating this acclamation to the deacon. This question has already been carefully studied and, therefore, the prescription of the *Missale Romanum*: "*Deinde (sacerdos) dicit: Mysterium fidei*"[30] (*Ordo Missae*, n. 93) is to be observed (see also also apostolic constitution, *Missale Romanum* of His Holiness, Pope Paul VI, of the 3 April, 1969).

(Private); S. C. Sacr. et Cult. Div., reply, 14 Jan., 1983, Prot. N. CD 1005/82; original English text; copy kindly sent to C.L.D. by the Office of the U.S. Apostolic delegate.

This reply appeared in *Canon Law Digest*.[31]

Anamnesis

After the memorial acclamation, the *Anamnesis* (Greek, "Remembrance") is said. The *General Instruction* describes it this way:

Anamnesis: In which the Church, fulfilling the command that she received from Christ the Lord through the Apostles, keeps the memorial of Christ, recalling especially his blessed Passion, glorious Resurrection, and Ascension into heaven.[32]

Offering

The *Anamnesis* is followed by the offering of Christ and his faithful to the Father:

Offering: By which, in this very memorial, the Church—and in particular the Church here and now gathered—offers in the

---

[30] [Then the priest says "The Mystery of Faith."]

[31] Vol. 10, p. 2.

[32] GIRM 79e.

Holy Spirit the spotless victim to the Father. The Church's intention, however, is that the faithful not only offer this spotless Victim but also learn to offer themselves, and so day by day to be consummated, through Christ the mediator, into unity with God and with each other, so that at last God may be all in all.[33]

Intercessions

The priest then intercedes with the Father that the fruit of the Eucharist may be applied to various groups:

Intercessions: By which expression is given to the fact that the Eucharist is celebrated in communion with the entire Church, of heaven as well as of earth, and that the offering is made for her and for all her members, living and dead, who have been called to participate in the redemption and the salvation purchased by Christ's body and blood.[34]

Included in the intercessions are references to the local bishop, who may have one or more auxiliaries, and these may require special adaptations to be made:

The priest continues the Eucharistic Prayer in accordance with the rubrics that are set forth in each of the prayers.

If the celebrant is a Bishop, in the prayers, after the words *Papa nostro N.* ("N., our Pope"), he adds, *et me, indigno famulo tuo* ("and me, your unworthy servant"). If, however, the Bishop is celebrating outside his own diocese, after the words *Papa nostro N.* ("N., our Pope"), he adds, *et me indigno famulo tuo, et fratre meo N., Episcopo huius Ecclesiae N.* ("me, your unworthy servant, and my brother N., the Bishop of this church of N.").

The diocesan Bishop or anyone equivalent to him in law must be mentioned by means of this formula: *una cum famulo*

---

[33] GIRM 79f.
[34] GIRM 79g.

tuo Papa nostro N. et Episcopo (or *Vicario, Prelato, Praefecto, Abbate*) ("together with your servant N., our pope, and N., our bishop [or vicar, prelate, prefect, abbot]").

It is permitted to mention coadjutor and auxiliary bishops in the Eucharistic Prayer, but not other bishops who happen to be present. When several are to be named, this is done with the collective formula *et Episcopo nostro N. eiusque Episcopis adiutoribus* (N., our Bishop and his assistant bishops).

In each of the Eucharistic Prayers, these formulas are to be modified according to the requirements of grammar.[35]

Final Doxology or *Per Ipsum*

The Eucharistic Prayer concludes with the Final Doxology, also known as the *Per Ipsum* (from its opening words in Latin ("Through him"):

Final Doxology: By which the glorification of God is expressed and is confirmed and concluded by the people's acclamation, "Amen."[36]

At this point, the rubrics do mandate that the Eucharist be elevated:

He [the priest] takes the chalice and the paten with the host and, elevating both, he says:

Through him, and with him, and in him,
O God, almighty Father,
In the unity of the Holy Spirit,
All glory and honor is yours,
For ever and ever.

---

[35] GIRM 149.
[36] GIRM 79h.

The people acclaim:

Amen.

Note that there is no specific amount of elevation specified, as there was during the words of Consecration. The priest does not have to hold the elements raised "slightly" above the altar. The absence of that direction suggests that this is a higher elevation.

If a deacon is present, he assists the priest by holding the chalice during the *Per Ipsum:*

> At the final doxology of the Eucharistic Prayer, the deacon stands next to the priest, holding the chalice elevated while the priest elevates the paten with the host, until the people have responded with the acclamation, "Amen."[37]

The Amen at the end of the *Per Ipsum* is one of the key moments of the faithful's participation in the Eucharistic Prayer, though they are not to say the *Per Ipsum* itself:

> [T]he assembly does not remain passive and inert; it unites itself to the priest in faith and silence and shows its concurrence by the various interventions provided for in the course of the Eucharistic Prayer: the responses to the Preface dialogue, the *Sanctus*, the acclamation after the Consecration, and the final Amen after the *Per Ipsum*. The *Per Ipsum* itself is reserved to the priest. This Amen especially should be emphasized by being sung, since it is the most important in the whole Mass.[38]

The reservation of the *Per Ipsum* to the priest was also stressed in *Ecclesia de Mysterio:*

> To promote the proper identity (of various roles) in this area, those abuses which are contrary to the provisions of canon 907

---

[37] GIRM 180.
[38] ID 4.

are to be eradicated. In eucharistic celebrations deacons and non-ordained members of the faithful may not pronounce prayers —e.g., especially the Eucharistic Prayer, with its concluding doxology [i.e., the *Per Ipsum*]—or any other parts of the liturgy reserved to the celebrant priest.[39]

See also *Redemptionis Sacramentum* 54 for another, more recent (2004) affirmation of this point.

---

[39] EM, Practical Provisions 6 §2.

9. Reception of Holy Communion

In the Communion rite that follows the Eucharistic Prayer, the faithful receive the body, blood, soul, and divinity of Jesus Christ, made truly present under the appearances of bread and wine. For this reason, the Communion rite has great importance and there are preliminary rites to prepare the faithful for Communion:

> Since the eucharistic celebration is the Paschal Banquet, it is desirable that in keeping with the Lord's command, his body and blood should be received by the faithful who are properly disposed as spiritual food. This is the sense of the Fraction and the other preparatory rites by which the faithful are led directly to Communion.[1]

It is also preferable that the faithful receive hosts consecrated during the Mass they are attending and that they partake of both the host and the chalice when permitted:

> It is most desirable that the faithful, just as the priest himself is bound to do, receive the Lord's body from hosts consecrated at the same Mass and that, in the instances when it is permitted, they partake of the chalice . . . so that even by means of the signs Communion will stand out more clearly as a participation in the sacrifice actually being celebrated.[2]

---

[1] GIRM 80.
[2] GIRM 85.

Who May Give and Receive Communion

Who May Give Communion

The ordinary ministers of Communion are bishops, priests, and deacons. If Communion is being given under both kinds, it is especially recommended that deacons fulfill their ministry by ministering the chalice to the faithful.[3]

Instituted acolytes are *de iure* (by law) extraordinary ministers of the Eucharist. Other lay persons can be authorized to act as extraordinary ministers of Holy Communion. For information on acolytes and when other lay people may be used as extraordinary ministers, see Chapter 3.

Only those serving as ordinary or extraordinary ministers may distribute Communion. The rest of the faithful at Mass cannot, even in the case of special events such as weddings:

> It is not licit for the faithful "to take . . . by themselves . . . and, still less, to hand . . . from one to another" the sacred host or the sacred chalice. Moreover, in this regard, the abuse is to be set aside whereby spouses administer Holy Communion to each other at a Nuptial Mass.[4]

Canon Law Requirements for Receiving Communion

The *Code of Canon Law* has a significant amount to say about who may receive the sacraments, including the Eucharist. The *Code*'s most basic statement on the matter is this:

> Sacred ministers cannot deny the sacraments to those who seek them at appropriate times, are properly disposed, and are not prohibited by law from receiving them [CIC 843 §1].

---

[3] See also GIRM 137.

[4] RS 94.

This canon lists three conditions that must be fulfilled for a minister to be required to give the sacraments to a person who requests them. The three conditions are (a) appropriate time, (b) proper disposition, and (c) lack of legal prohibition.

Appropriate Time

The notion of appropriate times can refer to such things as the time of day or the day of the week. For example, it would not be appropriate to ask the celebrant to hear one's confession after Mass has started; it would be perfectly fine to ask a different priest who is not celebrating or concelebrating Mass to hear it, however.[5] Similarly, under normal circumstances it would not be appropriate to ask a priest to administer the sacraments at two in the morning or while he is in the middle of an urgent task (though an emergency would take priority).

Regarding the Eucharist in particular, the appropriate time to receive it—though not the only time—is during Mass.

> It is highly recommended that the faithful receive Holy Communion during the eucharistic celebration itself. It is to be administered outside the Mass, however, to those who request it for a just cause, with the liturgical rites being observed [CIC 918].

When the canon speaks of the appropriate liturgical rites to be observed, it principally refers to a rite in the *Roman Ritual*

---

[5] While hearing confessions during Mass was discouraged in many quarters after Vatican II—lest the celebration of one sacrament detract from the celebration of the other—the Church eventually judged that offering the faithful the opportunity to confess their sins was so important that it warranted a return to the formerly common practice. Thus in the 2002 *motu proprio Misericordia Dei*, John Paul II urged "that confessions be especially available before Masses, and even during Mass if there are other priests available, in order to meet the needs of the faithful" (MD 2; see also RS 76).

titled "Holy Communion and Worship of the Eucharist Outside Mass."

This canon also sheds light on the reading of canon 843 with specific regard to receiving the Eucharist. The faithful are highly encouraged to receive the Eucharist during Mass, but Communion should also be administered to them outside Mass so long as there is a "just cause."

In canonical terms, a just cause is generally any reason that is not illegal. It does not even have to be a strong reason— just one that is not legally or morally forbidden. An example of a just cause would be to feed one's soul, spiritually. A just cause is among the lowest levels of justification that canon law recognizes. It is much lower, for example, than a requirement that there be a serious cause, much less a grave cause.

One situation when there is not only a just cause for receiving Communion outside of Mass but also a much stronger cause is when a sick person is in danger of death, unable to attend Mass, and unable to have Mass said where he is. The Church is very concerned that all Catholics receive the Eucharist as *viaticum* before they die. *Viaticum* is a form of Communion outside of Mass. It has a history going back to the early Church and has played a key role in preparation for death in Christian history.

The Code states:

> The Christian faithful who are in danger of death from any cause are to be nourished by Holy Communion in the form of *viaticum* [CIC 921 §1].

The Church is so concerned that it mandates the giving of *viaticum*, if possible, before the sick person goes into a coma or becomes mentally impaired:

> Holy *viaticum* for the sick is not to be delayed too long; those who have the care of souls are to be zealous and vigilant that

the sick are nourished by *viaticum* while fully conscious [CIC 922].

If the person has become mentally impaired or fallen into a coma, however, *viaticum* can still be given to the person, especially the precious blood under the form of wine, though a small fragment of the host can also be given to an unconscious person if it will dissolve in his mouth. If a feeding tube is in use, administration of either a fragment of the host or the precious blood may be done in this way provided that they do not linger in the tube and dissolve or become so mixed with other food that the Real Presence has vanished before they enter the recipient. This also applies to people who are not dying but who are unable to receive food normally, provided they have sufficient mental awareness to understand and consent to Communion.

Proper Disposition

Proper disposition includes deportment, attitude, holding the Church's faith regarding the sacrament, and the state of grace (for those sacraments that do not confer the state of grace; for the sacraments that ordinarily confer the state of grace, repentance is required).

The *Catechism of the Catholic Church* sheds light on what dispositions are proper:

> The Lord addresses an invitation to us, urging us to receive him in the sacrament of the Eucharist: "Truly, I say to you, unless you eat the flesh of the Son of man and drink his blood, you have no life in you" [John 6:53].
>
> To respond to this invitation we must prepare ourselves for so great and so holy a moment. Saint Paul urges us to examine our conscience: "Whoever, therefore, eats the bread or drinks the cup of the Lord in an unworthy manner will be guilty of profaning the body and blood of the Lord. Let a man examine

himself, and so eat of the bread and drink of the cup. For any one who eats and drinks without discerning the body eats and drinks judgment upon himself" [1 Cor. 11:27–29]. Anyone conscious of a grave sin must receive the sacrament of reconciliation before coming to Communion.

Before so great a sacrament, the faithful can only echo humbly and with ardent faith the words of the centurion: "*Domine, non sum dignus ut intres sub tectum meum, sed tantum dic verbo, et sanabitur anima mea*" ("Lord, I am not worthy that you should enter under my roof, but only say the word and my soul will be healed") [*Roman Missal*, response to the invitation to Communion; see also Matt. 8:8]. And in the Divine Liturgy of Saint John Chrysostom the faithful pray in the same spirit:

> O Son of God, bring me into communion today with your mystical supper. I shall not tell your enemies the secret, nor kiss you with Judas' kiss. But like the good thief I cry, "Jesus, remember me when you come into your kingdom."

To prepare for worthy reception of this sacrament, the faithful should observe the fast required in their Church [see also CIC, can. 919]. Bodily demeanor (gestures, clothing) ought to convey the respect, solemnity, and joy of this moment when Christ becomes our guest.[6]

Of the dispositions required to receive the Eucharist, the state of grace is the most fundamental. To receive the Eucharist while knowing that one does not have the state of grace is to commit grave sacrilege—a mortal sin if done with adequate reflection and sufficient consent.

Because of this, the Church has legally prohibited those who have unconfessed mortal sins from receiving the Eucharist except in very specific circumstances, and even then the person

---

[6] CCC 1384–87.

must make an act of perfect contrition to try to ensure the state of grace. The Code states:

> A person who is conscious of grave sin is not to celebrate Mass or receive the body of the Lord without previous sacramental confession unless there is a grave reason and there is no opportunity to confess; in this case the person is to remember the obligation to make an act of perfect contrition which includes the resolution of confessing as soon as possible [CIC 916].

A second disposition that the Church has mandated in its legislation concerns reverence for the Eucharist. One way that Christians have historically manifested their reverence for Christ's Presence in the Eucharist is by fasting before receiving it.

In the 1917 *Code of Canon Law*, the fast for the laity was to be from midnight to the time of Communion. However, in 1957, Pope Pius XII shortened it to three hours. Bishops later requested that it be shortened to one hour, and Pope Paul VI issued a concession on the eucharistic fast that was announced at a public session of Vatican II on November 21, 1964. The announcement stated:

> In view of the difficulties in many places regarding the eucharistic fast, Pope Paul VI, acceding to the requests of the bishops, grants that the fast from solid food is shortened to one hour before Communion in the case of both priests and faithful. The concession also covers use of alcoholic beverages, but with proper moderation being observed.[7]

Non-alcoholic drinks already had a one-hour rather than a three-hour fast.[8]

---

[7] AAS 57 (1965) 186, DOL 2117.
[8] See also DOL 2116.

The current (1983) *Code of Canon Law* frames the obligation this way:

> A person who is to receive the Most Holy Eucharist is to abstain for at least one hour before Holy Communion from any food and drink, except for only water and medicine [CIC 919 §1].

As this canon reveals, the eucharistic fast is currently reckoned from the time of Communion, not the time that Mass begins. One may take food within one hour of Mass, so long as one does not take it within one hour of the time that one will receive Communion.

The prohibition also contains exceptions for drinking water and taking medicine. Canon law does not make any requirement concerning a fast from these two. Under the Code, both may be taken at any time prior to Communion. In regard to medicine, the Code makes no requirement that there be a serious reason for taking it. Aspirin to relieve a mild headache is permitted, for medicine is not considered food. Also, if the medicine is one that is supposed to be taken with food then that is permitted (see below).

There is also no requirement that the faithful refrain from food or drink for any period following Communion.

In observing the eucharistic fast, the faithful should not be overly scrupulous. The fast gains its authority from Church law. There is nothing intrinsically sinful about having other things in one's stomach at the same time as the Eucharist. Food does no injury to Jesus under the sacramental species, and it is not intrinsically disrespectful. This is clear not only from the fact that there is no requirement to fast after Communion but also because the Code does not require priests to observe the fast for any Masses except the first one they celebrate during the day:

A priest who celebrates the Most Holy Eucharist two or three times on the same day can take something before the second or third celebration even if there is less than one hour between them [CIC 919 §2].

Because the Church's current law does not establish a canonical penalty or a specific moral gravity for violating the eucharistic fast, it should not be considered a grave matter and should not be the subject of scrupulosity. Thus, for example, if one is not entirely sure whether it has been a full hour since one last ate, this should not be an occasion of scruples to prevent one from receiving Communion. In fact, the point of reducing the eucharistic fast was to make it easier for the faithful to receive Communion more frequently.

A final change in the Church's law regarding the eucharistic fast concerns those who are aged or infirm and those who care for the aged or infirm. Prior to the 1983 Code, the aged and infirm were bound to observe a fast of about a quarter of an hour and those who took care of them were required only to observe this shorter fast if it was difficult for them to observe the normal, one-hour fast. The current *Code of Canon Law* removed these obligations and simply stated:

> The elderly, the infirm, and those who care for them can receive the Most Holy Eucharist even if they have eaten something within the preceding hour [CIC 919 §3].

The eucharistic fast is thus not binding on the aged, the infirm, or their caretakers.

This is also why one would be allowed to take food with medicine if it is the kind of medicine that should be taken with food. Medicine is a treatment for the infirm, and §3 of the canon makes it clear that the Church does not want food to prevent the infirm from being able to receive Communion.

If someone has a medical condition that eating food will help, they are not bound by the fast. In the same way, if they have a medical condition that food and medicine together will help, they similarly are not bound.

People with such conditions may choose to observe the fast anyway, but they are not bound to do so. (And they should not do so if it will pose a risk to their health.)[9]

Legal Prohibitions

RELIGIOUS AFFILIATION

The Code's most basic statement regarding who is legally impeded from receiving the sacraments is found in canon 844:

> Catholic ministers administer the sacraments licitly to Catholic members of the Christian faithful alone, who likewise receive them licitly from Catholic ministers alone, without prejudice to the prescripts of §§2, 3, and 4 of this canon, and can. 861, §2 [CIC 844 §1].[10]

In addition to the above requirements regarding who may receive the sacraments in general, there are also specific regulations dealing with the Eucharist. The most basic of these is this:

> Any baptized person not prohibited by law can and must be admitted to Holy Communion [CIC 912].

---

[9] For example, a diabetic who senses the need to eat before Mass should do so rather than risk the consequences of his blood sugar going too low. This should not be a source of scruple, which is why the Church exempted the elderly and the infirm in the first place.

[10] Canon 861 §2 explains that in an emergency situation, a person other than a bishop, priest, or deacon may baptize; this does not affect the question of who may receive baptism.

This is to be understood as including the conditions mentioned in 844 §1, which require the person to ask at an appropriate time and with the proper disposition.

Under 844 §1, non-Catholics are normally prohibited from receiving the sacraments from a Catholic priest, and Catholics are normally bound to receive them only from a Catholic minister. There are, however, some exceptions:

> Whenever necessity requires it or true spiritual advantage suggests it, and provided that danger of error or of indifferentism is avoided, the Christian faithful for whom it is physically or morally impossible to approach a Catholic minister are permitted to receive the sacraments of penance, Eucharist, and anointing of the sick from non-Catholic ministers in whose Churches these sacraments are valid [CIC 844 §2].

The churches where penance, the Eucharist, and the anointing of the sick are valid include the Eastern Orthodox churches as well as other Eastern churches, such as the Armenian Church and the Assyrian Church of the East. Also included in this category is the Polish National Catholic Church, which is based in the United States. However, since the Protestant communities have not preserved valid holy orders, the three sacraments are not valid in standard Protestant churches, including Anglican and Episcopalian churches, and a Catholic may not receive these sacraments from their ministers.

Indifferentism is a heresy that states that it does not matter what denomination one belongs to. The teaching of the Church is that, while it is possible for those who are not formal members of the Catholic Church to be saved, one's religious affiliation is not a matter of indifference, and one does have a grave obligation to enter the Catholic Church when one becomes aware of its role in God's plan. The *Catechism of the Catholic Church*, quoting Vatican II, states:

Basing itself on Scripture and Tradition, the Council teaches that the Church, a pilgrim now on earth, is necessary for salvation: the one Christ is the mediator and the way of salvation; he is present to us in his body which is the Church. He himself explicitly asserted the necessity of faith and baptism, and thereby affirmed at the same time the necessity of the Church which men enter through baptism as through a door. Hence they could not be saved who, knowing that the Catholic Church was founded as necessary by God through Christ, would refuse either to enter it or to remain in it.[11]

If receiving the sacraments in a non-Catholic church in which they are valid would lead one into indifferentism, then one should not receive the sacraments.

These same sacraments of the Eucharist, penance, and the anointing of the sick may also be given by Catholic priests to members of the Eastern (oriental) churches on certain conditions:

> Catholic ministers administer the sacraments of penance, Eucharist, and anointing of the sick licitly to members of Eastern churches which do not have full communion with the Catholic Church if they seek such on their own accord and are properly disposed. This is also valid for members of other Churches which in the judgment of the Apostolic See are in the same condition in regard to the sacraments as these Eastern churches [CIC 844 §3].

---

[11] CCC 846, citing Vatican II, *Lumen Gentium* 14. The *Catechism* adds: "This affirmation is not aimed at those who, through no fault of their own, do not know Christ and his Church: Those who, through no fault of their own, do not know the Gospel of Christ or his Church, but who nevertheless seek God with a sincere heart, and, moved by grace, try in their actions to do his will as they know it through the dictates of their conscience—those too may achieve eternal salvation" (CCC 847).

Non-Catholics belonging to the oriental churches thus are not legally prohibited from receiving the Eucharist if they ask on their own to receive it (e.g., they have not been pressured into requesting it). This does not apply to Anglicans or Episcopalians, since the Apostolic See has not judged them in the same condition as the oriental churches due to their lack of valid holy orders. They fall under the following section of the canon, which deals with Protestants generally:

> If the danger of death is present or if, in the judgment of the diocesan bishop or conference of bishops, some other grave necessity urges it, Catholic ministers administer these same sacraments licitly also to other Christians not having full communion with the Catholic Church, who cannot approach a minister of their own community and who seek such on their own accord, provided that they manifest Catholic faith in respect to these sacraments and are properly disposed [CIC 844 §4].

As this section of the canon makes clear, most Protestants (since they are non-Catholic Christians who do not belong to the oriental churches) are able to receive the Eucharist only in very limited circumstances. Five conditions must be met: (1) There must be the danger of death or a situation that the diocesan bishop or national conference of bishops has judged to be a case of grave necessity; (2) the non-Catholic must not be able to approach a minister of his own community; (3) he must ask on his own for the sacrament;[12] (4) he must manifest (display) Catholic faith in the sacrament (that is, believe what the Catholic Church believes concerning the sacrament); and

---

[12] Asking on their own does not mean that Catholics are prohibited from suggesting to them that they receive the sacraments. Letting them know that this is a possibility in their circumstances (when it is a possibility) is a spiritual work of mercy. What the Code wishes to avoid is forcing the sacraments on them against their will.

(5) he must be properly disposed. Since conditions (1), (2), and (4) are not often met, Protestants are legally prohibited from receiving the Eucharist in most circumstances.

Marriages and funerals at which non-Catholic Christians are present often occur in America. However, these do not meet the test set out in canon 844 §4 concerning non-Catholic Christians receiving Communion. Among other things (such as the necessity of sharing the Church's beliefs regarding the Eucharist), the canon permits such Communion only "if the danger of death is present or other grave necessity, in the judgment of the diocesan bishop or the conference of bishops." This condition is not met on a national basis for weddings and funerals since the conference of bishops has not declared these events to create a grave necessity for non-Catholics to receive Communion. Much less has the Holy See dispensed with the other requirements of 844 §4, which would be necessary to allow Protestants in general to receive Communion at these events.

John Paul II also noted that there can be no dispensation from these rules:

> These conditions, from which no dispensation can be given, must be carefully respected, even though they deal with specific individual cases, because the denial of one or more truths of the faith regarding these sacraments and, among these, the truth regarding the need of the ministerial priesthood for their validity, renders the person asking improperly disposed to legitimately receiving them.[13]

In giving penance, the Eucharist, and anointing to non-Catholics, sensitive ecumenical issues may emerge, and the heads of the local non-Catholic churches must be consulted before the diocesan bishop or national conference of bishops

---

[13] *Ecclesia de Eucharistica* 46.

enacts general norms regarding the distribution of these sacraments:

> For the cases mentioned in §§2, 3, and 4, the diocesan bishop or conference of bishops is not to issue general norms except after consultation at least with the local competent authority of the interested non-Catholic church or community [CIC 844 §5].

For the guidelines the U.S. National Conference of Catholic Bishops has established, see "U.S. Bishops' Guidelines for Receiving Communion" in the Bonus Materials.

Redemptionis Sacramentum adds:

> [W]hen Holy Mass is celebrated for a large crowd—for example, in large cities—care should be taken lest out of ignorance non-Catholics or even non-Christians come forward for Holy Communion, without taking into account the Church's magisterium in matters pertaining to doctrine and discipline. It is the duty of pastors at an opportune moment to inform those present of the authenticity and the discipline that are strictly to be observed.[14]

EXCOMMUNICATION, INTERDICT, AND MANIFEST GRAVE SIN

The Code also includes a prohibition concerning those who have been excommunicated or interdicted:

> Those who have been excommunicated or interdicted—after the imposition or declaration of the penalty—and others obstinately persevering in manifest grave sin are not to be admitted to Holy Communion [CIC 915].

Sometimes Catholics are scandalized when priests have given Communion to public figures who have reputations for immorality. But priests are not allowed to refuse a public figure

---

[14] RS 84.

Communion simply because he has a bad reputation or even because his past behavior has been scandalous. Only those "obstinately persevering in manifest grave sin" may be refused. This condition must be interpreted strictly, as a prior canon in the Code makes clear:

> Laws which establish a penalty, restrict the free exercise of rights, or contain an exception from the law are subject to strict interpretation [CIC 18].

In the case of canon 915, we have a canon that restricts the free exercise of the rights of the baptized to the sacraments in general and to Communion specifically (established in canons 844 §1 and 912, quoted above). Canon 915 therefore must be interpreted strictly, which means that whenever there is a doubt concerning whether a person fits the definition of one "obstinately persevering in manifest grave sin," then the question must be decided in favor of the person seeking Communion.

For a priest to deny someone Communion in this case, it must not only be true that the person sins but also that the person sins gravely, that the person's grave sins are publicly known (not just rumored or assumed to be occurring), that he is persevering in these publicly known sins, and that he is doing so obstinately—that is, that he is not innocently ignorant or partially ignorant or suffering from a psychological disorder that relieves him of full accountability for his actions.

As it stands, a priest is not allowed to refuse Communion to someone just because he is a notorious individual. A much stricter test must be met, and often the public does not have all the facts. For example, the public has no way of knowing if the notorious individual has just been to confession or what his confessor has told him in private.

A special situation exists in the case of politicians who vote contrary to Catholic moral principles on issues like abortion and euthanasia. In 2004, then-Cardinal Joseph Ratzinger circulated a memorandum that dealt with the subject at length (see "Worthiness to Receive Holy Communion—General Principles" in the Bonus Materials for the complete text of the memorandum). This document was provided privately to U.S. bishops but was subsequently leaked to the press.

It is an insightful reflection on the application of the Church's law regarding Communion and how it relates to politicians and voters who support abortion and euthanasia. Nevertheless, it does not itself have force of law for a variety of reasons: Cardinal Ratzinger was not yet pope, as the head of the CDF he did not have the ability to issue authoritative interpretations of canon law (that is the job of the Pontifical Council for Legislative Texts), and, since the document was circulated privately, it was never promulgated as law itself (promulgation is necessary for something to become law; as CIC 7 states: "A law is established when it is promulgated").

Despite the subsequent election of Cardinal Ratzinger as Pope Benedict XVI, the Holy See has not to date insisted that bishops uniformly deny Communion in the situations specified in the memorandum. Instead, it has allowed bishops to use their own judgment in the application of the law in their dioceses.

There has also been a notable debate among bishops regarding the application of canon 915. In this debate some have seemed to reduce the canon to a statement that those in manifest grave sin should not present themselves for Communion, while others have pointed out that the language of the canon itself requires the minister of Holy Communion to refuse to grant Communion to such individuals.

Also unclear is what kind of judgment an extraordinary

minister of Holy Communion should exercise regarding canon 915. It is not clear if the Holy See intends ordinary lay people who are administering Communion to decide on their own who is able to receive it worthily, or whether it would want them to deny Communion to specific individuals only on the instruction of their pastor or bishop.

Hopefully the Holy See will provide clarification on both these points in the future.

Multiple Receptions of Communion

Under the 1917 *Code of Canon Law*, it was permissible to receive Communion more than once a day only in very rare circumstances, such as when one was being given *viaticum*. Under the new Code, it is permissible to receive Communion twice a day, so long as one is assisting (worshipping) at the second Mass. This means that one could first receive Communion without assisting at Mass—for example, if one came into church right before Communion—but one must be assisting at Mass the second time in order to receive Communion.

The current *Code of Canon Law* states:

> A person who has already received the Most Holy Eucharist can receive it a second time on the same day only within the eucharistic celebration in which the person participates, without prejudice to the prescript of can. 921, §2 [CIC 917].

When the new Code was first released, there was some confusion about the meaning of this canon because in the Latin original the word translated as "a second time" is *iterum*, which can simply mean "again." Some thus thought a lay person might be able to receive Communion multiple times a day by attending multiple Masses a day. Consequently, the Pontifical Commission for the Authentic Interpretation of the Code of Canon Law (now called the Pontifical Council for Legislative Texts) clarified the canon by offering an authentic interpretation:

> *Dubium*: Whether, according to canon 917, one who has already received the Most Holy Eucharist may receive it again on the same day only a second time, or as often as one participates in the celebration of the Eucharist?
>
> *Responsum*: Affirmative to the first; negative to the second.[15]

This means that one's first Communion during the day might be (a) during a Mass that one is attending, (b) during a Mass where one is *present only* at Communion time, (c) at a public Communion service done in place of a Mass (common in areas where there is a deficiency of priests), or (d) at a private Communion service where only a person and the priest or extraordinary minister of Holy Communion are present (as when Communion is sent to the sick in hospitals).

One may receive Communion a second time, but only during a Mass that one is attending. (Participating in the Mass does not mean serving as a minister at the Mass; it requires only the level of participation that ordinary worshippers in the pews have.) There are a number of options for how one might receive Communion the first time during the day, but the second time must be in the context of a Mass one is attending.

An exception to this is found in canon 921 §2, which deals with those in danger of death:

> Even if they have been nourished by Holy Communion on the same day, however, those in danger of death are strongly urged to receive Communion again [CIC 921 §2].

---

[15] *Canon Law Digest* (1991) 11:208.

Thus if a person in danger of death has already received Communion once, he may receive it again, even if it is not in the context of a Mass being celebrated in his presence. However, if he remains in a critically ill situation, he should be given Communion only once a day unless he is able to make it to Mass for his second Communion of the day (not normally possible for one critically ill). The Code states:

> While the danger of death lasts, it is recommended that Holy Communion be administered often, but on separate days [CIC 921 §3].

First Communion and Confession

In the Latin Church it is normal to give First Communion to children who have reached the age of reason,[16] which is commonly reckoned to be around seven years old.[17] However, the age at which a child attains the sufficient use of reason varies from child to child. Thus:

> Where it happens, however, that a child who is exceptionally mature for his age is judged to be ready for receiving the sacrament, the child must not be denied First Communion provided he has received sufficient instruction.[18]

A special issue concerning who can go to Communion involves Latin rite children who are receiving their First Communion. May they be admitted to Communion before they are permitted to go to the sacrament of confession? The answer, apart from exceptional circumstances, is no.

---

[16] CIC 914; see also CIC 913 §2.
[17] CIC 11.
[18] RS 87.

In some places in the early 1970s, parishes had been experimenting with admitting children to First Communion before permitting them to go to first confession. However, in 1973 the Sacred Congregation for the Discipline of the Sacraments strictly prohibited this experimentation. The congregation promulgated a declaration in which it reaffirmed the ruling of a 1910 decree ordered by Pope Pius X. The decree was written by the same congregation and is known as *Quam Singulari*. It prohibited the practice of not admitting children to confession prior to First Communion.

Condemning a number of related errors, the decree stated:

> No less worthy of condemnation is that practice which prevails in many places prohibiting from sacramental confession children who have not yet made their first Holy Communion, or of not giving them absolution. Thus it happens that they, perhaps having fallen into serious sin, remain in that very dangerous state for a long time.
>
> But worse still is the practice in certain places which prohibits children who have not yet made their First Communion from being fortified by the holy *viaticum*, even when they are in imminent danger of death. . . .
>
> [D]aily approach to Communion is open to all, old and young, and two conditions only are required: the state of grace and a right intention.

The congregation then went on to explain that the age of discretion needed to receive these sacraments is the same for both confession and Communion:

> The abuses that we are condemning are due to the fact that they who distinguished one age of discretion for penance and another for the Eucharist did so in error. . . .
>
> [T]he age of discretion for confession is the time when one can distinguish between right and wrong, that is, when one

arrives at a certain use of reason, and so similarly, for Holy Communion is required the age when one can distinguish between the bread of the Holy Eucharist and ordinary bread— again the age at which a child attains the use of reason.

Finally, the congregation established a number of rules regarding the admission of children to Holy Communion and confession. They included:

> After careful deliberation on all these points, this Sacred Congregation of the Discipline of the Sacraments . . . has deemed it needful to prescribe the following rules, which are to be observed everywhere for the First Communion of children.
>
> 1. The age of discretion, both for confession and for Holy Communion, is the time when a child begins to reason, that is about the seventh year, more or less. From that time on begins the obligation of fulfilling the precept of both confession and Communion.
>
> 2. A full and perfect knowledge of Christian doctrine is not necessary either for first confession or for First Communion. Afterwards, however, the child will be obliged to learn gradually the entire catechism according to his ability. . . .
>
> 7. The custom of not admitting children to confession or of not giving them absolution when they have already attained the use of reason must be entirely abandoned. The Ordinary shall see to it that this condition ceases absolutely, and he may, if necessary, use legal measures accordingly.
>
> 8. The practice of not administering *viaticum* and extreme unction to children who have attained the use of reason, and of burying them with the rite used for infants, is a most intolerable abuse. The Ordinary should take very severe measures against those who do not give up the practice.

Based on this, in 1973 the Congregation for the Discipline of the Sacraments stated:

[N]ew practices [have recently been] introduced in some regions whereby reception of the Eucharist was permitted before reception of the sacrament of penance. . . .

The Congregations for the Discipline of the Sacraments and for the Clergy have considered this matter thoroughly and taken into account the views of the conferences of bishops. With the approval of Pope Paul VI, therefore, the two congregations by the present document declare that an end must be put to these experiments—which have now gone on for three years . . . and that thereafter the decree *Quam Singulari* must be obeyed everywhere by all.[19]

The Holy See has repeatedly reiterated this prohibition on admitting children to the Eucharist without permitting them to go to confession. The current *Code of Canon Law* states:

It is primarily the duty of parents and those who take the place of parents, as well as the duty of pastors, to take care that children who have reached the use of reason are prepared properly and, after they have made sacramental confession, are refreshed with this divine food as soon as possible. It is for the pastor to exercise vigilance so that children who have not attained the use of reason or whom he judges are not sufficiently disposed do not approach Holy Communion [CIC 914].

The age of reason, also determined by the Code, is established for canonical purposes as generally being seven years of age.[20] One cannot state that children in general past this age do not have sufficient reason for admission to the sacraments; one can say only that certain individual children have intellectual or emotional problems that deprive them of the reason that normal children have at this age.

Though it is not a work of canon law, the *Catechism of the*

---

[19] *Sanctus Pontifex*, May 24, 1973; AAS 65 (1973) 410; DOL 3141–42.
[20] CIC 11.

Catholic Church is even more forceful concerning the need for children to go to confession prior to First Communion:

> Children must go to the sacrament of penance before receiving Communion for the first time.[21]

Parents who wish their children to go to first confession prior to First Communion are sometimes told that the children must be properly catechized for confession before they may be admitted. This is not true. While the *Code of Canon Law* does require prior catechesis for "the sacraments of the living" —baptism, confirmation, the Holy Eucharist, holy orders, and marriage—it does not require prior catechesis for "the sacraments of the dead"—confession and anointing, which minister to those who are spiritually dead or in danger of physical death.

Canonist Edward Peters—currently a relator for the Supreme Tribunal of the Apostolic Signatura, the Church's highest court—discusses this point in the following question:

> Q: Our son is preparing for First Communion. When we spoke with the DRE [i.e., the Director of Religious Education] in our parish about his also receiving the sacrament of penance, we were told that he cannot make his confession because our parish does not offer catechesis for confession until two years after First Communion. This does not seem right to us.
>
> A: Telling a child (or the parents of a child inquiring on his behalf) that he cannot receive the sacrament of penance because "the parish does not offer catechesis for confession" until some future time is faulty in several respects. Let me outline just one serious problem with what you've been told.
>
> Strictly speaking, the 1983 *Code of Canon Law* does not require any catechesis prior to reception of the sacrament of penance.

---

[21] CCC 1457.

Unlike baptism (canon 865), confirmation (canon 889), Eucharist (canon 913), holy orders (canon 1028), or matrimony (canon 1063), all of which explicitly require various degrees of instruction prior to reception of the sacrament, the only thing required for reception of confession is contrition for sins (canon 987). No conscientious parent rejects a young child's attempt to say "sorry" for something just because that child has not yet been formally instructed in the notion of contrition and forgiveness, and the Church does not prevent her children from expressing sorrow for sins just because of a lack of prior instruction in the area. By the same token, and with the same reasoning, the other sacrament of healing, anointing of the sick, requires nothing by way of prior catechesis for licit reception (canon 1004).

Don't misunderstand me: I think catechesis for confession is a fine thing and it should be offered. It can deepen one's sense of personal sorrow for sin, heighten one's awareness of the obligation to avoid sin in the future, open one's eyes to the abundant mercy of God, and generally facilitate a fruitful reception of the sacrament. But to prevent a child from approaching the sacrament of penance simply because "we haven't taught him how to do it yet" is, at best, an unconvincing excuse for withholding a sacrament and, at worst, a violation of the child's fundamental right, as a member of the faithful, to approach his ministers for the sacraments in general (canon 213) and to access the graces of confession in particular (canon 991).[22]

While there is no canonical requirement for formal catechesis on confession, some catechesis is useful. It does not have to take place in a formal, classroom setting. The parents themselves may give this instruction.

It is the duty of the priest to make sure that the child is properly disposed for confession, but what counts as proper dispo-

---

[22] "Quick Questions," *This Rock*, October 1997, p. 41.

sition for the sacrament of penance is specified in the Code, and it does not include prior catechesis:

> To receive the salvific remedy of the sacrament of penance, a member of the Christian faithful must be disposed in such a way that, rejecting sins committed and having a purpose of amendment, the person is turned back to God [CIC 987].

To go to the sacrament of penance, one needs only to convert to God by repudiating one's sins and having a purpose of amendment. One does not need extensive catechesis in the different kinds or gravities of sins.

The Code is also specific about the duty of pastors not only to ensure that the faithful in their care have access to the sacraments in general but also to guarantee their access to confession in particular:

> All to whom the care of souls has been entrusted in virtue of some function are obliged to make provision so that the confessions of the faithful entrusted to them are heard when they reasonably seek to be heard and that they have the opportunity to approach individual confession on days and at times established for their convenience [CIC 986 §1].

This is important because once a person has attained the age of discretion, one has a positive obligation to confess one's grave sins at least annually.

> After having reached the age of discretion, each member of the faithful is obliged to confess faithfully his or her grave sins at least once a year [CIC 989].

For a pastor to deny a child of his parish the opportunity to confess his grave sins annually after that child has reached the age of discretion[23] is to prevent the child from doing something he has an obligation to do.

---

[23] See also CIC 11.

One situation in which children would not be going to confession prior to Communion would be when parents who belong to the Latin church have their child baptized in an Eastern rite Catholic parish (not the same as an Eastern Orthodox church). In many Eastern Catholic churches, infants receive baptism, confirmation (referred to as *chrismation*), and First Communion at the same time. Some parents belonging to Latin rite churches have chosen to have their infants baptized and confirmed and admitted to the Eucharist in an Eastern rite Catholic parish. The Eastern rite equivalent to the *Code of Canon Law*, a work known as the *Code of Canons of the Eastern Churches*, states:

> §1. All presbyters [priests] of the Eastern Churches can validly administer this sacrament [chrismation, or confirmation] either along with baptism or separately to all the Christian faithful of any Church *sui iuris* [with its own law], including the Latin church.
>
> §2. The Christian faithful of the Eastern Churches validly receive this sacrament also from presbyters of the Latin Church, according to the faculties with which these are endowed.
>
> §3. Any presbyter licitly administers this sacrament only to the Christian faithful of his own Church *sui iuris*; when it is a case of Christian faithful of other Churches *sui iuris*, he lawfully acts if they are his subjects, or those whom he lawfully baptizes in virtue of another title, or those who are in danger of death, and always with due regard for the agreements entered between the Churches *sui iuris* in this matter [CIC 696].

In the Latin church's *Code of Canon Law*, the word *subject* typically refers to one in the geographical region of a parish or church, whereas Eastern canon law operates predominantly personally rather than territorially.

A child baptized, confirmed, and admitted to the Eucharist in an Eastern rite Catholic church remains a member of the Latin church if he has Latin rite parents, since that would be the ecclesiastical title to which he was ascribed at his baptism. Unless special circumstances prevail, a child is always ascribed to the ritual church to which his parents belong.[24] Merely receiving baptism in an Eastern rite Catholic church "does not carry with it enrollment in that church."[25]

Manner of Receiving Communion

Because Christ himself is present under the sacred species, great reverence must be shown to them, and the Church has laid out specific rules concerning how Communion is to be received. For example, individuals may not administer Communion to themselves, a practice known as self-communication.

Self-Communication Not Permitted

Communicants may not pick up the sacred host from the ciborium or the sacred chalice from an altar or table. *Inaestimabile Donum* states:

> Communion is a gift of the Lord, given to the faithful through the minister appointed for this purpose. It is not permitted that the faithful should themselves pick up the consecrated bread and the sacred chalice, still less that they should hand them from one to another.[26]

The same concern about self-communication is expressed in the USCCB's 2001 *Norms for the Distribution and Reception of Holy Communion under Both Kinds in the Dioceses of the United States of America*, which was approved by the Holy See in 2002:

---

[24] See also canon 111 for rules governing when a child is a member of the Latin church.

[25] CIC 112 §2.

[26] ID 9.

The chalice may never be left on the altar or another place to be picked up by the communicant for self-communication (except in the case of concelebrating bishops or priests), nor may the chalice be passed from one communicant to another. There shall always be a minister of the chalice.[27]

Though they may not pick up the chalice, communicants do take the chalice from the priest or extraordinary minister of Holy Communion when receiving Communion under both kinds. Though the communicant may raise the chalice to his lips, it is not self-communication because the chalice was handed to him. It is not a liturgical abuse for the priest or extraordinary minister to hand the chalice to the communicant (see below).

Manner of Receiving the Host

The rubrics of the Mass state that at Communion time:

> [The priest] takes the paten or ciborium and approaches the communicants. The priest raises a host slightly and shows it to each of the communicants, saying:
>
> The body of Christ.
>
> The communicant replies:
>
> Amen.
>
> And receives Holy Communion.
>
> If a deacon also distributes Holy Communion, he does so in the same manner.

Although Communion on the tongue was the exclusive practice of the Latin rite of the Church until recently, Communion

---

[27] NDRHC 44.

in the hand was practiced in the early Church. For example, St. Cyril of Jerusalem instructed his newly baptized Christians:

> In approaching [Communion], therefore, come not with thy wrists extended or thy fingers spread; but make thy left hand a throne for the right, as for that which is to receive a king. And having hollowed thy palm, receive the body of Christ, saying over it, Amen. So then after having carefully hallowed thine eyes by the touch of the Holy Body, partake of it; giving heed lest thou lose any portion thereof; for whatever thou losest, is evidently a loss to thee as it were from one of thine own members.[28]

The former American Appendix to the *General Instruction* notes:

> On June 17, 1977, the Congregation of Sacraments and Divine Worship approved the request of the National Conference of Catholic Bishops to permit the optional practice of Communion in the hand.[29]

And according to the edition of the *General Instruction* currently in force in the United States:

> The priest then takes the paten or ciborium and goes to the communicants, who, as a rule, approach in a procession.
>
> The faithful are not permitted to take the consecrated bread or the sacred chalice by themselves and, still less, to hand them from one to another. The norm for reception of Holy Communion in the dioceses of the United States is standing. Communicants should not be denied Holy Communion because they kneel. Rather, such instances should be addressed pastorally, by providing the faithful with proper catechesis on the reasons for this norm.

---

[28] *Catechetical Lectures* 23:21.

[29] AGI 240. This document no longer has legal force, but it is being quoted here on a historical rather than legal point.

When receiving Holy Communion, the communicant bows his or her head before the sacrament as a gesture of reverence and receives the body of the Lord from the minister. The consecrated host may be received either on the tongue or in the hand, at the discretion of each communicant. When Holy Communion is received under both kinds, the sign of reverence is also made before receiving the precious blood.[30]

Note that the *General Instruction* states that the choice of receiving the host on the tongue or in the hand is "at the discretion of each communicant." A priest or other minister cannot require that people receive Communion in the hand. This is a liturgical abuse.

This choice applies also to extraordinary ministers of Holy Communion. Some priests are reported to have insisted that extraordinary ministers receive in the hand. This is not permitted. No exception is made for treating extraordinary ministers differently than other communicants in this regard.

Communion under Both Kinds

History of Communion under Both Kinds

In the early Church, it was common for the faithful to receive the Eucharist under the form of wine as well as under the form of bread (i.e., "under both kinds"). For example, St. Cyril of Jerusalem states:

> Then, after thou hast partaken of the body of Christ, draw near also to the cup of his blood; not stretching forth thine hands, but bending, and saying with an air of worship and reverence, Amen, hallow thyself by partaking also of the blood of Christ.[31]

---

[30] GIRM 160.
[31] *Catechetical Lectures* 23:22.

There were also many cases in the early Church where Communion was received only under the form of bread. In part, this was because it was often hard to hold celebrations of the liturgy. Receiving Communion under the form of bread allowed Christians to reserve the host in their houses[32] and receive daily Communion even when celebrations of the liturgy were not possible on a daily basis. Communion under one kind became the normal practice in many places by the late Middle Ages. When the Protestant reformers began to separate from communion with the Church, they often protested against the reception of Communion only under one kind, just as they protested against the use of Latin as a liturgical language.

In response, the Council of Trent protected the historical Christian teaching that Communion under one kind was valid by maintaining the standard practice whereby most people received Communion under one kind.

By the twentieth century, things had changed, and there was no movement within the Catholic Church denying the validity of Communion under only one kind. Thus the Second Vatican Council reviewed the situation and allowed for a greater use of Communion under both kinds. The *General Instruction of the Roman Missal* states:

> [T]he Second Vatican Council was able to give renewed consideration to what was established by Trent on Communion under both kinds. And indeed, since no one today calls into doubt in any way the doctrinal principles on the complete efficacy of eucharistic Communion under the species of bread alone, the Council thus gave permission for the reception of Communion

---

[32] It is not possible for the faithful to reserve the Eucharist in their own homes under current Church law apart from almost unheard of circumstances. See canons 934–44 of the *Code of Canon Law* for the regulations governing where the Eucharist may be reserved.

under both kinds on some occasions, because this clearer form of the sacramental sign offers a particular opportunity of deepening the understanding of the mystery in which the faithful take part.[33]

The discipline of Communion under both kinds has been restored in many parts of the Latin rite today. There has been no change in doctrine, however. The *General Instruction* states:

Sacred pastors should take care to ensure that the faithful who participate in the rite or are present at it are as fully aware as possible of the Catholic teaching on the form of Holy Communion as set forth by the Ecumenical Council of Trent. Above all, they should instruct the Christian faithful that the Catholic faith teaches that Christ, whole and entire, and the true sacrament, is received even under only one species, and consequently that as far as the effects are concerned, those who receive under only one species are not deprived of any of the grace that is necessary for salvation.

They are to teach, furthermore, that the Church, in her stewardship of the sacraments, has the power to set forth or alter whatever provisions, apart from the substance of the sacraments, that she judges to be most conducive to the veneration of the sacraments and the well-being of the recipients, in view of changing conditions, times, and places. At the same time, the faithful should be encouraged to seek to participate more eagerly in this sacred rite, by which the sign of the eucharistic banquet is made more fully evident.[34]

In the United States, it is frequently permissible to receive Communion under both kinds. In November 1970, the U.S. bishops approved the giving of Communion under both kinds at weekday Masses.[35] This permission was further extended in

---

[33] GIRM 14.

[34] GIRM 282.

[35] AGI 242:19.

the publication of the bishops' directory, *This Holy and Living Sacrifice: Directory for the Celebration and Reception of Communion under Both Kinds*, which was approved by the Holy See in 1984. This document stated that, in addition to weekday Masses:

Communion under both kinds is also permitted at parish and community Masses celebrated on Sundays and holy days of obligation in the dioceses of the United States.[36]

This Holy and Living Sacrifice was superseded by the U.S. bishops' 2001 document *Norms for the Distribution and Reception of Holy Communion under Both Kinds*, which was approved by the Holy See in 2002 and is the current law on the subject.

When Communion under Both Kinds May Be Offered

The current U.S. norms state:

23. The revised *Missale Romanum* [*Roman Missal*], third typical edition, significantly expands those opportunities when Holy Communion may be offered under both kinds. In addition to those instances specified by individual ritual books, the *General Instruction* states that Communion under both kinds may be permitted as follows:

a. For priests who are not able to celebrate or concelebrate.
b. For the deacon and others who perform some role at Mass.
c. For community members at their conventual Mass or what in some places is known as the "community" Mass, for seminarians, [and] for all who are on retreat or are participating in a spiritual or pastoral gathering.[37]

The *General Instruction* then indicates that:

[T]he diocesan Bishop may lay down norms for the distribution of Communion under both kinds for his own diocese, which

---

[36] HLS 21.
[37] NDRHC 23; cf. GIRM 283.

must be observed. . . . The diocesan Bishop also has the faculty
to allow Communion under both kinds, whenever it seems appropriate to the priest to whom charge of a given community
has been entrusted as [its] own pastor, provided that the faithful
have been well instructed and there is no danger of the profanation of the sacrament or that the rite would be difficult to carry
out on account of the number of participants or for some other
reason.[38]

In practice, the need to avoid obscuring the role of the priest
and the deacon as the ordinary ministers of Holy Communion
by an excessive use of extraordinary ministers might in some
circumstances constitute a reason either for limiting the distribution of Holy Communion under both species or for using
intinction instead of distributing the precious blood from the
chalice.

Norms established by the diocesan bishop must be observed
wherever the Eucharist is celebrated in the diocese, even in
the churches of religious orders and in celebrations with small
groups.[39]

The current law thus places the focus on norms created by
the diocesan bishop. It has the effect of bolstering his authority
in this area. *This Holy and Living Sacrifice* merely stated that "at
the discretion of the ordinary," Communion under both kinds
could be permitted in a long list of circumstances.[40] It did not
call upon the bishop to draw up specific norms for his diocese.
The revised law thus encourages the bishop to take a more
active role in deciding the circumstances in which the practice
will be allowed, as opposed to merely acquiescing to a long
existing list of circumstances. The result is that, in principle,

---

[38] Ibid.
[39] NDRHC 23–24.
[40] HLS 20.

Communion under both kinds is allowed at any Masses that the diocesan bishop thinks suitable, whether that be many or few. The only exceptions would be those at which permission is expressly granted in the law, such as for those individuals and groups listed in GIRM 283, quoted above.

Also significant is the statement that an excessive use of extraordinary ministers of Holy Communion can constitute a reason for limiting Communion under both kinds or using intinction. In other words, the argument that many extraordinary ministers must be used because Communion under both kinds is being offered doesn't necessarily hold. Rather than use so many and risk "obscuring the role of the priest and the deacon as the ordinary ministers," one should consider alternatives like having the ordinary ministers distribute by intinction or simply not having Communion under both kinds. The bishops thus appear to be trying to find a balance between the desire to offer Communion under both kinds and a desire not to have an excessive number of extraordinary ministers.

The document goes on to state:

> Extraordinary ministers of Holy Communion should receive sufficient spiritual, theological, and practical preparation to fulfill their role with knowledge and reverence. When recourse is had to extraordinary ministers of Holy Communion, especially in the distribution of Holy Communion under both kinds, their number should not be increased beyond what is required for the orderly and reverent distribution of the body and blood of the Lord. In all matters such extraordinary ministers of Holy Communion should follow the guidance of the diocesan bishop.[41]

Redemptionis Sacramentum adds:

> The chalice should not be ministered to lay members of Christ's faithful where there is such a large number of communicants

---

[41] NDRHC 28.

that it is difficult to gauge the amount of wine for the Eucharist and there is a danger that "more than a reasonable quantity of the blood of Christ remain to be consumed at the end of the celebration" [GIRM 285a]. The same is true wherever access to the chalice would be difficult to arrange, or where such a large amount of wine would be required that its certain provenance and quality could only be known with difficulty, or wherever there is not an adequate number of sacred ministers or extraordinary ministers of Holy Communion with proper formation, or where a notable part of the people continues to prefer not to approach the chalice for various reasons, so that the sign of unity would in some sense be negated.[42]

Regarding preparation for the distribution of Communion under both kinds, the *General Instruction* states:

For Communion under both kinds the following should be prepared:

a. If Communion from the chalice is carried out by communicants' drinking directly from the chalice, a chalice of a sufficiently large size or several chalices are prepared. Care should, however, be taken in planning lest beyond what is needed of the blood of Christ remains to be consumed at the end of the celebration.

b. If Communion is carried out by intinction, the hosts should be neither too thin nor too small, but rather a little thicker than usual, so that after being dipped partly into the blood of Christ they can still easily be distributed to each communicant.[43]

Redemptionis Sacramentum adds:

If one chalice is not sufficient for Communion to be distributed under both kinds to the priest concelebrants or Christ's faith-

---

[42] RS 102.
[43] GIRM 285.

ful, there is no reason why the priest celebrant should not use several chalices. For it is to be remembered that all priests in celebrating Holy Mass are bound to receive Communion under both kinds. It is praiseworthy, by reason of the sign value, to use a main chalice of larger dimensions, together with smaller chalices.

However, the pouring of the blood of Christ after the Consecration from one vessel to another is completely to be avoided, lest anything should happen that would be to the detriment of so great a mystery. Never to be used for containing the blood of the Lord are flagons, bowls, or other vessels that are not fully in accord with the established norms.[44]

Administration of the Precious Blood

The precious blood can be administered in a number of ways. According to the *General Instruction*:

> The blood of the Lord may be received either by drinking from the chalice directly, or by intinction, or by means of a tube or a spoon.[45]

Most Americans, at least in the Latin rite, are very unfamiliar with the reception of the precious blood through a tube or by a spoon. Indeed, the U.S. bishops' norms state:

> Distribution of the precious blood by a spoon or through a straw is not customary in the Latin dioceses of the United States of America.[46]

It is not prohibited to distribute the precious blood in this manner, but it is not common. Also, the reference to a "straw" is somewhat misleading. We are not talking about an ordinary

---

[44] RS 105–106.

[45] GIRM 245.

[46] NDRHC 48.

plastic or paper straw in this case, nor are we talking about an ordinary spoon.

Instead, we are talking about sacred vessels that are subject to the requirements to which all liturgical vessels are subject. For example, the previous edition of the *General Instruction* required that tubes be made of silver. This requirement is not found in the current edition, but the general laws regarding what liturgical vessels may be made of still apply. Under current law such tubes and spoons used at ordinary parish Masses would likely (though not necessarily) be made out of metal and plated with gold (see Chapter 12). The situation would be different in the case of administering Holy Communion to a person in danger of death in the hospital. If the right kind of liturgical tube or spoon were not available in an emergency such as that, the need to administer Communion as *viaticum* would take precedence.

Somewhat more familiar to Latin rite Americans is the distribution of the precious blood by intinction. The current U.S. bishops' norms state:

> Holy Communion may be distributed by intinction in the following manner: "the communicant, while holding the paten under the chin, approaches the priest who holds the vessel with the hosts and at whose side stands the minister holding the chalice. The priest takes the host, intincts the particle into the chalice and, showing it, says: 'The body and blood of Christ.' The communicant responds, 'Amen,' and receives the sacrament on the tongue from the priest. Afterwards, the communicant returns to his or her place" (Sacred Congregation for Divine Worship, *Sacramentali Communione: Instruction Extending the Practice of Communion under Both Kinds* [June 29, 1970], no. 6 [DOL 270, no. 2115]).

The communicant, including the extraordinary minister, is never allowed to self-communicate, even by means of intinction. Communion under either form, bread or wine, must always be given by an ordinary or extraordinary minister of Holy Communion.[47]

Redemptionis Sacramentum adds:

The communicant must not be permitted to intinct the host himself in the chalice, nor to receive the intincted host in the hand. As for the host to be used for the intinction, it should be made of valid matter, also consecrated; it is altogether forbidden to use non-consecrated bread or other matter.[48]

There has been a notable change in the law regarding intinction. The previous law for the Latin dioceses of the United States, *This Holy and Living Sacrifice*, stated:

Because of its ancient sign value *"ex institutione Christi"* ["of Christ's institution"], Communion from the cup or chalice is always to be preferred to any other form of ministering the precious blood.[49]

It also stated:

[This form] of receiving the precious blood . . . [is] not customary in the United States.[50]

So previously intinction, though not prohibited, was discouraged by being placed in the "not customary" category, like reception of the precious blood via a tube or spoon. In the new norms, however, this is not the case. Indeed, intinction is even encouraged as an option if the number of communicants would be so great that it would require an excessive number of extraordinary ministers.

---

[47] NDRHC 49–50.

[48] RS 104.

[49] HLS 44.

[50] HLS 51.

While intinction has been put on a higher footing, there is still something of a preference for receiving the precious blood from the chalice, though the language used to express this preference is much less forceful:

> Among the ways of ministering the precious blood as prescribed by the *General Instruction of the Roman Missal*, Communion from the chalice is generally the preferred form in the Latin Church, provided that it can be carried out properly according to the norms and without any risk of even apparent irreverence toward the blood of Christ.[51]

And, indeed, receiving the precious blood from the chalice is the normal way it is received in the Latin dioceses of the United States. When this occurs, the chalice is handed to the communicant:

> The chalice is offered to the communicant with the words "The blood of Christ," to which the communicant responds, "Amen."[52]

When the communicants drink from the cup, there is a brief purification performed after each one has received the precious blood:

> After each communicant has received the blood of Christ, the minister carefully wipes both sides of the rim of the chalice with a purificator. This action is a matter of both reverence and hygiene. For the same reason, the minister turns the chalice slightly after each communicant has received the precious blood.[53]

In no case may the faithful be required to receive the precious blood when Communion is offered from the chalice:

---

[51] NDRHC 42.
[52] NDRHC 43.
[53] NDRHC 45.

It is the choice of the communicant, not the minister, to receive from the chalice.[54]

There has also been a notable change in the law here. *This Holy and Living Sacrifice* stated:

> When Communion from the cup is offered to the assembly, it shall always be clear that it is the option of the communicant and not of the minister whether the communicant shall receive the consecrated wine. *Of course, pastors should encourage the whole assembly to receive Communion under both kinds.*[55]

As can be seen, the recommendation (assumption, even) that pastors should encourage everyone to receive from the chalice is gone. This omission suggests that the bishops (or the Holy See, which approved this document) do not want pastors putting pressure on people to receive our Lord under the form of wine, which could cause discomfort for them if they chose not to and were visibly seen to be "not going along with the group," or which could cause additional difficulties for people with a history of alcohol problems.

Children are allowed to receive the precious blood when it is offered to the faithful providing they are old enough and properly prepared:

> Children are encouraged to receive Communion under both kinds provided that they are properly instructed and that they are old enough to receive from the chalice.[56]

There has also been a notable change in the law here. According to *This Holy and Living Sacrifice*:

> Special care shall be given when children receive Communion from the chalice. Parents should be instructed that Communion

---

[54] NDRHC 46.
[55] HLS 48 (emphasis added).
[56] NDRHC 47.

under both kinds is an ancient tradition for children old enough to drink from a cup. However, children should have some familiarity with drinking wine at home before they are offered the chalice.[57]

There is no longer a recommendation that parents be "instructed" that it is an "ancient tradition" for "children old enough to drink from a cup" to receive the precious blood. This could put undue pressure on them. Also, the statement that children should already have experience drinking wine at home is gone. Matters are much more left to the discretion of parents—without encouraging pressure from parish sources.

With regard to posture during Communion—whether one can receive kneeling or standing—see the section on posture in Chapter 13.

---

[57] HLS 49.

10. Communion Rite

Lord's Prayer or Our Father

The Communion rite begins with the recitation of the Our Father. The *General Instruction* describes the significance of this prayer for the liturgy as follows:

> In the Lord's Prayer a petition is made for daily food, which for Christians means preeminently the eucharistic bread, and also for purification from sin, so that what is holy may, in fact, be given to those who are holy. The priest says the invitation to the prayer, and all the faithful say it with him; the priest alone adds the embolism, which the people conclude with a doxology. The embolism, enlarging upon the last petition of the Lord's Prayer itself, begs deliverance from the power of evil for the entire community of the faithful.
>
> The invitation, the prayer itself, the embolism, and the doxology by which the people conclude these things are sung or said aloud.[1]

The embolism is the prayer that immediately follows the Lord's Prayer, when the priest says:

> Deliver us Lord, we pray, from every evil,
> Graciously grant peace in our days,
> That, by the help of your mercy,
> We may always be free from sin
> And safe from all distress,
> As we await the blessed hope

---

[1] GIRM 81.

And the coming of our Savior, Jesus Christ.

Then follows the final doxology said by the people:

For the kingdom,
The power, and the glory are yours
Now and forever.

This is an ancient liturgical response. It appears in some ancient manuscripts as part of Matthew 6:13, though it was probably not in the original version of Matthew's Gospel but was
added by a scribe because of its use in the liturgy. It was not
part of the Latin liturgy prior to Vatican II, but it was restored
in the liturgical reform that followed the Council.

Concerning this final doxology, the *Catechism of the Catholic
Church* states:

> The final doxology, "For the kingdom, the power and the glory
> are yours, now and forever," takes up again, by inclusion, the
> first three petitions to our Father: the glorification of his name,
> the coming of his reign, and the power of his saving will. But
> these prayers are now proclaimed as adoration and thanksgiving,
> as in the liturgy of heaven (see also Rev. 1:6; 4:11; 5:13). The
> ruler of this world has mendaciously attributed to himself the
> three titles of kingship, power, and glory (see also Luke 4:5–
> 6). Christ, the Lord, restores them to his Father and our Father,
> until he hands over the kingdom to him when the mystery of
> salvation will be brought to its completion and God will be all
> in all (1 Cor. 15:24–28).[2]

One of the most commonly asked questions concerns the
holding of hands during the Our Father. The Holy See has not
ruled directly on this issue. In a response to a query, however,
the Holy See noted that holding hands "is a liturgical gesture
introduced spontaneously but on personal initiative; it is not

---

[2] CCC 2855.

in the rubrics."[3] For this reason, no one can be required to hold hands during the Our Father.

People also ask whether the embolism may be omitted, especially when the concluding doxology is sung. The answer is no. Priests are directed to say the embolism even in Masses without a congregation.[4] When the Lord's Prayer and its doxology are sung, the priest alone sings the embolism between the two. In 1972 the Sacred Congregation for Divine Worship issued an instruction that directed:

> After . . . the Eucharistic Prayer, all sing the acclamation, "Amen." Then the priest alone pronounces the invitation for the Lord's Prayer and all sing it with him. The priest alone continues [singing] with the embolism, and all join in the concluding doxology.[5]

Rite of Peace

Following the recitation of the Our Father is the Rite of Peace, which is a liturgical reflection of Jesus' exhortation to be reconciled with one's brother before presenting one's gift at the altar (Matt. 5:23–24). The *General Instruction* explains its purpose:

> The Rite of Peace follows, by which the Church asks for peace and unity for herself and for the whole human family, and the faithful express to each other their ecclesial communion and mutual charity before communicating in the sacrament.
>
> As for the sign of peace to be given, the manner is to be established by conferences of bishops in accordance with the culture and customs of the peoples. It is, however, appropriate

---

[3] *Notitiae* 11 [1975] 226; DOL 1502 n. R29.
[4] GIRM 266.
[5] *Ordo Cantus Missae* 15; DOL 4294.

that each person offer the sign of peace only to those who are nearest and in a sober manner.[6]

Regarding the manner in which the Rite of Peace is conducted, the rubrics state:

The priest, turned toward the people, extending and then joining his hands, adds:

The peace of the Lord be with you always.

The people reply:

And with your spirit.

Then, if appropriate, the deacon, or the priest, adds:

Let us offer each other the sign of peace.

And all offer one another a sign, in keeping with local customs, that expresses peace, communion, and charity. The priest gives the sign of peace to a deacon or minister.

There was a trend in which some priests conducted elaborate versions of the exchange of peace in which they left the sanctuary and greeted large numbers of people all over the church. This had the effect, at times deliberately so, of overshadowing the rite of Communion for which it was a preparation. This problem was noted at the 2005 Synod of Bishops on the Eucharist, and in his apostolic exhortation *Sacramentum Caritatis* that followed the synod, Pope Benedict XVI noted that:

[D]uring the Synod of Bishops there was discussion about the appropriateness of greater restraint in this gesture, which can be exaggerated and cause a certain distraction in the assembly just before the reception of Communion. It should be kept in mind that nothing is lost when the sign of peace is marked by

---

[6] GIRM 82.

a sobriety which preserves the proper spirit of the celebration, as, for example, when it is restricted to one's immediate neighbors.[7]

Accordingly, the rubrics now specify that the priest merely gives the sign of peace "to a deacon or minister" and the *General Instruction* adds:

> The priest may give the sign of peace to the ministers but always remains within the sanctuary, so as not to disturb the celebration. In the dioceses of the United States of America, for a good reason, on special occasions (for example, in the case of a funeral, a wedding, or when civic leaders are present) the priest may offer the sign of peace to a few of the faithful near the sanctuary. At the same time, in accord with the decisions of the conference of bishops, all offer one another a sign that expresses peace, communion, and charity. While the sign of peace is being given, one may say, *Pax Domini sit semper vobiscum* ("The peace of the Lord be with you always"), to which the response is "Amen."[8]

Note that the text says that while the sign of peace is being given "one *may* say" the greeting "The peace of the Lord be with you always." It proposes this as an example but does not mandate this formula. Neither is a particular way of expressing the sign mandated (handshake, hug, kiss, bow). While the U.S. bishops could determine these matters more precisely, they have chosen not to. The former American *Appendix to the General Instruction* stated:

> The conference of bishops has left the development of special modes of exchanging the sign of peace to local usage. Neither a specific form nor specific words are determined (November

---

[7] SCT 49.
[8] GIRM 154.

1969). See the statement of the Bishops' Committee on the Liturgy, *The Sign of Peace* (1977).[9]

The *Appendix* no longer has legal force, but what it says in this passage is an accurate description of the current state of law: The bishops have not established a national policy regarding the form or words for the sign of peace. Unless the local bishop has, the matter remains up to the individual person's discretion.

It also should be noted that the rubrics state, "Then, *if appropriate*, the deacon, or the priest" invites an individual exchange of a sign of peace. Many do not realize it, but the individual exchange of a sign of peace is optional. It is not a liturgical abuse to omit the individual exchange and conclude the Rite of Peace with the people's response, "And with your spirit," which is where it ended prior to the liturgical reform that followed Vatican II.

In fact, in some locations the individual exchange of peace has been omitted during flu season as a way of preventing infection. A 2009 document from the bishops' Committee on Divine Worship stated:

> In previous years, what has the Church done in localities where the outbreak of influenza is most significant?
>
> In those localities where the outbreak of the disease has been the most significant, bishops have introduced several liturgical adaptations in regard to such practices as the distribution of Holy Communion and the exchange of the sign of peace in order to limit the spread of contagion.[10]

Since the option of the individual exchange of peace was introduced after Vatican II, some have suggested that it be

---

[9] AGI 56b.

[10] *Ten Questions on Influenza/H1N1 (Swine Flu) and the Liturgy*, question 7.

moved to another location in the Mass (e.g., the beginning of the Liturgy of the Eucharist) so that it does not disturb or distract people as they are mentally preparing to receive the Lord in Holy Communion. At the 2005 Synod of Bishops on the Eucharist, this was suggested in the "Propositions" that the synod fathers drafted for Pope Benedict XVI:

PROPOSITION 23: THE SIGN OF PEACE

The greeting of peace in the Holy Mass is an expressive sign of great value and depth (see also John 14:27). However, in certain cases, it assumes a dimension that could be problematic, when it is too prolonged or even when it causes confusion, just before receiving Communion.

Perhaps it would be useful to assess if the sign of peace should take place at another moment of the celebration, taking into account ancient and venerable customs.

And in his post-synodal apostolic exhortation, Pope Benedict XVI wrote:

Taking into account ancient and venerable customs and the wishes expressed by the synod fathers, I have asked the competent curial offices to study the possibility of moving the sign of peace to another place, such as before the presentation of the gifts at the altar. To do so would also serve as a significant reminder of the Lord's insistence that we be reconciled with others before offering our gifts to God (see also Matt. 5:23 ff.); see also *Propositio* 23.[11]

As of this writing, no decision has been announced regarding the proposal to move the sign of peace. Presumably it is still under study at the Holy See.[12]

---

[11] SCT footnote 150.

[12] As part of its study of this issue, the Congregation for Divine Worship and the Discipline of the Sacraments has apparently been polling the

Fraction, Commingling, and Agnus Dei

The fraction rite, or "breaking of the bread," follows the Rite of Peace. "Breaking of the bread" is an ancient term for the eucharistic liturgy. Though it can mean just sharing a meal together, its eucharistic usage goes back to apostolic days, following Christ's breaking of the bread at the Last Supper (Acts 2:42, 46; see also Luke 22:19). This use of the term *bread* follows Christ's own description of himself as "the Bread of Life" (John 6:48) and St. Paul's references to the Eucharist *according to appearances*, such as, "The bread which we break, is it not a participation in the body of Christ?" (1 Cor. 10:16).

At the time when the priest's host is broken, he also drops a small part of it into the chalice. This is called the commingling. It originally developed from a practice known as the *fermentum*, whereby a fragment from one host was broken off and sent to another celebration of the Eucharist to reveal the continuity of the Church in the eucharistic sacrifice. This custom fell out of use over time, and other interpretations of the significance of the commingling have been offered, such as that it signifies the reunification of Christ's body and blood in his glorious, resurrected body.

While the fraction rite and commingling are taking place, the prayer *Agnus Dei* or "Lamb of God" is sung or recited.

---

national bishops' conferences. According to the BCDW *Newsletter*, a survey of the U.S. bishops was conducted at the November 2008 meeting of the bishops' conference. Of the eighty-nine bishops who responded, 66 percent favored moving the sign of peace after the Prayer of the Faithful and before the Presentation of the Gifts, 32 percent favored leaving it where it is now, and 2 percent proposed other solutions (BCDW *Newsletter*, November–December 2008, p. 42).

The U.S. norms for distributing Holy Communion under both kinds note:

> As the *Agnus Dei* or Lamb of God is begun, the Bishop or priest alone, or with the assistance of the deacon, and if necessary of concelebrating priests, breaks the eucharistic bread. Other empty ciboria or patens are then brought to the altar if this is necessary. The deacon or priest places the consecrated bread in several ciboria or patens, if necessary, as required for the distribution of Holy Communion. If it is not possible to accomplish this distribution in a reasonable time, the celebrant may call upon the assistance of other deacons or concelebrating priests.[13]

Note that it is the priest or deacon who distributes the hosts among several ciboria—not a lay person.

The *General Instruction* offers the following description of this part of the Mass:

> The priest breaks the eucharistic bread, assisted, if the case calls for it, by the deacon or a concelebrant. Christ's gesture of breaking bread at the Last Supper, which gave the entire eucharistic action its name in apostolic times, signifies that the many faithful are made one body (1 Cor. 10:17) by receiving Communion from the one bread of life which is Christ, who died and rose for the salvation of the world. The fraction or breaking of bread is begun after the sign of peace and is carried out with proper reverence, though it should not be unnecessarily prolonged, nor should it be accorded undue importance. This rite is reserved to the priest and the deacon.
>
>   The priest breaks the bread and puts a piece of the host into the chalice to signify the unity of the body and blood of the Lord in the work of salvation, namely, of the living and glorious

---

[13] NDRHC 37.

body of Jesus Christ. The supplication *Agnus Dei* is, as a rule, sung by the choir or cantor with the congregation responding; or it is, at least, recited aloud. This invocation accompanies the fraction and, for this reason, may be repeated as many times as necessary until the rite has reached its conclusion, the last time ending with the words *dona nobis pacem* ("grant us peace").[14]

Personal Preparation for Communion

Both the priest and the people now make a personal act of preparation to receive Communion:

> The priest prepares himself by a prayer, said quietly, that he may fruitfully receive Christ's body and blood. The faithful do the same, praying silently.
>
> The priest next shows the faithful the eucharistic bread, holding it above the paten or above the chalice, and invites them to the banquet of Christ. Along with the faithful, he then makes an act of humility using the prescribed words taken from the Gospels.[15]

At this point the priest shows the host to the people. The rubrics of the *Roman Missal* specify:

> *The priest genuflects, takes the host and, holding it slightly raised above the paten or above the chalice, while facing the people, says aloud:*
>
> Behold the Lamb of God,
> Behold him who takes away the sins of the world.
> Blessed are those who called to the supper of the Lamb.
>
> *And together with the people he adds once:*
>
> Lord, I am not worthy
> That you should enter under my roof,

---

[14] GIRM 83.
[15] GIRM 84.

But only say the word
And my soul shall be healed.

This contains a number of interesting changes. The first and least obvious is that the priest now has the option of holding the host above the chalice. This was not the case before. He had only the option of holding it over the paten. Yet for years while this law was in force there were pictures of John Paul II elevating the host above the chalice. It was no surprise, then, that when the *Roman Missal* was revised, John Paul II made provision for a practice that he himself had been following for years.

More obvious are the changes in the words used by the priest and people. Both have been translated more literally so that they reflect the biblical passages they are based on. The priest's part is based on John the Baptist's declaration "Behold, the Lamb of God, who takes away the sin of the world!" (John 1:29).

It is also based on an angel's statement in Revelation: "Write this: Blessed are those who are invited to the marriage supper of the Lamb" (Rev. 19:9).

Meanwhile, the people's response is based on the words of the centurion who asked Jesus to heal his servant: "Lord . . . I am not worthy to have you come under my roof. . . . But say the word, and let my servant be healed" (Luke 7:6–7).

Reception of Communion

The priest then takes Communion. The rubrics specify the manner in which he is to do this:

The priest, facing the altar, says quietly:

May the body of Christ
keep me safe for eternal life.

And he reverently consumes the body of Christ.
Then he takes the chalice and says quietly:

> May the blood of Christ
> keep me safe for eternal life.

And he reverently consumes the blood of Christ.

The rubrics specify what the priest is to say as his private prayer and that he is to say it quietly. It is not a problem if he can be faintly heard (if he is wearing a sensitive microphone, it may be very difficult for him not to be heard), but he should not deliberately project his voice, nor should he change the words of the prayer—e.g., "May the body/blood of Christ bring us to everlasting life."

It is also important that he receive Communion first, before the faithful do, as the following rubrics indicate:

> *After this [i.e., his own Communion], he takes the paten or ciborium and approaches the communicants. The priest raises a host slightly and shows it to each of the communicants, saying:*

> The body of Christ.

> *The communicant replies:*

> Amen.

> *And receives Holy Communion.*
> *If a deacon also distributes Holy Communion, he does so in the same manner.*

Sequence of Communion

It is clear from a variety of sources that the priest is to receive Communion prior to the faithful.[16] It is also clear that the deacon is to receive Communion after the priest and before the people:

---

[16] E.g., GIRM 158–60.

After the priest's Communion, the deacon receives Communion under both kinds from the priest himself and then assists the priest in distributing Communion to the people. If Communion is given under both kinds, the deacon himself administers the chalice to the communicants; and, when the distribution is completed, he immediately and reverently consumes at the altar all of the blood of Christ that remains, assisted if necessary by other deacons and priests.[17]

It is, therefore, not permitted for the deacon and the priest to receive Communion at the same time.

It is even less appropriate, and also not permitted, for extraordinary ministers of Holy Communion to receive at the same time as the priest.

> To avoid creating confusion, certain practices are to be avoided and eliminated where such have emerged in particular churches [including] extraordinary ministers receiving Holy Communion apart from the other faithful as though concelebrants.[18]

The strong statement—that the practice of having extraordinary ministers receive Communion at the same time as the priest, apart from the rest of the faithful, must be eliminated—shows how serious the Holy See is on this matter.

This concern with the sequence in which Communion is received is prompted by a pair of opposing tendencies that have emerged in recent years. The natural sequence—and the one that the Church intends—is for the reception of Holy Communion to flow hierarchically, from the main celebrant and any concelebrating priests to the deacon and then to the laity. However, in recent years some priests have delayed their own reception of Communion (as well as that of the deacons

---

[17] GIRM 182.
[18] EM, Practical Provisions 8 §2.

assisting them) until after the laity in a misguided expression of humility. Others have advanced the reception of Holy Communion by extraordinary ministers to the time that they themselves receive it out of a misguided attempt to promote lay people to something like the status they themselves hold. Both errors are to be avoided.

Redemptionis Sacramentum thus contains a forceful statement regarding when the priest celebrant is to receive Communion:

> A priest must communicate at the altar at the moment laid down by the *Missal* each time he celebrates Holy Mass, and the concelebrants must communicate before they proceed with the distribution of Holy Communion. The priest celebrant or a concelebrant is never to wait until the people's Communion is concluded before receiving Communion himself.[19]

The American norms make explicit when extraordinary ministers should receive Communion:

> If extraordinary ministers of Holy Communion are required by pastoral need, they should not approach the altar before the priest has received Communion. After the priest has concluded his own Communion, he distributes Communion to the extraordinary ministers, assisted by the deacon, and then hands the sacred vessels to them for distribution of Holy Communion to the people.[20]

The American norms also stress that deacons and extraordinary ministers must receive Communion at the times indicated for them:

> All receive Holy Communion in the manner described by the *General Instruction to the Roman Missal*, whether priest concelebrants . . . deacons . . . or extraordinary ministers of Holy

---

[19] RS 97.
[20] NDRHC 38.

Communion. . . . Neither deacons nor lay ministers may ever receive Holy Communion in the manner of a concelebrating priest. The practice of extraordinary ministers of Holy Communion waiting to receive Holy Communion until after the distribution of Holy Communion is not in accord with liturgical law.[21]

After all who will be distributing Holy Communion have received it, the vessels are given to the deacons and extraordinary ministers for the distribution of Holy Communion to the rest of the congregation:

After all [ordinary and extraordinary] eucharistic ministers have received Communion, the bishop or priest celebrant reverently hands vessels containing the body or the blood of the Lord to the deacons or extraordinary ministers who will assist with the distribution of Holy Communion. The deacon may assist the priest in handing the vessels containing the body and blood of the Lord to the extraordinary ministers of Holy Communion.[22]

Avoiding Profanation

The Holy See is quite concerned that the danger of profaning the Eucharist be avoided during the Communion rite. As a result, certain safeguards are required. For example, when the faithful receive Communion in the hand, they must consume it immediately:

[S]pecial care should be taken to ensure that the host is consumed by the communicant in the presence of the minister, so that no one goes away carrying the eucharistic species in his

---

[21] NDRHC 39.
[22] NDRHC 40.

hand. If there is a risk of profanation, then Holy Communion should not be given in the hand to the faithful.[23]

Similarly, even when Communion is not being given in the hand:

The Communion plate for the Communion of the faithful should be retained, so as to avoid the danger of the sacred host or some fragment of it falling.[24]

Communion Chant

During the reception of Communion, it is typical that a Communion chant is sung:

While the priest is receiving the sacrament, the Communion chant is begun. Its purpose is to express the communicants' union in spirit by means of the unity of their voices, to show joy of heart, and to highlight more clearly the "communitarian" nature of the procession to receive Communion. The singing is continued for as long as the sacrament is being administered to the faithful. If, however, there is to be a hymn after Communion, the Communion chant should be ended in a timely manner.

Care should be taken that singers, too, can receive Communion with ease.

In the dioceses of the United States of America there are four options for the Communion chant: (1) the antiphon from the *Roman Missal* or the Psalm from the Roman Gradual as set to music there or in another musical setting; (2) the seasonal antiphon and Psalm of the Simple Gradual; (3) a song from another collection of psalms and antiphons, approved by the United States Conference of Catholic Bishops or the diocesan

---

[23] RS 92.
[24] RS 93.

Bishop, including psalms arranged in responsorial or metrical forms; (4) a suitable liturgical song chosen in accordance with no. 86 [of the GIRM]. This is sung either by the choir alone or by the choir or cantor with the people.

If there is no singing, however, the Communion antiphon found in the *Missal* may be recited either by the faithful, or by some of them, or by a lector. Otherwise the priest himself says it after he has received Communion and before he distributes Communion to the faithful.[25]

Purification of Vessels

Following the distribution of Holy Communion, the vessels need to be purified. A basic description of the process is given in the *General Instruction*:

When the distribution of Communion is finished, the priest himself immediately and completely consumes at the altar any consecrated wine that happens to remain; as for any consecrated hosts that are left, he either consumes them at the altar or carries them to the place designated for the reservation of the Eucharist.

Upon returning to the altar, the priest collects any fragments that may remain. Then, standing at the altar or at the credence table, he purifies the paten or ciborium over the chalice then purifies the chalice, saying quietly, *Quod ore sumpsimus* ("Lord, may I receive"), and dries the chalice with a purificator. If the vessels are purified at the altar, they are carried to the credence table by a minister. Nevertheless, it is also permitted, especially if there are several vessels to be purified, to leave them suitably covered on a corporal, either at the altar or at the credence table, and to purify them immediately after Mass following the dismissal of the people.[26]

---

[25] GIRM 86–87.
[26] GIRM 163.

Although the above passage speaks in terms of the priest performing these tasks, it is possible for others to do so. The rubrics state:

> When the distribution of Communion is over, the priest or a deacon or an acolyte purifies the paten over the chalice and also the chalice itself.

This also applies if the vessels are purified after Mass:

> The sacred vessels are purified by the priest, the deacon, or an instituted acolyte after Communion or after Mass, insofar as possible at the credence table. The purification of the chalice is done with water alone or with wine and water, which is then drunk by whoever does the purification. The paten is usually wiped clean with the purificator.
>
> Care must be taken that whatever may remain of the blood of Christ after the distribution of Communion is consumed immediately and completely at the altar.[27]

The American norms state:

> When more of the precious blood remains than was necessary for Communion, and if not consumed by the bishop or priest celebrant, "the deacon immediately and reverently consumes at the altar all of the blood of Christ which remains; he may be assisted, if needs dictate, by other deacons and priests" [GIRM 287]. When there are extraordinary ministers of Holy Communion, they may consume what remains of the precious blood from their chalice of distribution with permission of the diocesan bishop.[28]

One thing to note is that, while deacons and acolytes can perform the purification, others cannot. This is not something that

---

[27] GIRM 279.
[28] NDRHC 52.

extraordinary ministers of Holy Communion or altar servers can do:

> The sacred vessels are to be purified by the priest, the deacon or an instituted acolyte. The chalice and other vessels may be taken to a side table, where they are cleansed and arranged in the usual way. Other sacred vessels that held the precious blood are purified in the same way as chalices. Provided the remaining consecrated bread has been consumed or reserved and the remaining precious blood has been consumed, "it is permissible to leave the vessels . . . suitably covered and at a side table on a corporal, to be cleansed immediately after Mass following the dismissal of the people."[29]

There is actually a bit of a story to the fact that only priests, deacons, and instituted acolytes can purify the vessels:

> On March 22, 2002, the Congregation for Divine Worship and the Discipline of the Sacraments granted an indult to the USCCB to allow extraordinary ministers of Holy Communion to purify the sacred vessels used during the liturgy. In a letter accompanying the indult (Prot. No. 1382/01/L, March 22, 2002), the Congregation approved the indult *ad experimentum* [for purposes of experiment] for three years.
>
> With the impending expiration of the indult, the Bishops' Committee on the Liturgy surveyed the bishops of the United States regarding the practice of extraordinary ministers of Holy Communion purifying sacred vessels. An overwhelming majority of bishops deemed the practice pastorally useful and free from abuse.
>
> The committee, therefore, recommended that the president of the conference, Bishop William Skylstad, request a permanent indult from the Congregation of Divine Worship and the Discipline of the Sacraments for this continued practice. Accordingly, in a March 9, 2005, letter to Cardinal Francis Arinze, Prefect

---

[29] NDRHC 53; quoting GIRM 182.

of the Congregation for Divine Worship and the Discipline of the Sacraments, a renewal of the indult was requested.[30]

So what happened? Despite the "overwhelming majority" favoring the practice,[31] Rome said no.

On October 13, 2006, Bishop William Skylstad, president of the United States Conference of Catholic Bishops, informed all Bishop members of the conference that he had received a response to his request for an extension of an indult permitting extraordinary ministers of Holy Communion to assist with the purification of sacred vessels at Mass.

In a recent letter to the Conference President, Cardinal Francis Arinze, Prefect of the Congregation for Divine Worship and the Discipline of the Sacraments (Prot. no. 468/05/L), reported that he had brought the matter to the attention of our Holy Father [Benedict XVI] on June 9, 2006, and received a response in the negative.[32]

Consequently, the BCL *Newsletter* published the following:

6. May an extraordinary minister of Holy Communion assist in the purification of sacred vessels?

In accord with the Holy Father's recent decision, as reported in Cardinal Arinze's letter of October 12, 2006 (Prot. no. 468/05/L), an extraordinary minister of Holy Communion may not assist in the purification of sacred vessels. This extraordinary ministry was created exclusively for those instances where there are not enough ordinary ministers to distribute Holy Communion, due to the consummate importance of assuring that the faithful have the opportunity to receive Holy Communion at Mass, even when it is distributed under both species. (See also RS, no. 102.)

---

[30] BCL *Newsletter*, March–April 2005, p. 13.

[31] Of the 119 bishops who responded, 115 (97%) favored making the practice permanent (BCL *Newsletter*, October–November 2005, p. 41).

[32] BCL *Newsletter*, October 2006, p. 37.

7. What about those instances where there are many chalices and only one priest to purify them?

When there are insufficient priests, deacons, or instituted acolytes to purify the additional chalices during Mass, the purification may take place immediately after the Mass has concluded. If such purification by ordinary ministers proves pastorally problematic, consideration should be given to distribution of Holy Communion by intinction or to the distribution of Holy Communion under the form of consecrated bread alone. Priests should also keep in mind potential health risks associated with intinction, especially in the coming flu season.[33]

When the vessels are being purified, and at all other times, great care must be taken with particles or drops of the Eucharist:

> Whenever a fragment of the host adheres to his fingers, especially after the fraction or the Communion of the faithful, the priest is to wipe his fingers over the paten or, if necessary, wash them. Likewise, he should also gather any fragments that may have fallen outside the paten.[34]
>
> If a host or any particle should fall, it is to be picked up reverently. If any of the precious blood is spilled, the area where the spill occurred should be washed with water, and this water should then be poured into the sacrarium in the sacristy.[35]

A sacrarium is a special sink in the sacristy that leads down into the earth rather than into the sewer system. Sacraria have been in use in Catholic churches for a very long time. They are used to dispose of *water* that has been used to purify the liturgical vessels and linens. The *General Instruction* states:

---

[33] Ibid., p. 40.
[34] GIRM 278.
[35] GIRM 280.

The practice is to be kept of building a sacrarium in the sacristy, into which are poured the water from the purification of sacred vessels and linens.[36]

Redemptionis Sacramentum adds:

Let pastors take care that the linens for the sacred table, especially those which will receive the sacred species, are always kept clean and that they are washed in the traditional way. It is praiseworthy for this to be done by pouring the water from the first washing, done by hand, into the church's sacrarium or into the ground in a suitable place. After this a second washing can be done in the usual way.[37]

The sacred species themselves may *not* be put into a sacrarium. The sacred species must be consumed or reserved or, in exceptional instances, dissolved so that the Real Presence no longer remains and the resulting *water* disposed of through the sacrarium.

Dissolving the sacred species of wine, for example, is indicated in GIRM 280 (above) when the precious blood has been spilled. One would dissolve a particle of a host, for example, if it had become so soiled (such as by regurgitation) that it is inedible. In both cases, by dissolving the sacred species, the appearances of bread and wine, and thus the Real Presence, no longer remain and only water is left. Only this water, not species concealing the Real Presence, may be put into a sacrarium.

The American norms state:

The reverence due to the precious blood of the Lord demands that it be fully consumed after Communion is completed and never be poured into the ground or the sacrarium.[38]

---

[36] GIRM 334.

[37] RS 120.

[38] NDRHC 55.

In fact, there are severe canonical penalties for putting the sacred species (undissolved) into the sacrarium:

> In accordance with what is laid down by the canons, "one who throws away the consecrated species or takes them away or keeps them for a sacrilegious purpose, incurs a *latae sententiae* excommunication reserved to the Apostolic See; a cleric, moreover, may be punished by another penalty, not excluding dismissal from the clerical state" [CIC 1367]. To be regarded as pertaining to this case is any action that is voluntarily and gravely disrespectful of the sacred species. Anyone, therefore, who acts contrary to these norms, for example casting the sacred species into the sacrarium or in an unworthy place or on the ground, incurs the penalties laid down.[39]

The Holy See also clarified what is to be done with particles of the Eucharist that are recovered:

> *Dubium*: *The GIRM no. 237*[40] *says that particles of the eucharistic bread are to be collected after the Consecration, but it is not clear what is to be done about them.*

> *Responsum*: The GIRM no. 237 must be taken in context with other articles that deal with the same point. The description of the basic form of celebration says clearly: "After Communion the priest returns to the altar and collects any remaining particles. Then, standing at the side of the altar or at the side table, he purifies the paten or ciborium over the chalice, then purifies the chalice . . . and dries it with a purificator" (GIRM no. 120[41]). The Order of Mass with a congregation no. 138[42] says: "After

---

[39] RS 107.

[40] This refers to section 237 of the previous edition of the GIRM. It corresponds to section 278 (quoted above) in the current edition.

[41] The former GIRM 120 corresponds to part of GIRM 162 in the current edition.

[42] The former GIRM 138 corresponds to GIRM 183 in the current edition.

Communion the priest or deacon purifies the paten over the chalice and the chalice itself." The Order of Mass without a congregation no. 31 says: "Then the priest purifies the chalice over the paten and the chalice itself." The point, therefore, is quite clear.[43]

Reservation of the Eucharist

For information on the tabernacle—the place where the Eucharist is reserved—see Chapter 12.

The reservation of hosts is standard and generally does not give rise to many questions. However, the reservation of the precious blood is another matter. As noted in the previous section, any of the precious blood that remains after communion is to be consumed entirely—under normal circumstances.

The American norms state:

> The precious blood may not be reserved, except for giving Communion to someone who is sick. Only sick people who are unable to receive Communion under the form of bread may receive it under the form of wine alone at the discretion of the priest. If not consecrated at a Mass in the presence of the sick person, the blood of the Lord is kept in a properly covered vessel and is placed in the tabernacle after Communion. The precious blood should be carried to the sick in a vessel that is closed in such a way as to eliminate all danger of spilling. If some of the precious blood remains after the sick person has received Communion, it should be consumed by the minister, who should also see to it that the vessel is properly purified.[44]

---

[43] *Notitiae* 8 (1972) 195; DOL 1627 n. R41.
[44] NDRHC 54.

Silence after Communion

In many parishes, after Communion has been administered, it is normal to pause for a few moments of silent prayer. However, this is not the only option:

> When the distribution of Communion is finished, as circumstances suggest, the priest and faithful spend some time praying privately. If desired, a psalm or other canticle of praise or a hymn may also be sung by the entire congregation.[45]

Elsewhere the *General Instruction* states:

> Afterwards [i.e., after Communion], the priest may return to the chair. A sacred silence may now be observed for some period of time, or a psalm or another canticle of praise or a hymn may be sung.[46]

Note that the priest *may* return to the chair; he does not have to do so. This is important to note because it is the practice in some places for people to kneel following Communion until the priest sits down or until the Holy Eucharist has been reserved in the tabernacle. These are permitted practices, but they are not mandated by law.

As we will see in Chapter 13, there is no mandated posture following Communion. Individuals may stand, sit, or kneel at their preference; they may do whatever they feel best promotes their own personal devotion to Christ in the Eucharist. One should not scruple about when to begin sitting after Communion.

If there is not a pause for silent prayer at this time, the faithful are urged to express their gratitude and devotion by making an

---

[45] GIRM 88.
[46] GIRM 164.

act of thanksgiving after they have received their Lord in Holy Communion. Many times people fail to do this. Some even leave the church building as soon as they receive Communion. As a result, the Holy See has stated that:

> The faithful are to be recommended not to omit to make a proper thanksgiving after Communion. They may do this during the celebration with a period of silence, with a hymn, psalm or other song of praise, or also after the celebration, if possible by staying behind to pray for a suitable time.[47]

Prayer after Communion

After the silence or the song following Communion, or after the purification of the vessels (if this is done during Mass), the priest then invites the faithful to prayer, which closes the Communion rite. The rubrics of the *Roman Missal* state:

> *Then, standing at the altar or at the chair and facing the people, with his hands joined, the priest says:*
>
> Let us pray.
>
> *All pray in silence with the priest for a while, unless silence has just been observed. Then the priest, with hands extended, says the prayer after Communion, at the end of which the people acclaim:*
>
> Amen.

---

[47] ID 17.

11. Concluding Rites

Just as Mass is begun with certain rites, normally it is also brought to a close with certain rites.

The concluding rites consist of:

a. Brief announcements, if they are necessary.

b. The priest's greeting and blessing, which on certain days and occasions is enriched and expressed in the prayer over the people or another more solemn formula.

c. The dismissal of the people by the deacon or the priest, so that each may go out to do good works, praising and blessing God.

d. The kissing of the altar by the priest and the deacon, followed by a profound bow to the altar by the priest, the deacon, and the other ministers.[1]

The concluding rites do not always occur, however:

If, however, another liturgical action follows the Mass, the concluding rites, that is, the greeting, the blessing, and the dismissal, are omitted.[2]

In most cases, a second liturgical service does not follow, and so the concluding rites take place. They may, however, be preceded by parish announcements:

When the prayer after Communion is concluded, brief announcements to the people may be made, if they are needed.[3]

---

[1] GIRM 90.

[2] GIRM 170.

[3] GIRM 166.

If there is a deacon present, he also may make the announcements:

Once the prayer after Communion has been said, the deacon makes brief announcements to the people, if indeed any need to be made, unless the priest prefers to do this himself.[4]

The priest then greets and blesses the people:

Then the Priest, extending his hands, greets the people, saying, *The Lord be with you*. They reply, *And with your spirit*. The Priest, joining his hands again and then immediately placing his left hand on his breast, raises his right hand and adds, *May Almighty God bless you* and, as he makes the Sign of the Cross over the people, he continues, *the Father, and the Son, and the Holy Spirit*. All reply, *Amen*.

On certain days and occasions this blessing, in accordance with the rubrics, is expanded and expressed by a Prayer over the People or another more solemn formula.

A Bishop blesses the people with the appropriate formula, making the Sign of the Cross three times over the people.[5]

Immediately after the Blessing, with hands joined, the Priest adds, *Ite, missa est (Go forth, the Mass is ended)* and all reply, *Thanks be to God*.[6]

If a deacon is present, he may give the dismissal instead of the priest:

If a Prayer over the People or a formula of Solemn Blessing is used, the deacon says, *Bow down for the blessing*. After the priest's blessing, the deacon, with hands joined and facing the people,

---

[4] GIRM 184.

[5] Cf. *Ceremonial of Bishops* [*Caeremoniale Episcoporum*], *editio typica*, 1984, nos. 1118–21.

[6] GIRM 167–68.

dismisses the people, saying, *Ite, missa est* (*Go forth, the Mass is ended*).[7]

Under the previous translation of the Mass, there was only one option for the priest or deacon to say at the conclusion of the Mass: "The Mass is ended, go in peace." With the release of the new translation, not only were these words changed, but several new options approved by Pope Benedict XVI have also been added. The current rubrics state:

Then the deacon, or the priest himself, with hands joined and facing the people, says:

Go forth, the Mass is ended.

Or:

Go and announce the Gospel of the Lord.

Or:

Go in peace, glorifying the Lord by your life.

Or:

Go in peace.

The people reply:

Thanks be to God.

Then the priest venerates the altar as usual with a kiss, as at the beginning. After making a profound bow with the ministers, he withdraws.

If there is a deacon present, he also kisses the altar:

Then, together with the priest, the deacon venerates the altar with a kiss, makes a profound bow, and departs in a manner similar to the procession beforehand.[8]

---

[7] GIRM 185.
[8] GIRM 186.

12. Liturgical Furnishings and Vestments

General Considerations

Because of the sacred functions carried out in a church and because it is a place for the public worship and honor of God, it is important that, to the best of the community's ability, the church honor God by its design and furnishings. The same is true of the articles and vestments used in the liturgy itself.

As a result, the Church has laid down some general norms for this area. For example, the *Ceremonial of Bishops* states:

> Vestments, church furnishings, and decorative objects that have been handed down from the past are not to be treated carelessly, but kept in good condition. When anything new needs to be provided, it should be chosen to meet the standards of contemporary art, but not out of a desire for novelty.[1]

Often, works of art will be used in the furnishings of a church. These may be freestanding images or paintings or they may be part of some other furnishing. For example, a baptismal font may have a bas-relief carving on its side depicting a scene or scenes from the Bible. Regardless of whether art is freestanding or part of another furnishing, the Church is very concerned that it be of the highest quality:

---

[1] CB 37.

Consequently, the Church constantly seeks the noble assistance of the arts and admits the artistic expressions of all peoples and regions. In fact, just as she is intent on preserving the works of art and the artistic treasures handed down from past centuries and, insofar as necessary, on adapting them to new needs, so also she strives to promote new works of art that are in harmony with the character of each successive age.

On account of this, in commissioning artists and choosing works of art to be admitted into a church, what should be required is that true excellence in art that nourishes faith and devotion and accords authentically with both the meaning and the purpose for which it is intended.[2]

With this said, we may look at the regulations the Church provides for specific furnishings and articles.

Baptismal and Holy Water Fonts

A church's baptismal font is an important liturgical furnishing, for it is through the sacrament of baptism that people become members of the Church.

The baptistery, or area where the baptismal font is located, should be reserved for the sacrament of baptism and should be worthy to serve as a place where Christians are reborn in water and the Holy Spirit. The baptistery may be situated in a chapel either inside or outside the church or in some part of the church easily seen by the faithful; it should be large enough to accommodate a good number of people.

The baptismal font, or the vessel in which on occasion the

---

[2] GIRM 289.

water is prepared for the celebration of the sacraments in the sanctuary, should be spotlessly clean and of pleasing design.[3]

In some churches, the baptismal font is positioned at the main entrance so that people may dip their fingers in its water and make the sign of the cross, reminding themselves of their entrance into the Church by baptism.

In many churches, however, the baptismal font is located elsewhere and small holy water fonts take its place at the entrances to the church. The *Ceremonial of Bishops* states:

> It is an old and honored practice for all who enter a church to dip their hand in a font (stoup) of holy water and sign themselves with the sign of the cross as a reminder of their baptism.[4]

Following the Mass of the Lord's Supper on Holy Thursday, the fonts are emptied of water until they are refilled with the water blessed at Easter. *Paschales Solemnitatis* states:

> Mass is to be celebrated on Easter Day with great solemnity. It is appropriate that the penitential rite on this day take the form of a sprinkling with water blessed at the Vigil, during which the antiphon *Vidi aquam* or some other song of baptismal character should be sung. The fonts at the entrance to the church should also be filled with the same water.[5]

In some places holy water has been removed from the fonts prior to Holy Thursday (e.g., at the beginning of Lent). Sometimes it has even been replaced by sand as part of a misguided evocation of the desert and spiritual dryness. Neither of these practices is called for in the rubrics, nor are they in keeping with the Church's intent. A private reply from the Congregation for Divine Worship in 2000 speaks to this point:

---

[3] BC 995.

[4] CB 110.

[5] PS 97.

Congregation de Cultu Divino et Disciplina Sacramentorum
Prot. N. 569/00/L

March 14, 2000

Dear Father:

This Congregation for Divine Worship has received your letter sent by fax in which you ask whether it is in accord with liturgical law to remove the holy water from the fonts for the duration of the season of Lent.

This Dicastery is able to respond that the removing of holy water from the fonts during the season of Lent is not permitted, in particular, for two reasons:

1. The liturgical legislation in force does not foresee this innovation, which in addition to being *praeter legem* [Latin, "apart from the law"] is contrary to a balanced understanding of the season of Lent, which though truly being a season of penance, is also a season rich in the symbolism of water and baptism, constantly evoked in liturgical texts.

2. The encouragement of the Church that the faithful avail themselves frequently [of] her sacraments and sacramentals is to be understood to apply also to the season of Lent. The "fast" and "abstinence" which the faithful embrace in this season does not extend to abstaining from the sacraments or sacramentals of the Church. The practice of the Church has been to empty the holy water fonts on the days of the Sacred Triduum in preparation of the blessing of the water at the Easter Vigil, and it corresponds to those days on which the Eucharist is not celebrated (i.e., Good Friday and Holy Saturday).

Hoping that this resolves the question and with every good wish and kind regard, I am,

Sincerely yours in Christ,
Mons. Mario Marini
Undersecretary

Candles

Candles play an important role in churches. In the old days they were used as both a source of light and a sign of reverence. Today we use electric lighting, but candles remain important as a sign of reverence and prayer.

> The candles, which are required at every liturgical service out of reverence and on account of the festiveness of the celebration . . . are to be appropriately placed either on or around the altar in a way suited to the design of the altar and the sanctuary so that the whole may be well balanced and not interfere with the faithful's clear view of what takes place at the altar or what is placed on it.[6]

Candles or lamps are also used to indicate the reservation of the Eucharist in the tabernacle (see below).

Chairs

During parts of the liturgy, the priest celebrating Mass is directed to sit. Accordingly, the *General Instruction* states:

> The chair of the priest celebrant must signify his office of presiding over the gathering and of directing the prayer. Thus the best place for the chair is in a position facing the people at the head of the sanctuary, unless the design of the building or other circumstances impede this: for example, if the great distance would interfere with communication between the priest and the gathered assembly, or if the tabernacle is in the center behind the altar. Any appearance of a throne, however, is to be avoided. It is appropriate that, before being put into liturgical

---

[6] GIRM 307.

use, the chair be blessed according to the rite described in the *Roman Ritual*.

Likewise, seats should be arranged in the sanctuary for concelebrating priests as well as for priests who are present for the celebration in choir dress but who are not concelebrating.

The seat for the deacon should be placed near that of the celebrant. Seats for the other ministers are to be arranged so that they are clearly distinguishable from those for the clergy and so that the ministers are easily able to fulfill the function entrusted to them.[7]

The faithful are also directed to sit during much of the Mass, and so the *General Instruction* makes mention of their seating accommodations as well:

Places should be arranged with appropriate care for the faithful so that they are able to participate in the sacred celebrations visually and spiritually, in the proper manner. It is expedient for benches or seats usually to be provided for their use. The custom of reserving seats for private persons, however, is reprehensible. Moreover, benches or chairs should be arranged, especially in newly built churches, in such a way that the people can easily take up the postures required for the different parts of the celebration and can easily come forward to receive Holy Communion.

Care should be taken that the faithful be able not only to see the priest, the deacon, and the lectors but also, with the aid of modern technical means, to hear them without difficulty.[8]

Note that the *General Instruction* stresses that the faithful's seats are to be set up so that they can take the different postures—sitting, standing, kneeling—used in the liturgy. We will come back to this in the section on posture in Chapter 13.

---

[7] GIRM 310.
[8] GIRM 311.

Images

Though the practice arose much earlier, the Second Council of Nicaea (787) dogmatically defined the liceity of using images of Christ and the saints in church. Since that time images —whether in the forms of mosaics, paintings, stained glass, icons, bas-reliefs, or statuary—have been a constant feature of Catholic churches.

This was also emphasized at the Second Vatican Council:

> The practice of placing sacred images in churches so that they may be venerated by the faithful is to be maintained. Nevertheless there is to be restraint regarding their number and prominence so that they do not create confusion among the Christian people or foster religious practices of doubtful orthodoxy.[9]

Correspondingly, the *General Instruction of the Roman Missal* states:

> In the earthly liturgy, the Church participates, by a foretaste, in that heavenly liturgy which is celebrated in the holy city of Jerusalem toward which she journeys as a pilgrim, and where Christ is sitting at the right hand of God; and by venerating the memory of the saints, she hopes one day to have some part and fellowship with them.
>
> Thus, images of the Lord, the Blessed Virgin Mary, and the saints, in accordance with the Church's most ancient tradition, should be displayed for veneration by the faithful in sacred buildings and should be arranged so as to usher the faithful toward the mysteries of faith celebrated there. For this reason, care should be taken that their number not be increased indiscriminately and that they be arranged in proper order so as not to distract the faithful's attention from the celebration itself. There should

---

[9] SC 125.

usually be only one image of any given saint. Generally speaking, in the ornamentation and arrangement of a church as far as images are concerned, provision should be made for the devotion of the entire community as well as for the beauty and dignity of the images.[10]

Generally there are fewer images displayed in churches now than there were a few decades ago. This is in keeping with the Church's regulations. However, the Church has not in any way mandated a total absence of images or a minimalist approach to their use. Note, for example, that the *General Instruction* states that "there should usually be only one image of any given saint"—implying that there can sometimes be more than one and seemingly presupposing that there will be multiple saints represented in the church.

From the very beginning of the liturgical reform, concern was shown that images remain a part of Catholic life. In 1965, Cardinal Giacomo Lercaro, president of the Concilium, wrote a letter to the presidents of the national conferences of bishops in which he stated:

> In the adaptation of churches to the demands of liturgical renewal there has sometimes been exaggeration regarding sacred images. At times, it is true, some churches have been cluttered with images and statues, but to strip bare and do away with absolutely everything is to risk the opposite extreme.[11]

The current *Code of Canon Law* is firm in stating that images are to be placed in churches:

> The practice of displaying sacred images in churches for the reverence of the faithful is to remain in effect. Nevertheless, they

---

[10] GIRM 318.

[11] *Le renouveau liturgique*, June 20, 1965; *Notitiae* 1 (1965), 257–264; DOL 417.

are to be exhibited in moderate number and in suitable order so that the Christian people are not confused nor occasion given for inappropriate devotion [CIC 1188].

The Code is also specific about properly preserving images that are treasures from the past:

> If they are in need of repair, precious images, that is, those distinguished by age, art, or veneration, which are exhibited in churches or oratories for the reverence of the faithful, are never to be restored without the written permission of the ordinary; he is to consult experts before he grants permission [CIC 1189].

Musical Instruments

What instruments may be used at Mass? It is not possible to give an entirely clear answer to this. The Church's current laws regarding music and musical instruments have not been developed with the same kind of rigor that other aspects of the laws have.

One reason may be that music in church is performed live. The ability to play music competently is a specialized skill—even more so now that we have recorded music and most people no longer know how to play instruments. Consequently, a certain amount of deference is shown to musicians. It is easy to imagine a pastor thinking, "Well, I don't really like that hymn, but it's a favorite of the only organist I've got."

Another reason is that music is a very subjective experience about which people have different views—sometimes strongly disagreeing with each other. It also varies by culture, and the Holy See is reluctant to impose a single, highly detailed standard regarding sacred music on cultures around the world.

In practice the Holy See has left much to the discretion of national bishops' conferences, local bishops, and local pastors.

While there has been an effort to tighten the rules, as of this writing the effort has produced limited results.

It is not possible, therefore, to give a detailed list of permitted or prohibited instruments. But here is what can be said.

First, Vatican II's Constitution on the Sacred Liturgy states:

> In the Latin Church the pipe organ is to be held in high esteem, for it is the traditional musical instrument that adds a wonderful splendor to the Church's ceremonies and powerfully lifts up the spirit to God and to higher things.
>
> But other instruments also may be admitted for use in divine worship, with the knowledge and consent of the competent territorial authority. . . . This applies, however, only on condition that the instruments are suitable, or can be made suitable, for sacred use, are in accord with the dignity of the place of worship, and truly contribute to the uplifting of the faithful.[12]

The Sacred Congregation for Rites further elaborated this in the instruction *Musicam Sacram*:

> One criterion for accepting and using musical instruments is the genius and traditions of the particular peoples. At the same time, however, instruments that are generally associated and used only with worldly music are to be absolutely barred from liturgical services and religious devotions. All musical instruments accepted for divine worship must be played in such a way as to meet the requirements of a liturgical service and to contribute to the beauty of worship and the building up of the faithful.[13]

The former *Appendix to the General Instruction* is no longer in force but it provides background on how this was applied here in the United States:

> The conference of bishops has decreed that musical instruments other than the organ may be used in liturgical services provided

---

[12] SC 120.

[13] *Notitiae* 3 (1967) 87–105, 63; DOL 4184.

they are played in a manner that is suitable to public worship (November 1967; see *Constitution on the Liturgy*, art. 120). This decision deliberately refrains from singling out specific instruments. Their use depends on circumstances, the nature of the congregation, etc. In particular cases, if there should be doubt as to the suitability of the instruments, it is the responsibility of the diocesan bishop, in consultation with the diocesan liturgical and music commissions, to render a decision.[14]

What the current law says is this:

While the organ is to be accorded pride of place, other wind, stringed, or percussion instruments may be used in liturgical services in the dioceses of the United States of America, according to longstanding local usage, provided they are truly apt for sacred use or can be rendered apt.[15]

Ambo

Concerning the placement of the ambo, the *General Instruction* states:

The dignity of the word of God requires that the church have a place that is suitable for the proclamation of the word and toward which the attention of the whole congregation of the faithful naturally turns during the Liturgy of the Word.

It is appropriate that this place be ordinarily a stationary ambo and not simply a movable lectern. The ambo must be located in keeping with the design of each church in such a way that the ordained ministers and lectors may be clearly seen and heard by the faithful.

From the ambo only the readings, the Responsorial Psalm, and the Easter Proclamation (*Exsultet*) are to be proclaimed; it may be used also for giving the homily and for announcing the

---

[14] AGI 275.
[15] GIRM 393.

intentions of the Prayer of the Faithful. The dignity of the ambo requires that only a minister of the Word should go up to it.

It is appropriate that a new ambo be blessed according to the rite described in the *Roman Ritual* before it is put into liturgical use.[16]

Altar

The altar is the most important furnishing in a church. It is where the eucharistic sacrifice takes place. Through world history—whether in early Yahwism, in Judaism, in Christianity, or even in non-Christian religions—an altar has always been, in a special way, where man goes to meet and have fellowship with the divine.

On Christian altars, Christ is presented as a living sacrifice to God. He does not suffer or die again, for he did that once for all on the cross. However, the sacrifice of the cross is made sacramentally present on the altar, and in the Eucharist Christ presents himself to the Father as a living sacrifice, just as we are directed to do (Rom. 12:1).

The *General Instruction* states:

> The altar on which the sacrifice of the cross is made present under sacramental signs is also the table of the Lord to which the people of God is called together to participate in the Mass, as well as the center of the thanksgiving that is accomplished through the Eucharist.[17]

Because of its special importance, the Church has requirements about the construction, maintenance, and use of altars. Among the most important of these is whether an altar is fixed or movable and where it is to be located. The Code states:

---

[16] GIRM 309.
[17] GIRM 296.

§1. An altar, or a table upon which the eucharistic sacrifice is celebrated, is called fixed if it is so constructed that it adheres to the floor and thus cannot be moved; it is called movable if it can be removed.

§2. It is desirable to have a fixed altar in every church, but a fixed or a movable altar in other places designated for sacred celebrations [CIC 1235].

The *General Instruction* adds:

The altar should be built apart from the wall, in such a way that it is possible to walk around it easily and that Mass can be celebrated at it facing the people, which is desirable wherever possible. The altar should, moreover, be so placed as to be truly the center toward which the attention of the whole congregation of the faithful naturally turns. The altar is usually fixed and is dedicated.[18]

Note that this text states that it is "desirable whenever possible" to celebrate the Mass facing the people. This establishes a preference in the ordinary form for celebrating Mass in this fashion, but it is legitimate to celebrate Mass *ad orientem* (Latin, "to the east"), meaning that the priest faces in the same direction as the people for much of the celebration, a position that highlights his role as their representative before God. This is the traditional position for the priest, and it is still the usual practice in the extraordinary form.

Still, it can be done in the ordinary form, and there are specific places in the *General Instruction* where it indicates that the priest is to perform certain actions "facing the people," meaning that he would need to turn around at these points in the Mass if he otherwise faces the same direction they do. The points where he is specifically directed to face the people are

---

[18] GIRM 299.

when greeting the congregation in the Introductory Rites,[19] at the *Orate, fratres* just before the Eucharistic Prayer,[20] when he says "The peace of the Lord be with you always,"[21] when he says, "Behold the Lamb of God,"[22] and when he says the Prayer after Communion.[23] It is implicit that he faces the people when away from the altar, such as when preaching the homily or at the chair.[24]

The material out of which an altar is made is also important. In the case of a fixed altar, the regulations are more specific:

> In keeping with the Church's traditional practice and the altar's symbolism, the table of a fixed altar is to be of stone and indeed of natural stone. In the dioceses of the United States of America, however, wood which is worthy, solid, and well crafted may be used, provided that the altar is structurally immobile. The supports or base for upholding the table, however, may be made of any sort of material, provided it is worthy and solid.[25]

In the case of a movable altar, more leeway is allowed:

> A movable altar may be constructed of any noble and solid materials suited to liturgical use, according to the traditions and usages of the different regions.[26]

For many centuries, churches have typically had relics of the saints contained under their main altar. This custom remains today:

---

[19] GIRM 124.
[20] GIRM 146.
[21] GIRM 154.
[22] GIRM 157.
[23] GIRM 165.
[24] See GIRM 310.
[25] GIRM 301.
[26] GIRM 301.

The practice of placing relics of saints, even those not martyrs, under the altar to be dedicated is fittingly retained. Care should be taken, however, to ensure the authenticity of such relics.[27]

The *Code of Canon Law* also mandates this:

The ancient tradition of placing relics of martyrs or other saints under a fixed altar is to be preserved, according to the norms given in the liturgical books [CIC 1237 §2].

The altar is also to be covered with a special cloth:

Out of reverence for the celebration of the memorial of the Lord and for the banquet in which the body and blood of the Lord are offered on an altar where this memorial is celebrated, there should be at least one white cloth, its shape, size, and decoration in keeping with the altar's design. When, in the dioceses of the United States of America, other cloths are used in addition to the altar cloth, then those cloths may be of other colors possessing Christian honorific or festive significance according to longstanding local usage, provided that the uppermost cloth covering the *mensa* (i.e., the altar cloth itself) is always white in color.[28]

And, finally, the altar is to be used only in divine worship:

§1. An altar, whether fixed or movable, must be reserved for divine worship alone, to the absolute exclusion of any profane use.

§2. A body is not to be buried beneath an altar; otherwise, it is not permitted to celebrate Mass on the altar [CIC 1239].

---

[27] GIRM 302.
[28] GIRM 304.

Altar Cross

The cross is the most important symbol in Christian history. The *Ceremonial of Bishops* explains:

> Of all the sacred images, the "figure of the precious life-giving cross of Christ" is preeminent, because it is the symbol of the entire paschal mystery. The cross is the image most cherished by the Christian people and the most ancient; it represents Christ's suffering and victory, and at the same time, as the Fathers of the Church have taught, it points to his Second Coming.[29]

The cross has historically been associated with the altar because of its preeminence as a Christian symbol and because it represents or depicts the sacrifice of the cross that is made sacramentally present on the altar. However, in recent years some parishioners report that in their churches there is either no cross near the altar or there is an image of the resurrected Christ instead. Neither of these is permissible. The Church mandates the presence of a cross:

> There is also to be a cross, with the figure of Christ crucified upon it, either on the altar or near it, where it is clearly visible to the assembled congregation. It is appropriate that such a cross, which calls to mind for the faithful the saving Passion of the Lord, remain near the altar even outside of liturgical celebrations.[30]

Note that it is required that the altar cross have "the figure of Christ crucified upon it." A bare cross or a cross with Christ depicted in some other way (e.g., a resurrected Christ) does not fulfill this requirement.

---

[29] CB 1011.
[30] GIRM 308.

Eucharistic Vessels

The specific vessels used for celebrating the Eucharist are also governed by regulations:

> Among the requisites for the celebration of Mass, the sacred vessels are held in special honor, especially the chalice and paten in which the bread and wine are offered and consecrated and from which they are consumed.
>
> Sacred vessels are to be made from precious metal. If they are made from metal that rusts or from a metal less precious than gold, then ordinarily they should be gilded on the inside.
>
> In the dioceses of the United States of America, sacred vessels may also be made from other solid materials that, according to the common estimation in each region, are precious, for example, ebony or other hard woods, provided that such materials are suited to sacred use and do not easily break or deteriorate. This applies to all vessels which hold the hosts, such as the paten, the ciborium, the pyx, the monstrance, and other things of this kind.[31]

Because of abuses in this area, *Inaestimabile Donum* took pains to stress that some materials are not appropriate and that the judge of which materials are appropriate is the national conference of bishops and not the individual priest or liturgist:

> Particular respect and care are due to the sacred vessels, both the chalice and paten for the celebration of the Eucharist, and the ciboria for the Communion of the faithful. The form of the vessels must be appropriate for the liturgical use for which they are meant. The material must be noble, durable, and in every case adapted to sacred use. In this sphere, judgment belongs to the episcopal conference of the individual regions.

---

[31] GIRM 327–29.

Use is not to be made of simple baskets or other receptacles meant for ordinary use outside the sacred celebrations, nor are the sacred vessels to be of poor quality or lacking any artistic style.[32]

Redemptionis Sacramentum adds:

Reprobated . . . is any practice of using for the celebration of Mass common vessels, or others lacking in quality, or devoid of all artistic merit or which are mere containers, as also other vessels made from glass, earthenware, clay, or other materials that break easily. This norm is to be applied even as regards metals and other materials that easily rust or deteriorate.

Before they are used, sacred vessels are to be blessed by a priest according to the rites laid down in the liturgical books. It is praiseworthy for the blessing to be given by the diocesan Bishop, who will judge whether the vessels are worthy of the use to which they are destined.[33]

The *General Instruction* comments on what kinds of patens may be used:

For the Consecration of hosts, a large paten may appropriately be used; on it is placed the bread for the priest and the deacon as well as for the other ministers and for the faithful.[34]

It also deals with vessels meant to contain the precious blood:

As regards chalices and other vessels that are intended to serve as receptacles for the blood of the Lord, they are to have bowls of nonabsorbent material. The base, on the other hand, may be made of other solid and worthy materials.[35]

---

[32] ID 16.
[33] RS 117–118.
[34] GIRM 331.
[35] GIRM 330.

The Holy See has also stressed the use of a veil for the chalice:

> *Dubium*: In a great many places the veil is hardly ever used to cover the chalice prepared at a side table before Mass. Have any recent norms been given to suppress use of the veil?

> *Responsum*: There is no norm, not even a recent one, to change the GIRM no. 80c, which reads: "The chalice should be covered with a veil, which may always be white."[36]

Tabernacle

One of the most controversial issues concerning liturgical furnishings is the proper placement of the tabernacle in which the Eucharist is reserved. Sometimes liturgical consultants insist on moving the tabernacle on the basis of a document called *Environment and Art in Catholic Worship* (see "Guide to the Church's Liturgical Documents" in the Bonus Materials).

Section 78 of this document states that the tabernacle should be placed in a separate chapel. However, this document has no legal authority. Neither the U.S. Conference of Catholic Bishops nor the Holy See approved it, and the approval of both would be required to give it legal force.

Msgr. Peter J. Elliott, noted author of the guidebook *Ceremonies of the Modern Roman Rite*, suggests the reason for the document's recommendation concerning the placement of the tabernacle:

> A partial reading of authorities and consequent dogmatism is evident in *Environment and Art in Catholic Worship*, 1978, nos. 78, 79. To be fair to the authors, their opinions reflect the era of the 1970s and were presented before *Inaestimabile Donum* and

---

[36] *Notitiae* 14 (1978) 594, no. 16, 1470.

the new *Code*. But this dated document continues to circulate, endorsed and unmodified.[37]

Inaestimabile Donum, which the Holy See released after *Environment and Art*, has a more flexible attitude toward the placement of the tabernacle:

> The tabernacle in which the Eucharist is kept can be located on an altar, or away from it, in a spot in the church which is very prominent, truly noble, and duly decorated, or in a chapel suitable for private prayer and for adoration by the faithful.[38]

The *Code of Canon Law* states:

> §1. The Most Holy Eucharist is to be reserved habitually in only one tabernacle of a church or oratory.
>
> §2. The tabernacle in which the Most Holy Eucharist is reserved is to be situated in some part of the church or oratory which is distinguished, conspicuous, beautifully decorated, and suitable for prayer [CIC 938].

A problem with many eucharistic adoration chapels is that they are not conspicuous and in a prominent place in the church but out of the way and not easily accessible. It is reported that at times closets have been converted into a "side chapel" for Jesus in the Eucharist.

For a time it was unclear who had the final say regarding the placement of the tabernacle, but this matter was clarified with the release of the new *General Instruction*, which states:

> In accordance with the structure of each church and legitimate local customs, the Most Blessed Sacrament should be reserved in a tabernacle in a part of the church that is truly noble, prominent, readily visible, beautifully decorated, and suitable for prayer.

---

[37] CMRR 325, n. 1.

[38] ID 24.

The one tabernacle should be immovable, be made of solid and inviolable material that is not transparent, and be locked in such a way that the danger of profanation is prevented to the greatest extent possible. Moreover, it is appropriate that, before it is put into liturgical use, it be blessed according to the rite described in the *Roman Ritual*.

It is more in keeping with the meaning of the sign that the tabernacle in which the Most Holy Eucharist is reserved not be on an altar on which Mass is celebrated.

Consequently, it is preferable that the tabernacle be located, according to the judgment of the diocesan Bishop:

a. Either in the sanctuary, apart from the altar of celebration, in a form and place more appropriate, not excluding on an old altar no longer used for celebration . . .

b. Or even in some chapel suitable for the faithful's private adoration and prayer and which is organically connected to the church and readily visible to the Christian faithful.[39]

The diocesan bishop is thus the one who has ultimate responsibility for determining the placement of the tabernacle, not a liturgical consultant or even a pastor.

The *General Instruction* also notes:

In accordance with traditional custom, near the tabernacle a special lamp, fueled by oil or wax, should be kept alight to indicate and honor the presence of Christ.[40]

Liturgical Vestments

The wearing of special clothing for ministering at a liturgy has roots going back thousands of years. It is mentioned, for example, in Exodus 28, where the Lord tells Moses:

---

[39] GIRM 314–15.
[40] GIRM 316.

Make sacred garments for your brother Aaron, to give him dignity and honor. Tell all the skilled men to whom I have given wisdom in such matters that they are to make garments for Aaron, for his consecration, so he may serve me as priest [Ex. 28:2–3].

This practice is still honored today. The *General Instruction* states:

In the Church, which is the body of Christ, not all members have the same office. This variety of offices in the celebration of the Eucharist is shown outwardly by the diversity of sacred vestments, which should therefore be a sign of the office proper to each minister. At the same time, however, the sacred vestments should also contribute to the beauty of the sacred action itself. It is appropriate that the vestments to be worn by priests and deacons, as well as those garments to be worn by lay ministers, be blessed according to the rite described in the *Roman Ritual* before they put into liturgical use.[41]

Not all vestments are suitable, however, and so attention must be paid to their design and to the materials of which they are made:

Regarding the design of sacred vestments, conferences of bishops may determine and propose to the Apostolic See adaptations that correspond to the needs and the usages of their regions.

In addition to the traditional materials, natural fabrics proper to each region may be used for making sacred vestments; artificial fabrics that are in keeping with the dignity of the sacred action and the person wearing them may also be used. The conference of bishops will be the judge in this matter.

It is fitting that the beauty and nobility of each vestment derive not from abundance of overly lavish ornamentation but rather from the material that is used and from the design.

---

[41] GIRM 335.

Ornamentation on vestments should, moreover, consist of figures, that is, of images or symbols, that evoke sacred use, avoiding thereby anything unbecoming.[42]

The subject of liturgical vestments is complicated by the fact that many people are unfamiliar with the names for different vestments. We may see them all the time at Mass, but we often don't know what they are called. See the Glossary for definitions.

Some vestments are based on clothing that was common in ancient times. The alb, for example, is based on a Greco-Roman tunic, the chasuble on a tunic cover, and the cope on a Roman raincoat. Owing to the dignified nature of liturgy, these forms of clothing retained their use at Mass (although in a modified form) when their secular counterparts fell out of fashion. This is similar to how, on formal occasions in our society, dignified clothing is worn that used to be common in secular society but is otherwise now out of fashion (e.g., top hats and long coattails).

Use of Vestments

In some areas, priests wearing minimal vestments, such as a stole over plainly visible street clothes—even shorts—have disturbed parishioners. The Congregation for Divine Worship forbade this practice in its instruction of September 5, 1970:

> The vestment common to ministers of every rank is the alb. The abuse is here repudiated of celebrating or even concelebrating Mass with stole only over the monastic cowl or over ordinary clerical garb, to say nothing of street clothes. Equally forbidden is the wearing of the stole alone over street clothes when carrying out other ritual acts, for example, the laying on of hands

---

[42] GIRM 342–44.

at ordinations, administering the other sacraments, giving blessings.[43]

Ecclesia de Mysterio stresses that the ordained must wear all of the liturgical vestments prescribed for them and that the faithful may wear only those liturgical vestments proper to them in the roles they fulfill at Mass:

> In the same way, the use of sacred vestments which are reserved to priests or deacons (stoles, chasubles, or dalmatics) at liturgical ceremonies by non-ordained members of the faithful is clearly unlawful.
>
> Every effort must be made to avoid even the appearance of confusion which can spring from anomalous liturgical practices. As the sacred ministers are obliged to wear all of the prescribed liturgical vestments, so too the non-ordained faithful may not assume that which is not proper to them.[44]

Redemptionis Sacramentum adds that the faithful also are not to wear clothing that resembles those vestments that are particularly reserved to the clergy:

> [I]t is never licit for lay persons to assume the role or the vesture of a priest or a deacon or other clothing similar to such vesture.[45]

The *General Instruction* offers a more thorough discussion of liturgical vestments. It also affirms that the most basic vestment worn by different kinds of ministers is the alb:

> The sacred garment common to ordained and instituted ministers of any rank is the alb, to be tied at the waist with a cincture unless it is made so as to fit even without such. Before the alb is put on, should this not completely cover the ordinary clothing

---

[43] *Notitiae* 7 (1971) 10–26, 8c, DOL 526; see also RS 126.

[44] EM, Practical Provisions 6 §2.

[45] RS 153.

at the neck, an amice should be put on. The alb may not be replaced by a surplice, not even over a cassock, on occasions when a chasuble or dalmatic is to be worn or when, according to the norms, only a stole is worn without a chasuble or dalmatic. . . .

In the dioceses of the United States of America, acolytes, altar servers, lectors, and other lay ministers may wear the alb or other suitable vesture or other appropriate and dignified clothing.[46]

The priest who is celebrating Mass is normally to wear a chasuble:

The vestment proper to the priest celebrant at Mass and other sacred actions directly connected with Mass is, unless otherwise indicated, the chasuble, worn over the alb and stole. . . .

The stole is worn by the priest around his neck and hanging down in front.[47]

In special situations, a priest may also wear a cope:

The cope is worn by the priest in processions and other sacred actions, in keeping with the rubrics proper to each rite.[48]

Deacons are to be vested differently:

The vestment proper to the deacon is the dalmatic, worn over the alb and stole. The dalmatic may, however, be omitted out of necessity or on account of a lesser degree of solemnity. . . .

The stole . . . is worn by the deacon over his left shoulder and drawn diagonally across the chest to the right side, where it is fastened.[49]

---

[46] GIRM 336–39.
[47] GIRM 337, 340.
[48] GIRM 341.
[49] GIRM 338, 340.

One final note: Some have inquired about the appropriate vestment for extraordinary ministers of Holy Communion. Regarding this issue, the Holy See has said:

> The [extraordinary] minister who is to distribute Communion is to wear either the liturgical vestment in use locally or clothing befitting this sacred ministry.[50]

This means that, according to section 339 of the *General Instruction* (quoted above), extraordinary ministers could wear the alb or suitable street clothes (and what is suitable is generally left to the judgment of the pastor).

Proper Colors for Vestments

The Church uses different-colored vestments through the course of the year. The *General Instruction* explains why:

> The purpose of a variety in the color of the sacred vestments is to give effective expression even outwardly to the specific character of the mysteries of faith being celebrated and to a sense of Christian life's passage through the course of the liturgical year.[51]

It goes on to list the specific times that particular colors are to be used:

> As to the color of sacred vestments, the traditional usage is to be retained, namely:
>
> a. White is used in the Offices and Masses during the Easter and Christmas seasons; also on celebrations of the Lord other than of his Passion, of the Blessed Virgin Mary, of the holy angels, and of saints who were not martyrs; on the Solemnities

---

[50] *Notitiae* 9 (1973) 167; DOL 2951.
[51] GIRM 345.

of All Saints (1 November) and of the Nativity of Saint John the Baptist (24 June); and on the Feasts of Saint John the Evangelist (27 December), of the Chair of Saint Peter (22 February), and of the Conversion of Saint Paul (25 January).

b. Red is used on Palm Sunday of the Lord's Passion and on Good Friday, on Pentecost Sunday, on celebrations of the Lord's Passion, on the feasts of the apostles and evangelists, and on celebrations of martyr saints.

c. Green is used in the Offices and Masses of Ordinary Time.

d. Violet or purple is used in Advent and in Lent. It may also be worn in Offices and Masses for the Dead (see also below).

e. Besides violet, white or black vestments may be worn at funeral services and at other Offices and Masses for the Dead in the dioceses of the United States of America.

f. Rose may be used, where it is the practice, on *Gaudete* Sunday (Third Sunday of Advent) and on *Laetare* Sunday (Fourth Sunday of Lent).

g. On more solemn days, sacred vestments may be used that are festive, that is, more precious, even if not of the color of the day.

h. Gold- or silver-colored vestments may be worn on more solemn occasions in the dioceses of the United States of America.[52]

Redemptionis Sacramentum provides a clarifying note on sections (g) and (h):

A special faculty is given in the liturgical books for using sacred vestments that are festive or more noble on more solemn occasions, even if they are not of the color of the day. However, this faculty, which is specifically intended in reference to vestments made many years ago, with a view to preserving the Church's patrimony, is improperly extended to innovations by which forms and colors are adopted according to the inclina-

---

[52] GIRM 346.

tion of private individuals, with disregard for traditional practice, while the real sense of this norm is lost to the detriment of the tradition. On the occasion of a feast day, sacred vestments of a gold or silver color can be substituted as appropriate for others of various colors, but not for purple or black.[53]

The appropriate liturgical color also may be affected by the type of Mass being celebrated:

> Ritual Masses are celebrated in their proper color, in white, or in a festive color; Masses for Various Needs, on the other hand, are celebrated in the color proper to the day or the season or in violet if they are of a penitential character, for example, no. 31 (in Time of War or Conflict), no. 33 (in Time of Famine), or no. 38 (for the Forgiveness of Sins); Votive Masses are celebrated in the color suited to the Mass itself or even in the color proper to the day or the season.[54]

Some have asked about the practice of priests wearing blue vestments during Advent and Lent instead of purple. While wearing a bluish purple would not be proscribed, pure blue is not permitted. Lent and Advent are penitential seasons, and purple is the authorized color for them. Though blue vestments are used in some countries on certain occasions (e.g., Spain and Bavaria on certain Marian days), blue is not an approved liturgical color in the Latin dioceses of the United States. A priest or even an individual bishop cannot change this on his own authority.

---

[53] RS 127.
[54] GIRM 347.

13. Liturgical Postures and Actions

Just as there are certain prayers that are proper to the ordained and other prayers that are proper to the laity, so there are certain postures and actions that are proper to the ordained and others that are proper to the laity. This was stressed in *Ecclesia de Mysterio*. After indicating that certain prayers of the Mass are reserved to priests, it states:

> Neither may deacons or non-ordained members of the faithful use gestures or actions which are proper to the same priest celebrant. It is a grave abuse for any member of the non-ordained faithful to "quasi-preside" at the Mass while leaving only that minimal participation to the priest which is necessary to secure validity.[1]

Fortunately, cases in which members of the laity "quasi-preside" are not common. However, there have been many times when the laity assume postures proper to the priest (such as standing when they are supposed to be kneeling) or use gestures proper to the priest (such as praying with arms outstretched during a presidential prayer).

Posture During Mass

There are three basic postures used by the faithful during Mass: standing, sitting, and kneeling. For a table showing the sequence in which they are assumed, see "Table of Postures

---

[1] EM, Practical Provisions 6 §2.

During Mass" in the Bonus Materials. Here we will look at the law regarding posture in more detail.

Standing

According to the *General Instruction*:

> The faithful should stand from the beginning of the Entrance chant, or while the priest approaches the altar, until the end of the Collect; for the *Alleluia* chant before the Gospel; while the Gospel itself is proclaimed; during the Profession of Faith and the Prayer of the Faithful; from the invitation, *Orate, fratres* ("Pray, brethren"), before the prayer over the offerings until the end of Mass, except at the places indicated below.[2]

In some places, especially where there is a very small congregation in attendance, the priest invites the members of the congregation (or some of them, such as teenagers in a Mass for teens) to stand with him around the altar during the Eucharistic Prayer. The Holy See has given the following ruling on this practice:

> *Dubium*: At the presentation of gifts at a Mass with congregation, persons (lay or religious) bring to the altar the bread and wine which are to be consecrated. These gifts are received by the priest celebrant. All those participating in the Mass accompany this group procession in which the gifts are brought forward. They then stand around the altar until Communion time. Is this procedure in conformity with the spirit of the law and of the Roman Missal?

> *Responsum*: Assuredly, the eucharistic celebration is the act of the entire community, carried out by all the members of the liturgical assembly. Nevertheless, everyone must have and also must observe his or her own place and proper role: "In liturgical celebrations each one, minister or lay person, who has an

---

[2] GIRM 43.

office to perform, should do all of, but only, those parts which pertain to that office by the nature of the rite and the principles of liturgy" [SC art. 29].

During the Liturgy of the Eucharist, only the presiding celebrant remains at the altar. The assembly of the faithful take their place in the Church outside the *presbyterium*, which is reserved for the celebrant or concelebrants and altar ministers.[3]

Sitting

According to the *General Instruction*:

They should, however, sit while the readings before the Gospel and the Responsorial Psalm are proclaimed and for the homily and while the preparation of the gifts at the Offertory is taking place; and, as circumstances allow, they may sit or kneel while the period of sacred silence after Communion is observed.[4]

Kneeling

According to the *General Instruction*:

In the dioceses of the United States of America, [the faithful] should kneel beginning after the singing or recitation of the *Sanctus* until after the Amen of the Eucharistic Prayer, except when prevented on occasion by reasons of health, lack of space, the large number of people present, or some other good reason. Those who do not kneel ought to make a profound bow when the priest genuflects after the Consecration. The faithful kneel after the *Agnus Dei* unless the diocesan Bishop determines otherwise.[5]

This means that in the United States people are to kneel *after* the *Sanctus* ("Holy, Holy, Holy . . .") and remain kneeling un-

---

[3] *Notitiae* 17 (1981) 61.

[4] GIRM 43.

[5] GIRM 43.

til *after* the Amen of the Eucharistic Prayer, also known as the Great Amen, which follows the priest's *Per Ipsum* ("Through him, and with him, and in him . . .").

People are not to stand up before or during the Great Amen, which is the climax of the congregation's participation in the Eucharistic Prayer. This special solemnity is why, in America, the congregation remains kneeling during the Amen.

For some years it was controversial whether the faithful in America were to kneel during the second elevation of the host, when the priest (using the new translation) says:

> Behold the Lamb of God,
> Behold him who takes away the sins of the world.
> Blessed are those called to the supper of the Lamb

and the people respond:

> Lord, I am not worthy
> That you should enter under my roof,
> But only say the word
> And my soul shall be healed.

The rubrics did not call for kneeling at this point, nor did the *General Instruction*, yet it was common for parishes to do this. The 2002 American edition of the *General Instruction* finally cleared matters up by stating that the faithful should kneel at this point unless the local bishop decides to have them stand.[6]

The subject of one's posture when receiving Communion has also been controversial. Historically it was customary in the Latin Church for the faithful to kneel to receive Communion, typically at an altar rail. Even after the removal of altar rails from most parishes, many of the faithful continued to kneel. A controversy ensued when some priests and other ministers

---

[6] If the diocesan bishop decides against kneeling at this point, then the posture of the faithful would default back to standing, which an earlier portion of GIRM 43 had mandated for the latter portions of Mass except where noted.

insisted that they stand to receive Holy Communion. As a result, in the instruction *Inaestimabile Donum*, the Holy See stated:

> With regard to the manner of going to Communion, the faithful can receive it either kneeling or standing, in accordance with the norms laid down by the episcopal conference: When the faithful communicate kneeling, no other sign of reverence towards the Blessed Sacrament is required, since kneeling is itself a sign of adoration. When they receive Communion standing, it is strongly recommended that, coming up in procession, they should make a sign of reverence before receiving the Sacrament. This should be done at the right time and place, so that the order of people going to and from Communion is not disrupted.[7]

Since *Inaestimabile Donum*, the subject of posture when receiving Communion has been contentious. For a number of years there were many reports of priests and others attempting to force Communicants to stand in order to receive, at times publicly chastising them or even refusing to administer Communion if they did not.

Eventually, the United States bishops sought to resolve the matter by establishing an official posture for receiving Communion in their dioceses: standing. This was proposed as one of the U.S. adaptations for the 2002 edition of the GIRM, but the Holy See desired additional protections for those who wished to receive kneeling. The resulting text stated:

> The norm for reception of Holy Communion in the dioceses of the United States is standing. Communicants should not be denied Holy Communion because they kneel. Rather, such instances should be addressed pastorally, by providing the faithful with proper catechesis on the reasons for this norm.[8]

This text sought to strike a balance between what the U.S. bishops requested—establishing standing as the posture for re-

---

[7] ID 11.
[8] GIRM 160, 2002 ed.

ceiving Communion—and the Holy See's desire to protect the piety of those who wish to receive kneeling. The bottom line was that the official posture became standing and that catechesis was to be given to the faithful on this point, but if communicants choose to kneel they were not to be denied Holy Communion.

Problematic reports continued to emerge, with the faithful who choose to receive kneeling stating that they were being pressured to stand through the pastoral catechesis this text mentions. The Holy See chose to further protect the right of the U.S. faithful to receive kneeling by deleting this language and leaving the decision to kneel entirely up to the individual communicant. The version of the GIRM implemented in 2011 thus states:

> The norm established for the Dioceses of the United States of America is that Holy Communion is to be received standing, unless an individual member of the faithful wishes to receive Communion while kneeling (Congregation for Divine Worship and the Discipline of the Sacraments, Instruction *Redemptionis Sacramentum*, 25 March 2004, no. 91).[9]

The normal posture for receiving Communion in the United States is thus standing, but if they wish the faithful are free to receive kneeling, without being hassled about it. This section of the revised GIRM also references a norm provided in *Redemptionis Sacramentum* that indicates the faithful are not to be denied Communion if they choose to kneel or stand, regardless of what the national norm may be:

> [I]t is not licit to deny Holy Communion to any of Christ's faithful solely on the grounds, for example, that the person wishes to receive the Eucharist kneeling or standing.[10]

---

[9] GIRM 160, 2011 ed.
[10] RS 91.

A final posture controversy involves the period following Communion. In 1974, the Holy See gave the following reply:

Dubium: After Communion should the faithful be seated or not?

Responsum: After Communion they may either kneel, stand, or sit. Accordingly the GIRM no. 21[11] gives this rule: "The people sit . . . if this seems useful during the period of silence after Communion." Thus it is a matter of option, not obligation. The GIRM no. 121[12] should, therefore, be interpreted to match no. 21.[13]

You may have noticed that the posture controversies we have been discussing all involve the same posture: standing. It is as if there is an attempt to get people up on their feet as much as possible, as soon as possible (e.g., getting them to stand before or during the Great Amen instead of at its end), and eliminating to the extent possible sitting and especially kneeling. This is indeed the case. In the liturgical reform that followed Vatican II, it became fashionable in some circles to hold that standing is a superior, more dignified way of showing respect than the traditional posture of kneeling. The latter was held to be too servile (a posture that subjects used to reverence royalty) or simply too traditional.

It is no surprise, then, that some liturgists would try to mandate standing for the period after Communion as well. This was done in two forms: (1) claiming that upon returning from Commuion the faithful should stand for the rest of the Mass, or, if it was pointed out that sitting and kneeling were allowed, (2) claiming that upon returning from Communion the faithful should stand until the priest returns to the chair and sits down.

---

[11] The former GIRM 21 corresponds to GIRM 43 in the new edition.

[12] The former GIRM 121 corresponds to GIRM 164 in the new edition.

[13] *Notitiae* 10 (1974) 407; DOL 1411 n. R2.

As we saw earlier, though, the priest does not necessarily return to the chair,[14] and the idea that the faithful are to stay standing if he is standing is simply false. There is nothing in the law that mandates that. What current law does say is that "as circumstances allow, they may sit or kneel while the period of sacred silence after Communion is observed."

There were doubts raised about this, though, and so the Bishops' Committee on Liturgy queried the Holy See, resulting in the following clarification:

5 June 2003

Prot. n. 855/03/L

Dubium: In many places, the faithful are accustomed to kneeling or sitting in personal prayer upon returning to their places after individually received Holy Communion during Mass. Is it the intention of the *Missale Romanum, editio typica tertia* [*Roman Missal*, third typical edition], to forbid this practice?

Responsum: *Negative, et ad mentem* [No, and for a reason]. The *mens* [reason] is that that the prescription of the *Institutio Generalis Missalis Romani* [GIRM], no. 43, is intended, on one hand, to ensure within broad limits a certain uniformity of posture within the congregation for the various parts of the celebration of the Holy Mass, and on the other, to not regulate posture rigidly in such a way that those who wish to kneel or sit would no longer be free.

Francis Cardinal Arinze
Prefect

Note in particular that the *dubium* is asking about what posture the faithful may assume "upon returning to their places after individually received Holy Communion," not "after the priest returns to the chair" or "after the distribution of Holy

---

[14] See p. 231.

Communion ends." As soon as they get back to their places they are free to sit or kneel if they wish.

This is a very helpful reply in clarifying the mind of the Holy See. For years, liturgists had been trying to compel the faithful to assume nontraditional postures as much as possible. They would appeal to things in the previous edition of the *General Instruction* that said things like:

> The uniformity in standing, kneeling, or sitting to be observed by all taking part is a sign of the community and the unity of the assembly; it both expresses and fosters the spiritual attitude of those taking part.
>
> For the sake of uniformity in movement and posture, the people should follow the directions given during the celebration by the deacon, the priest, or another minister.[15]

The faithful would be told, "It is important to express our unity by all having the same posture, and you are supposed to follow the directions we are giving"—even when the directions were contrary to the *General Instruction* and the rubrics.

Cardinal Arinze's reply is most helpful by clarifying that the Holy See intends "to ensure within broad limits a certain uniformity of posture within the congregation for the various parts of the celebration" while also seeking "to not regulate posture rigidly" and take away the freedom of those who wish to kneel or sit after returning from Communion.

Also helpful was the revision of the *General Instruction*, which now states:

> With a view to a uniformity in gestures and postures during one and the same celebration, the faithful should follow the directions which the deacon, lay minister, or priest gives *according to whatever is indicated in the Missal.*[16]

---

[15] GIRM, 2nd ed., 20–21.

[16] GIRM 43 (emphasis added).

This revision makes it clear that the faithful are bound only to follow gesture and posture directions that are in accord with what the *Missal* says, not contrary to it or optional.

One way that has been used to discourage kneeling is to remove the kneelers from a church (or not put them in when a church is built or renovated). The faithful would then be told, "We have no kneelers, so we're going to stand instead." Church law does not require the presence of kneelers, but it does require the practice of kneeling. It is simply a question of how comfortable the parish wants to make the parishioners while they kneel in accordance with the Church's law. The Holy See has ruled that the absence of kneelers is not a sufficient reason for the congregation to remain standing or sitting:

> *Dubium*: In some places kneelers have been taken out of the churches. Thus, the people can only stand or sit and this detracts from the reverence and adoration due to the Eucharist.

> *Responsum*: The appointments of a place of worship have some relationship to the customs of the particular locale. For example, in the East there are carpets; in the Roman basilicas, only since modern times, there are usually chairs without kneelers, so as to accommodate large crowds. There is nothing to prevent the faithful from kneeling on the floor to show their adoration, no matter how uncomfortable this may be. In cases where kneeling is not possible (see GIRM no. 21[17]), a deep bow and a respectful bearing are signs of the reverence and adoration to be shown at the time of the Consecration and Communion.[18]

Finally, though kneelers are not mentioned, the Church does state that the places where the faithful sit should be set up so that people can easily assume the different postures the liturgy requires.

---

[17] The former GIRM 21 corresponds to GIRM 43 in the new edition.

[18] *Notitiae* 14 (1978) 302–303, no. 4; DOL 1411 n. R2.

Places should be arranged with appropriate care for the faithful so that they are able to participate in the sacred celebrations visually and spiritually, in the proper manner. It is expedient for benches or seats usually to be provided for their use. The custom of reserving seats for private persons, however, is rep-rehensible. Moreover, benches or chairs should be arranged, especially in newly built churches, in such a way that the people can easily take up the postures required for the different parts of the celebration and can easily come forward to receive Holy Communion.

Care should be taken that the faithful be able not only to see the priest, the deacon, and the lectors but also, with the aid of modern technical means, to hear them without difficulty.[19]

Thus it is not appropriate to jam the chairs or pews so close together that it is impossible to kneel.

Kneelers are specifically mentioned in the U.S. bishops' document *Built of Living Stones*, which states:

Since the liturgy requires various postures and movements, the space and furniture for the congregation should accommodate them well. Styles of benches, pews, or chairs can be found that comfortably accommodate the human form. Kneelers or kneeling cushions should also be provided so that the whole congregation can easily kneel when the liturgy calls for it. Parishes will want to choose a seating arrangement that calls the congregation to active participation and that avoids any semblance of a theater or an arena.[20]

Since *Built of Living Stones* is a document giving guidelines rather than a legal one, it does not establish a requirement for kneelers or kneeling cushions but rather a preference.

---

[19] GIRM 311.
[20] *Built of Living Stones* § 86.

Acts of Reverence

Genuflections

Genuflecting is a way of showing reverence that has been an important part of Christian ritual for centuries. The *General Instruction* explains it this way:

> A genuflection, made by bending the right knee to the ground, signifies adoration, and therefore it is reserved for the Most Blessed Sacrament, as well as for the holy cross from the solemn adoration during the liturgical celebration on Good Friday until the beginning of the Easter Vigil.[21]

The priest is called upon to genuflect at specific points during the Liturgy of the Eucharist:

> During Mass, three genuflections are made by the priest celebrant: namely, after the showing of the host, after the showing of the chalice, and before Communion. Certain specific features to be observed in a concelebrated Mass are noted in their proper place.[22]

If there is a tabernacle, additional genuflections are required:

> If, however, the tabernacle with the Most Blessed Sacrament is present in the sanctuary, the priest, the deacon, and the other ministers genuflect when they approach the altar and when they depart from it, but not during the celebration of Mass itself.[23]

The laity are also called upon to genuflect:

---

[21] GIRM 274.

[22] GIRM 274.

[23] GIRM 274.

No one who enters a church should fail to adore the Blessed Sacrament either by visiting the Blessed Sacrament chapel or at least by genuflecting.[24]

This requirement is reflected in *Inaestimabile Donum* as well:

The venerable practice of genuflecting before the Blessed Sacrament, whether enclosed in the tabernacle or publicly exposed, as a sign of adoration, is to be maintained. This act requires that it be performed in a recollected way. In order that the heart may bow before God in profound reverence, the genuflection must be neither hurried nor careless.[25]

Those passing in front of the tabernacle also normally genuflect as well:

Otherwise all who pass before the Most Blessed Sacrament genuflect, unless they are moving in procession.

Ministers carrying the processional cross or candles bow their heads instead of genuflecting.[26]

Bows

Another traditional way of expressing reverence is the bow. The *General Instructions* explains:

A bow signifies reverence and honor shown to the persons themselves or to the signs that represent them. There are two kinds of bows: a bow of the head and a bow of the body.

a. A bow of the head is made when the three divine Persons are named together and at the names of Jesus, of the Blessed Virgin Mary, and of the saint in whose honor Mass is being celebrated.

---

[24] CB 71.
[25] ID 26.
[26] GIRM 274.

b. A bow of the body, that is to say a profound bow, is made to the altar; during the prayers *Munda cor meum* ("Almighty God, cleanse my heart") and *In spiritu humilitatis* ("Lord God, we ask you to receive)"; in the Creed at the words *Et incarnatus est* ("by the power of the Holy Spirit . . . made man"); in the Roman Canon at the words *Supplices te rogamus* ("Almighty God, we pray that your angel"). The same kind of bow is made by the deacon when he asks for a blessing before the proclamation of the Gospel. In addition, the priest bows slightly as he speaks the words of the Lord at the Consecration.[27]

Priests, deacons, and ministers are called upon to make profound bows at several points in the liturgy, as indicated above. The laity are also required to make a profound bow at certain points.

A deep bow is made to the altar by all who enter the sanctuary (chancel), leave it, or pass before the altar.[28]

As noted above in the section on genuflecting, a profound bow or bow of the body is not made by those carrying articles for use in the Mass. Instead, they bow their heads.

One bow the laity makes that calls for special attention occurs during the Profession of Faith. This is a profound bow, or bow of the body[29] that is made to reverence the Incarnation of Christ. If the Nicene Creed is being said, the rubrics state:

At the words that follow up to and including "and became man," all bow:

And by the Holy Spirit was incarnate
Of the Virgin Mary,
And became man.

---

[27] GIRM 275.
[28] CB 72.
[29] See GIRM 275b above.

If the Apostles' Creed is being used, the rubrics state:

At the words that follow up to and including "the Virgin Mary," all bow:

Who was conceived by the Holy Spirit,
Born of the Virgin Mary,

As noted, on certain days during the year there is to be a genuflection instead. The *General Instruction* states:

The Creed is sung or recited by the priest together with the people (see also above, no. 68ss) with everyone standing. At the words *et incarnatus est* ("by the power of the Holy Spirit . . . became man") all make a profound bow; *but on the Solemnities of the Annunciation* [March 25] *and of the Nativity of the Lord* [December 25], *all genuflect.*[30]

Kiss

A kiss is a traditional sign of greeting and reverence that goes back in Christian history to the days of the apostles. Thus St. Paul tells his readers, "Greet one another with a holy kiss" (Rom. 16:16; 1 Cor. 16:20; 2 Cor. 13:12) or to "Greet all the brethren with a holy kiss" (1 Thess. 5:26), and St. Peter states: "Greet one another with the kiss of love" (1 Pet. 5:14).

This is the basis of the sign of peace during Mass, but since kissing is not universally used as a greeting in our culture, other more common greetings such as handshakes are typically used instead. Kissing as a sign of reverence is still used in the Mass, as priests and deacons are directed to kiss the altar and the Book of the Gospels:

According to traditional practice, the altar and the Book of the Gospels are venerated by means of a kiss. Where, however, a

---

[30] GIRM 137 (emphasis added).

sign of this kind is not in harmony with the traditions or the culture of some region, it is for the conference of Bishops to establish some other sign in its place, with the consent of the Apostolic See.[31]

Praying with Arms Outstretched

One final gesture of reverence is praying with arms outstretched, which is the traditional posture of prayer for priests and bishops during the liturgy:

> Customarily in the Church a bishop or presbyter addresses prayers to God while standing and with hands slightly raised and outstretched.
>
> This practice appears already in the tradition of the Old Testament and was taken over by Christians in memory of the Lord's Passion: "Not only do we raise our hands, but we hold them outstretched so that by imitating the Lord in his Passion, we bear witness to him as we pray."[32]

As we saw at the beginning of this chapter, *Ecclesia de Mysterio* prohibits the laity from mimicking the gestures appropriate to a priest, and that would suggest that people should not pray with arms outstretched, particularly during the presidential prayers:

> Among the parts assigned to the priest, the foremost is the Eucharistic Prayer, which is the high point of the entire celebration. Next are the orations: that is to say, the collect, the prayer over the offerings, and the prayer after Communion. These prayers are addressed to God in the name of the entire holy people and all present, by the priest who presides over the assembly in the

---

[31] GIRM 273.
[32] CB 104, citing Tertullian, *De Oratione*, 14.

person of Christ. It is with good reason, therefore, that they are called the Presidential Prayers.[33]

However, there is at least one situation in which the question remains somewhat murky: The Lord's Prayer is not one of the presidential prayers. The priest does not pray it on behalf of the people who listen and then respond, "Amen." Instead, the people say the Lord's Prayer with the priest. Yet the rubrics call for the priest to say the Lord's Prayer with arms outstretched. In this case, this posture—known as the *orans* (Latin, "praying") position—is not being associated with one of the presidential prayers reserved to the priest. Some have suggested that the faithful pray with arms outstretched here, though neither the U.S. bishops nor the Holy See has said anything regarding such a practice.

An alternative suggestion would be that the rubrics should be changed so that the priest no longer prays with arms outstretched during this prayer, for it is no longer presidential. It used to be, prior to the liturgical reforms of Pius XII,[34] and the rubric directing the priest to use the *orans* position may just be an artifact of an earlier age when this prayer was presidential. By including the people among those who say this prayer, one might argue, the priest should no longer use the *orans* position, the same way he does not use it at other points in the Mass where he prays with the people (e.g., the *Confiteor*, the *Gloria*, and the Creed).[35]

One of the reasons the issue of the laity using the *orans* position has come up is that it has been proposed as an alterna-

---

[33] GIRM 30.

[34] *Canon Law Digest* V:587.

[35] For an excellent discussion of this issue and its history, see Edward Peters, "Another Look at the *Orans* Issue," at *canonlaw.info/liturgysacraments_orans.htm*.

tive to another common practice in the United States: the laity holding hands during the Our Father.

Holding Hands

Despite how common it is in many areas, there is no authorization in the Church's liturgical law for the laity to hold hands, either during the Our Father or at any other time during Mass. Holding hands is simply not an approved liturgical posture. As we noted at the beginning of the book, "the liturgical books approved by competent authority are to be observed faithfully; accordingly, no one is to add, omit, or alter anything in them on one's own authority."[36] And as the Second Vatican Council stated: "No person, even if he be a priest, may add, remove, or change anything in the liturgy on his own authority."[37] Consequently, on its face, introducing a new liturgical posture like holding hands violates Church law.

Rome clearly knows about this practice, yet it hasn't said anything about it in official documents. In 2002 the U.S. bishops considered asking Rome to allow the laity to use the *orans* position (seemingly as a way of discouraging hand-holding) but the measure did not get the two-thirds vote needed.[38]

My own sense is that Rome hasn't addressed the issue yet because it considers the matter relatively minor, it is busy addressing other issues, and some in Rome may view this as a matter of local custom. The Holy See probably does not have a strong objection to individual families deciding to hold hands on their own, but it would definitely have a problem with priests or

---

[36] CIC 846 § 1.

[37] SC 22.

[38] See Edward McNamara, "Holding Hands at the Our Father?," at *ewtn.com/library/liturgy/zlitur10.htm*.

other ministers *telling* people to hold hands. The thing most likely to prompt a clarification would be Rome's desire not to have people feel compelled to hold hands, which is something they definitely don't want. The more reports the Congregation for Divine Worship and the Discipline of the Sacraments gets of people feeling forced to hold hands with strangers, and even being told to do so by priests, the more likely they are to come back with a negative judgment on this.

Liturgical Dance

In 1975, the Congregation for the Sacraments and Divine Worship prepared a document titled *Religious Dance: An Expression of Spiritual Joy*,[39] which it described as a "qualified and authoritative sketch" of the subject and said it was to be considered "an authoritative point of reference for every discussion on the matter."

Although the document noted that religious dance plays a positive role in many cultures:

> [D]ance has never been made an integral part of the official worship of the Latin Church. If local churches have accepted the dance, sometimes even in the church building, that was on the occasion of feasts in order to manifest sentiments of joy and devotion. But that always took place outside of liturgical services. Conciliar decisions have often condemned the religious dance because it conduces little to worship and because it could degenerate into disorder.

The document also names a number of specific cultures where religious dance plays or has played a role in the liturgy:

---

[39] *Notitiae* 11 [1975] 202–205.

Concretely: There are cultures in which this is possible insofar as dancing is still reflective of religious values and becomes a clear manifestation of them. Such is the case of the Ethiopians. In their culture, even today, there is the religious ritualized dance, clearly distinct from the martial dance and from the amorous dance. The ritual dance is performed by priests and levites before beginning a ceremony and in the open air in front of the church. The dance accompanies the chanting of psalms during the procession. When the procession enters the church, then the chanting of the psalms is carried out with and accompanied by bodily movement.

The same thing is found in the Syriac liturgy by means of chanting of psalms.

In the Byzantine liturgy, there is an extremely simplified dance on the occasion of a wedding when the crowned spouses make a circular revolution around the lectern together with the celebrant.

Such is the case of the Israelites: In the synagogue their prayer is accompanied by a continuous movement to recall the precept from tradition: "When you pray, do so with all your heart, and all your bones." And for primitive peoples the same observation can be made.

But the document is forceful in stating that this does not mean religious dance can be used in the liturgy in Western culture:

However, the same criterion and judgment cannot be applied in the Western culture.

Here dancing is tied with love, with diversion, with profaneness, with unbridling of the senses: Such dancing, in general, is not pure.

For that reason it cannot be introduced into liturgical celebrations of any kind whatever: that would be to inject into the liturgy one of the most desacralized and desacralizing elements; and so it would be equivalent to creating an atmosphere of profaneness which would easily recall to those present and to the participants in the celebration worldly places and situations.

In some places a kind of ballet or "interpretive dance" has been tried in liturgy, but the document indicates that this is equally prohibited:

> Neither can acceptance be had of the proposal to introduce into the liturgy the so-called artistic ballet because there would be presentation here also of a spectacle at which one would assist, while in the liturgy one of the norms from which one cannot prescind is that of participation.
>
> Therefore, there is a great difference in cultures: what is well received in one culture cannot be taken on by another culture.
>
> The traditional reserve of the seriousness of religious worship, and of the Latin worship in particular, must never be forgotten.

This does not mean that religious dance cannot be done at all. It can be done but only when three conditions are met: (1) It does not take place during Mass, (2) it does not take place in strictly liturgical areas (e.g., in the sanctuary or nave of a church), and (3) priests do not participate in it. The document specifies:

> If the proposal of the religious dance in the West is really to be made welcome, care will have to be taken that in its regard a place be found outside of the liturgy, in assembly areas which are not strictly liturgical. Moreover, the priests must always be excluded from the dance.

In 1994 the Holy See stated concerning those cultures where dance and dance-like movements have ritual significance:

> Among some peoples, singing is instinctively accompanied by hand clapping, rhythmic swaying, and dance movements on the part of the participants. Such forms of external expression can

have a place in the liturgical actions of these peoples on condition that they are always the expression of true communal prayer of adoration, praise, offering and supplication, and not simply a performance.[40]

Another consideration is that, as we have noted before, no one is allowed to introduce new elements into the Mass on his own authority. This includes dancing.

---

[40] *Instruction on Inculturation and the Roman Liturgy* 42.

14. Liturgical Abuses

The previous chapters have been intended as a resource for both priests and laity. This one is intended primarily for laity who encounter liturgical abuses and do not know how to deal with them.

Liturgical abuses occur when those who celebrate the liturgy—whether priests, deacons, or other ministers—violate the Church's liturgical law. Because fallen human beings are sinful and prone to error, abuses of the liturgy have occurred in every age of the Church. When the liturgy was celebrated in Latin, many of these abuses went unnoticed (at least in the centuries after people ceased to understand Latin). But with the shift to vernacular languages like English, liturgical abuses are far more noticeable.

Add to that the unsettled state of affairs that followed the Second Vatican Council and there was a recipe for widespread liturgical abuse, resulting in the shock and alienation of many of the faithful. In an apostolic letter commemorating the twenty-fifth anniversary of *Sacrosanctum Concilium*, John Paul II wrote:

> It must be recognized that the application of the liturgical reform has met with difficulties due especially to an unfavorable environment marked by a tendency to see religious practice as something of a private affair, by a certain rejection of institutions, by a decrease in the visibility of the Church in society, and by a calling into question of personal faith. It can also be supposed that the transition from simply being present, very often in a rather passive and silent way, to a fuller and more active participation has been for some people too demanding.

Different and even contradictory reactions to the reform have resulted from this. Some have received the new books with a certain indifference, or without trying to understand or help others to understand the reasons for the changes; others, unfortunately, have turned back in a one-sided and exclusive way to the previous liturgical forms which some of them consider to be the sole guarantee of certainty in faith. Others have promoted outlandish innovations, departing from the norms issued by the authority of the Apostolic See or the bishops, thus disrupting the unity of the Church and the piety of the faithful, and even on occasion contradicting matters of faith. . . .

On occasion there have been noted illicit omissions or additions, rites invented outside the framework of established norms; postures or songs which are not conducive to faith or to a sense of the sacred; abuses in the practice of general absolution; confusion between the ministerial priesthood, linked with ordination, and the common priesthood of the faithful, which has its foundation in baptism.

It cannot be tolerated that certain priests should take upon themselves the right to compose Eucharistic Prayers or to substitute profane readings for texts from Sacred Scripture. Initiatives of this sort, far from being linked with the liturgical reform as such, or with the books which have issued from it, are in direct contradiction to it, disfigure it, and deprive the Christian people of the genuine treasures of the liturgy of the Church.

It is for the bishops to root out such abuses, because the regulation of the liturgy depends on the bishop within the limits of the law and because "the life in Christ of his faithful people in some sense is derived from and depends upon him" (SC 41).[1]

John Paul II wrote this in 1988—after the liturgical abuse crisis had been building for years. It would continue for years longer, but the Holy See began implementing a policy designed to slow and reverse the crisis one step at a time. It began taking

---

[1] *Vincesimus Quintus Annus* 11, 13.

a progressively firmer line on the liturgy and used the release of new documents—such as the *General Instruction* of the new edition of the *Roman Missal* in 2002—as occasions to reaffirm liturgical law and break with the past.

The translation of the whole *Roman Missal* represents another such opportunity. However, the forces responsible for the liturgical abuse crisis can be expected to do everything in their power to subvert this. Even before its release they were sharply critical of the new translation and tried to slow it down or stop its implementation. It would only be natural to expect a new eruption of liturgical dissent and disobedience once it finally begins to be used in parishes. Consequently, we will look at liturgical abuses and how to deal with them.

We should remember a plea issued by John Paul II in 1980:

> Above all I wish to emphasize that the problems of the liturgy, and in particular of the eucharistic liturgy, must not be an occasion for dividing Catholics and for threatening the unity of the Church. This is demanded by an elementary understanding of that sacrament which Christ has left us as the source of spiritual unity. And how could the Eucharist, which in the Church is the *sacramentum pietatis* ["sacrament of tenderness"], *signum unitatis* ["sign of unity"], *vinculum caritatis* ["bond of love"], form between us at this time a point of division and a source of distortion of thought and of behavior, instead of being the focal point and constitutive center, which it truly is in its essence, of the unity of the Church herself?[2]

The Rights of the Laity

The starting point for understanding liturgical abuses is understanding why they are abuses and who they abuse. A liturgical

---

[2] DC 13.

abuse is an instance in which the liturgy is conducted out of accord with the Church's liturgical law. It is not merely a misuse of dead text on a page in a lectionary or a *Missal*. In the first place, it is an abuse of Jesus Christ because it involves the refusal to perform the rites that his Church—and specifically the successor of his vicar St. Peter—have lawfully approved. Consequently, such acts also abuse the sanctity of the Church, whose holiness is shown forth through the correct celebration of its rites.

In addition, liturgical abuses are offenses against the faithful who attend the liturgy. The faithful have a right by canon law to experience the liturgy as the Church has designed and intended it. If those who plan or conduct a liturgy tamper with the Church's design for it, they are abusing the faithful by denying them their right to an authentic liturgy.

> The faithful have a right to a true liturgy, which means the liturgy desired and laid down by the Church, which has in fact indicated where adaptations may be made as called for by pastoral requirements in different places or by different groups of people. Undue experimentation, changes, and creativity bewilder the faithful.[3]

This right is reflected in the *Code of Canon Law:*

> The Christian faithful have the right to worship God according to the prescripts of their own rite approved by the legitimate pastors of the Church and to follow their own form of spiritual life so long as it is consonant with the doctrine of the Church [CIC 214].

Redemptionis Sacramentum is particularly forceful in stating the right of the faithful to have their bishop deal with liturgical abuses:

---

[3] ID, Introduction.

It is the right of the Christian people themselves that their diocesan Bishop should take care to prevent the occurrence of abuses in ecclesiastical discipline, especially as regards the ministry of the Word, the celebration of the sacraments and sacramentals, the worship of God and devotion to the saints.[4]

It also states:

[L]et everyone do all that is in their power to ensure that the most holy sacrament of the Eucharist will be protected from any and every irreverence or distortion and that all abuses be thoroughly corrected. This is a most serious duty incumbent upon each and every one, and all are bound to carry it out without any favoritism.[5]

Who Can Change the Liturgy?

Liturgical abuses generally involve the omission of a mandatory part of the liturgy, the addition to the liturgy of something the Church has not authorized, or the change of a liturgical text to say something other than what the Church has authorized. This raises the question of who is able to authorize changes in the liturgy. Because the liturgy is the public or corporate worship the Church gives to God, those whom God has given charge of the Church (see also 1 Thess. 5:12; Heb. 13:17) have the responsibility of regulating the liturgy to make sure that it is conducted properly.

The way the liturgy is regulated at the present time is spelled out in the *Code of Canon Law:*

§1. The direction of the sacred liturgy depends solely on the authority of the Church, which resides in the Apostolic See and, according to the norm of law, the diocesan bishop.

---

[4] RS 24.
[5] RS 183.

§2. It is for the Apostolic See to order the sacred liturgy of the universal Church, publish liturgical books and review their translations in vernacular languages, and exercise vigilance that liturgical regulations are observed faithfully everywhere.

§3. It pertains to the conferences of bishops to prepare and publish, after the prior review of the Holy See, translations of liturgical books in vernacular languages, adapted appropriately within the limits defined in the liturgical books themselves.

§4. Within the limits of his competence, it pertains to the diocesan bishop in the Church entrusted to him to issue liturgical norms which bind everyone [CIC 938].

The pattern is for the Holy See to structure and amend the basic texts of the liturgy, the conference of bishops to translate and adapt them to its own jurisdiction, and the diocesan bishop to issue additional, more specific liturgical norms.

An example of the latter would be what time the Easter Vigil will be celebrated in a particular diocese. However, the local bishop may not make norms that conflict with those that have been established by the Holy See. Similarly, the conference of bishops must obtain the confirmation, or *recognitio*, of the Holy See before any translations or adaptations it has proposed may to be used. (This is what is meant by "the prior review of the Holy See" in some documents.)

This means that no one—whether lector, extraordinary minister of Holy Communion, deacon, priest, bishop, or even a national conference of bishops—is able to authorize changes in the liturgy that conflict with what has been approved by the Holy See. The Holy See must ratify any such changes and adaptations before they can be put into practice. Thus the *Code of Canon Law* states:

§1. In celebrating the sacraments the liturgical books approved by competent authority are to be observed faithfully;

accordingly, no one is to add, omit, or alter anything in them on one's own authority [CIC 846 §1].

Inaestimabile Donum also stresses this:

One who offers worship to God on the Church's behalf in a way contrary to that which is laid down by the Church with God-given authority and which is customary in the Church is guilty of falsification.

The use of unauthorized texts means a loss of the necessary connection between the *lex orandi* ["the law of prayer"] and the *lex credendi* ["the law of belief"]. The Second Vatican Council's admonition in this regard must be remembered: "No person, even if he be a priest, may add, remove, or change anything in the Liturgy on his own authority" [SC 22]. And Paul VI of venerable memory stated that: "Anyone who takes advantage of the reform to indulge in arbitrary experiments is wasting energy and offending the ecclesial sense" (Paul VI, address of August 22, 1973, *L'Osservatore Romano*, August 23, 1973).[6]

Pope John Paul II also stressed:

The priest . . . cannot consider himself a "proprietor" who can make free use of the liturgical text and of the sacred rite as if it were his own property, in such a way as to stamp it with his own arbitrary personal style. At times this latter might seem more effective, and it may better correspond to subjective piety; nevertheless, objectively it is always a betrayal of that union which should find its proper expression in the sacrament of unity.

Every priest who offers the holy sacrifice should recall that during this sacrifice it is not only he with his community that is praying but the whole Church, which is thus expressing in this sacrament her spiritual unity, among other ways by the use of the approved liturgical text. To call this position "mere insistence on uniformity" would only show ignorance of the objective

---

[6] ID, Introduction.

requirements of authentic unity and would be a symptom of harmful individualism.[7]

A new section in the current edition of the *General Instruction* deals with the adaptation of the liturgy. This section had no predecessor in the previous editions, and it seeks to resolve questions about what kinds of adaptations the diocesan bishop and the conference of bishops may make to the liturgy.
Concerning the diocesan bishop, it states:

> The diocesan Bishop, who is to be regarded as the high priest of his flock, and from whom the life in Christ of the faithful under his care in a certain sense derives and upon whom it depends, must promote, regulate, and be vigilant over the liturgical life in his diocese. It is to him that in this Instruction is entrusted the regulating of the discipline of concelebration . . . and the establishing of norms regarding the function of serving the priest at the altar . . . the distribution of Holy Communion under both kinds . . . and the construction and ordering of churches. . . . With him lies responsibility above all for fostering the spirit of the sacred liturgy in the priests, deacons, and faithful.[8]

It then notes that certain other adaptations are not within his authority:

> The adaptations spoken of below that call for a wider degree of coordination are to be decided, in accord with the norm of law, by the conferences of bishops.[9]

Redemptionis Sacramentum also notes that the bishop should not issue regulations that remove the liberty of pastors and others in exercising legitimate options presented in the liturgy:

---

[7] DC 12.

[8] GIRM 387.

[9] GIRM 388.

It pertains to the diocesan Bishop, then, "within the limits of his competence, to set forth liturgical norms in his diocese, by which all are bound" [CIC 838 §4]. Still, the Bishop must take care not to allow the removal of that liberty foreseen by the norms of the liturgical books so that the celebration may be adapted in an intelligent manner to the church building, or to the group of the faithful who are present, or to particular pastoral circumstances in such a way that the universal sacred rite is truly accommodated to human understanding.[10]

Concerning the conference of bishops, the *General Instruction* states:

It is the competence of the conferences of bishops in the first place to prepare and approve an edition of this *Roman Missal* in the authorized vernacular languages, for use in the regions under their care, once their decisions have been accorded the *recognitio* of the Apostolic See.

The *Roman Missal*, whether in Latin or in lawfully approved vernacular translations, is to be published in its entirety.

It is up to the conferences of bishops to decide on the adaptations indicated in this *General Instruction* and in the Order of Mass and, once their decisions have been accorded the *recognitio* of the Apostolic See, to introduce them into the *Missal* itself. These adaptations include:

• The gestures and posture of the faithful . . . ;

• The gestures of veneration toward the altar and the Book of the Gospels . . . ;

• The texts of the chants at the entrance, at the presentation of the gifts, and at Communion . . . ;

• The readings from Sacred Scripture to be used in special circumstances . . . ;

---

[10] RS 21.

- The form of the gesture of peace . . . ;
- The manner of receiving Holy Communion . . . ;
- The materials for the altar and sacred furnishings, especially the sacred vessels, and also the materials, form, and color of the liturgical vestments. . . .

Directories or pastoral instructions that the conferences of bishops judge useful may, with the prior *recognitio* of the Apostolic See, be included in the *Roman Missal* at an appropriate place.[11]

An individual bishop could not, therefore, declare that in his diocese specific gestures and postures different than those approved by the national conference and the Holy See are to be used, or that the sign of peace should take a different form, or that people should receive Communion in a different manner.

Concerning further adaptations, the *General Instruction* provides:

Finally, if the participation of the faithful and their spiritual welfare require variations and profounder adaptations in order for the sacred celebration to correspond with the culture and traditions of the different nations, then Conferences of Bishops may propose these to the Apostolic See in accordance with article 40 of the Constitution on the Sacred Liturgy for introduction with the Apostolic See's consent, especially in the case of nations to whom the Gospel has been more recently proclaimed. The special norms handed down by means of the *Instruction on the Roman Liturgy and Inculturation* should be attentively observed.

As regards the procedures in this matter, these should be observed:

Firstly, a detailed preliminary proposal should be set before the Apostolic See, so that, after the necessary faculty has been granted, the detailed working out of the individual points of adaptation may proceed.

---

[11] GIRM 389–90.

Once these proposals have been duly approved by the Apostolic See, experiments should be carried out for specified periods and at specified places. When the period of experimentation is concluded, the Conference of Bishops shall decide, if the case requires, upon pursuing the adaptations and shall submit a mature formulation of the matter to the judgment of the Apostolic See.[12]

However, the *General Instruction* indicates caution in proposing new adaptations for use in specific cultures around the world (a process known as "inculturation"):

Before, however, proceeding to new adaptations, especially those more thoroughgoing, great care should be taken to promote the proper instruction of clergy and faithful in a wise and orderly fashion, so as to take advantage of the faculties already foreseen and to implement fully the pastoral norms concerning the spirit of a celebration. . . .

The Roman rite constitutes a notable and precious part of the liturgical treasure and patrimony of the Catholic Church. Its riches are of benefit to the universal Church, so that were they to be lost, the Church would be seriously harmed. . . .

The norm established by the Second Vatican Council—that in the liturgical reform there should be no innovations unless required in order to bring a genuine and certain benefit to the Church, and taking care that any new forms adopted should in some way grow organically from forms already existing—must also be applied to efforts at the inculturation of the same Roman rite. Inculturation, moreover, requires a necessary length of time, lest the authentic liturgical tradition suffer contamination due to haste and a lack of caution.

Finally, the purpose of pursuing inculturation is not in any way the creation of new families of rites but [it] aims rather at meeting the needs of a particular culture in such a way that

---

[12] GIRM 395.

adaptations introduced either in the *Missal* or in combination with other liturgical books are not at variance with the distinctive character of the Roman rite.

And so, the *Roman Missal*, even if in different languages and with some variety of customs, must be preserved in the future as an instrument and an outstanding sign of the integrity and unity of the Roman rite.[13]

Finally, *Redemptionis Sacramentum* notes:

The reprobated practice by which priests, deacons or the faithful here and there alter or vary at will the texts of the sacred liturgy that they are charged to pronounce must cease. For in doing thus, they render the celebration of the sacred liturgy unstable and not infrequently distort the authentic meaning of the liturgy.[14]

Sometimes, when a Mass is being celebrated for a particular group of the faithful, there is an idea that the normal requirements of liturgical law are suspended (e.g., because this is a "teen Mass" or a "healing Mass" or a Mass for a particular spiritual movement—none of which are categories that liturgical law recognizes). This idea is false:

While it is permissible that Mass should be celebrated for particular groups according to the norm of law, these groups are nevertheless not exempt from the faithful observance of the liturgical norms.[15]

Bizarre Abuses

Liturgical abuses come in a bewildering variety. Some are so bizarre that they include situations the Holy See could not have

---

[13] 396–99.

[14] RS 59.

[15] RS 114.

foreseen in its rubrics and could only correct afterward. Like humorist Jean Kerr giving her children a long list of things not to do but neglecting to tell them not to eat the daisies on the dining room table, there are a certain number of liturgical "Please don't eat the daisies" situations that can be dealt with only in hindsight.

For example, one sometimes hears about a "traveling Mass" in which part is celebrated in one location, then people move to another location, where the next part of the Mass is celebrated. The *General Instruction* and the rubrics clearly envision the Mass being celebrated at a single place and time, but they do not explicitly address the "traveling Mass" situation, and so it is left to documents like *Redemptionis Sacramentum*, which states:

> In the celebration of Mass, the Liturgy of the Word and the Liturgy of the Eucharist are intimately connected to one another and form one single act of worship. For this reason it is not licit to separate one of these parts from the other and celebrate them at different times or places. Nor is it licit to carry out the individual parts of Holy Mass at different times of the same day.[16]

Another bizarre, unforeseeable abuse is trying to turn the Eucharist into a full meal or banquet. Again, *Redemptionis Sacramentum* states:

> The celebration of holy Mass is not to be inserted in any way into the setting of a common meal, nor joined with this kind of banquet. Mass is not to be celebrated without grave necessity on a dinner table nor in a dining room or banquet hall, nor in a room where food is present, nor in a place where the participants during the celebration itself are seated at tables. If out of grave necessity Mass must be celebrated in the same place

---

[16] RS 60.

where eating will later take place, there is to be a clear interval of time between the conclusion of Mass and the beginning of the meal, and ordinary food is not to be set before the faithful during the celebration of Mass.[17]

Sometimes Masses have been linked to political rallies or other secular events:

It is not permissible to link the celebration of Mass to political or secular events, nor to situations that are not fully consistent with the magisterium of the Catholic Church.[18]

At times even elements of non-Christian religions (e.g., New Age concepts or Native American prayers) have been introduced into it:

Finally, it is strictly to be considered an abuse to introduce into the celebration of Holy Mass elements that are contrary to the prescriptions of the liturgical books and taken from the rites of other religions.[19]

Another bizarre set of abuses concern distributing unconsecrated hosts or other items in the manner of Holy Communion:

The practice is reprobated whereby either unconsecrated hosts or other edible or inedible things are distributed during the celebration of holy Mass or beforehand after the manner of Communion, contrary to the prescriptions of the liturgical books. For such a practice in no way accords with the tradition of the Roman rite and carries with it the danger of causing confusion among Christ's faithful concerning the eucharistic doctrine of the Church. Where there exists in certain places by concession a particular custom of blessing bread after Mass for distribution,

---

[17] RS 77.
[18] RS 78.
[19] RS 79.

proper catechesis should very carefully be given concerning this action. In fact, no other similar practices should be introduced, nor should unconsecrated hosts ever be used for this purpose.[20]

Also:

It is never lawful for a priest to celebrate in a temple or sacred place of any non-Christian religion.[21]

And:

The abuse is reprobated by which the celebration of holy Mass for the people is suspended in an arbitrary manner contrary to the norms of the *Roman Missal* and the healthy tradition of the Roman rite, on the pretext of promoting a "fast from the Eucharist."[22]

And finally:

"A cleric who loses the clerical state in accordance with the law . . . is prohibited from exercising the power of order" [CIC 274]. It is therefore not licit for him to celebrate the sacraments under any pretext whatsoever save in the exceptional case set forth by law [i.e., hearing confession of one in danger of death; CIC 976; 986 §2], nor is it licit for Christ's faithful to have recourse to him for the celebration. . . . Moreover, these men should neither give the homily nor ever undertake any office or duty in the celebration of the sacred liturgy, lest confusion arise among Christ's faithful and the truth be obscured.[23]

---

[20] RS 96.
[21] RS 109.
[22] RS 115.
[23] RS 168.

Reasons for Liturgical Abuses

Why do liturgical abuses occur? *Inaestimabile Donum* explained the main cause of liturgical abuses in this way:

> Most of the difficulties encountered in putting into practice the reform of the liturgy, and especially the reform of the Mass, stem from the fact that neither priests nor faithful have perhaps been sufficiently aware of the theological and spiritual reasons for which the changes have been made, in accordance with the principles laid down by the Council.[24]

It went on to stress the role of priests in correcting the problem:

> Priests must acquire an ever deeper understanding of the authentic way of looking at the Church, of which the celebration of the liturgy, and especially of the Mass, is the living expression. Without an adequate biblical training, priests will not be able to present to the faithful the meaning of the liturgy as an enactment, in signs, of the history of salvation. Knowledge of the history of the liturgy will likewise contribute to an understanding of the changes which have been introduced, and introduced not for the sake of novelty but as a revival and adaptation of authentic and genuine tradition.[25]

Finally, it stressed the role of liturgical commissions and centers in correcting the problem of liturgical abuses:

> In the implementation of the liturgical reform, great responsibility falls upon national and diocesan liturgical commissions and liturgical institutes and centers, especially in the work of translating the liturgical books and training the clergy and faithful

---

[24] ID, Conclusion.
[25] Ibid.

in the spirit of the reform desired by the Council. The work of these bodies must be at the service of the ecclesiastical authority, which should be able to count upon their faithful collaboration. Such collaboration must be faithful to the Church's norms and directives and free of arbitrary initiatives and particular ways of acting that could compromise the fruits of the liturgical renewal.[26]

How to Deal with Liturgical Abuses

When responding to a violation of the Church's liturgical law, one should follow a definite sequence of steps:

1. Pray for Guidance and for a Spirit of Humility and Love

Liturgical abuse is a complex and important subject that has the potential to stir up strong, unpleasant emotions on all sides. For these reasons, whenever one confronts a situation in which one believes a liturgical abuse may exist, one should always pray for guidance in determining whether there is an abuse and, if so, what to do about it.

To avoid the hostile and painful emotions that discussing liturgical abuses can stir up, one should also pray that one will maintain a spirit of humility and love toward all who are involved in the situation. One must determine that one *will* approach others with these attitudes, and one should pray that they will also respond in a humble and loving way.

---

[26] ID, Conclusion.

2. Determine Whether a Liturgical Abuse Is Actually Occurring

Often people run into situations in which a priest, deacon, or minister is doing something they do not like or are simply unfamiliar with but is not actually a liturgical abuse. Before making an issue of a practice, for the sake of one's reputation and to avoid needless division and conflict, one must first determine whether an abuse is being committed.

The test for that is not our personal preferences but the Church's liturgical law. In many instances, one finds liturgical practices that are unfamiliar or unsettling but do not violate any norms or are actually provided as an option.

Many of the Church's laws and regulations pertaining to liturgical abuses are discussed in this book. However, there is no substitute for consulting the original sources or obtaining the counsel of experts. For information on possible liturgical abuses not covered in this book, see "Where to Go for More Help" below.

3. Determine Whether to Take Action Concerning the Abuse

Although any liturgical abuse is a violation of one's right to an authentic celebration of the liturgy,[27] sometimes one needs to be humble and, out of Christian charity, allow one's rights to be violated. In other words, one needs to turn the other cheek (Matt. 5:39). I generally advise people that they should not make an issue of minor abuses unless they have a good rapport with the person committing them and can point out minor things without offending or making the person angry.

---

[27] CIC 214; ID, Introduction.

If one does not have that special rapport, it is important to engage only over major liturgical abuses—for the very practical reason that one has only a limited number of "bullets" to shoot before one is branded a "troublemaker" in the parish. Once that happens, the chance of getting an abuse corrected diminishes, and one's relationship with the person may be poisoned, with negative spiritual effects on both parties. It may also be important to save one's "ammo" in case grave theological or liturgical problems arise in the future.

In deciding whether to take action about a liturgical abuse, one must weigh, among other things, whether more harm or good will be done by bringing it up. We must decide to act not on the fact that we are right and that an abuse should not continue but on whether taking action will help or harm the local church.

In the case of very serious abuses (e.g., use of invalid matter for the Eucharist), the benefit to the parish demands that something be done (because it is not a valid Eucharist and the people are not receiving and adoring Jesus Christ). However, in the case of minor liturgical abuses, it may cause more harm than good to try to correct them. Often it is a judgment call and only individuals with personal knowledge of the parish, of the people involved, and of the type of abuse being committed will be able to determine whether action should or should not be taken, though one should also consider consulting the organizations mentioned below in the "Where to Go for More Help" section.

One of the valuable things about the instruction *Redemptionis Sacramentum* is that it contains a section that seeks to rank, in broad strokes, liturgical abuses by their severity. At the high end of the spectrum are those termed *graviora delicta* (Latin, "more grave offenses"). Below this are a set of abuses classified as "grave matters," and below this are "other abuses." The list is not complete, and by nature can't be, but it is nevertheless a valuable tool in determining the relative gravity of different abuses. For a detailed look at the classifications it makes, see "Liturgical Abuses by Severity" in the Bonus Materials.

4. Approach the Person Committing the Abuse

If one decides to take action concerning the liturgical abuse, one should usually begin by speaking to the person doing it, whether that is a lector, extraordinary minister of Holy Communion, deacon, priest, or pastor. Do not begin by going over someone's head. That is not only less likely to produce results, but it can be a defect in Christian charity, which always seeks to cure a problem on the lowest level possible. Only if the abuse is not corrected and one determines that it is worth pursuing it further should one move up the chain of authority.

While there are rare, imaginable exceptions to this rule, I have become more and more convinced over the years of the necessity of following Jesus' instruction to begin with the offender and not to go behind his back or over his head (see also Matt. 18:15–17). One should continually apply the Golden Rule: "Whatever you wish that men would do to you, do so to them" (Matt. 7:12). Ask yourself at each step, "If I were the other person, how would *I* want this handled?"

One consequence of this is that, when approaching the person, it is important to be as respectful and friendly as possible. Not only will this increase the chances of having the abuse corrected, but it is necessary in Christian charity. One should try to be as relaxed and non-threatening as possible.

One might try sending a one-page letter to the person to request that the abuse be corrected.

If one is talking to a priest—in person or by letter—one should speak to him as kindly as one would when correcting one's own father (see also 1 Tim. 5:1).

One should also approach the person committing the abuse

with specific documentation showing where in the Church's liturgical law the abuse is prohibited. One should not simply say, "What you are doing is wrong." It would be better to say, "Here (in this quotation from an official text), it says that the practice is not allowed. Is there a more recent ruling you can show me, and, if not, could we do it this way?"

Following the advice of Matthew 18:15–17, one might initially approach the priest alone and, if he does not respond to the request to have the abuse corrected, one should then take a few others from the congregation to ask for it to be corrected —or, considering how our culture does things, it might be better to have several people sign a common letter. This will make him aware that the matter is of concern to more than one person in the congregation and should be taken more seriously.

5. Appeal to a Higher Authority

Only if these efforts fail should one go over the head of the person committing the abuse and talk to the pastor of the parish, and only if that fails should one appeal still higher. If the pastor of the parish is unresponsive then one may consider speaking to the dean (the head of the local deanery) before speaking to the bishop's office.

Redemptionis Sacramentum states:

> Any Catholic, whether priest or deacon or lay member of Christ's faithful, has the right to lodge a complaint regarding a liturgical abuse to the diocesan Bishop or the competent Ordinary equivalent to him in law, or to the Apostolic See on account of the primacy of the Roman pontiff. It is fitting, however, insofar as possible, that the report or complaint be submitted first to the diocesan Bishop. This is naturally to be done in truth and charity.[28]

---

[28] RS 184.

Concerning the role of the bishop, *Redemptionis Sacramentum* states:

"Since he must safeguard the unity of the universal Church, the Bishop is bound to promote the discipline common to the entire Church and therefore to insist upon the observance of all ecclesiastical laws. He is to be watchful lest abuses encroach upon ecclesiastical discipline, especially as regards the ministry of the Word, the celebration of the sacraments and sacramentals, the worship of God and the veneration of the saints" [CIC 392].

Hence whenever a local Ordinary or the Ordinary of a religious Institute or of a society of apostolic life receives at least a plausible notice of a delict or abuse concerning the Most Holy Eucharist, let him carefully investigate, either personally or by means of another worthy cleric, concerning the facts and the circumstances as well as the imputability.

Delicts against the faith as well as *graviora delicta* committed in the celebration of the Eucharist and the other sacraments are to be referred without delay to the Congregation for the Doctrine of the Faith, which "examines [them] and, if necessary, proceeds to the declaration or imposition of canonical sanctions according to the norm of common or proper law" [John Paul II, *Pastor Bonus*, art. 52].

Otherwise the Ordinary should proceed according the norms of the sacred canons, imposing canonical penalties if necessary, and bearing in mind in particular that which is laid down by canon 1326.[29] If the matter is serious, let him inform the Congregation for Divine Worship and the Discipline of the Sacraments.[30]

---

[29] This canon provides that a judge may punish certain offenders more gravely than the law or precept has established (e.g., one displaying obstinate ill will after the imposition of a penalty) and that additional penalties and penances can be added when a person has incurred an offense *latae sententiae* (i.e., automatically, by the commission of the act itself).

[30] RS 177–80.

If one goes to the bishop's office, it is important to provide specific documentation of the abuse. One is much more likely to get action if one can say, "On the following five dates the priest did this . . ." than if one says, "Recently my priest did something that was kind of funny during Mass."

Another form of documentation that has begun to play a role in recent years is video. With the widespread use of smartphones and other video and audio recording devices, a significant number of people witnessing liturgical abuses have simply taped them. Some have posted videos of shocking liturgical abuses to YouTube and other online video services. While the statement that pictures don't lie isn't as true as it used to be, such recordings can provide powerful confirmation of exactly what was said and done.

It is understandable that many (especially those committing the abuses) would object to such recordings, and there may be state laws affecting what can be taped (particularly if the taping is done surreptitiously and is of a private rather than public event), but the technology is so widespread that these recordings are here to stay. It is inevitable that they will continue and that their role will grow, which is not a bad thing. Sunshine is a good antidote for problems that grow in the dark, and people who are following the Church's laws have nothing to fear from such recordings.

At the same time, let me offer a few cautions:

- First, it is not worth using recordings to document minor abuses. Only use them for grave issues.

- Second, do not immediately post them online. Work your way up the chain of command using the recordings as evidence for the people to whom you present the problem (the pastor, the bishop, etc.).

- Third, do not threaten to post them online. Making threats will cause a "circle the wagons" reaction and make it less likely that you will get the problem successfully addressed.

• Fourth, if you do determine that the only way to get results is to post online, do so only after exhausting other lines of recourse.

• Fifth, consider what would actually be accomplished by posting online. Would it really help? Or would it just get people mad and possibly alienate them from the Church?

• Sixth, ask yourself in an objective and emotionally dispassionate way if there is any possibility that what is in the recording could be understood another way or involve a slip of the tongue or an accident or a case in which a person was doing his best to get through a delicate or confusing situation? If there are alternative interpretations, you are better off not publishing an ambiguous video.

• Finally, if you do post online, do not edit the recording in such a way that there is doubt about what happened. Too many edits, or edits in the wrong places, will only generate questions about how the recording has been manipulated. Show the whole context, and make extremely sure that you are correct about everything you claim in the video.

If you are writing a letter to the bishop's office, you should also cite the official text in which the abuse is prohibited and ask for a citation of another document, if there is one, that has changed the rule. Then look up that work, if any. You should always be willing to acknowledge that you have made a mistake and that there may be a more recent regulation, and you should look it up oneself.

If it is necessary to speak to the bishop's office, you should attempt to be even more respectful, polite, and friendly than when you went to the priest. You should also explain that several members of the congregation (whom you name in the letter) have contacted the priest, yet the abuse has not been corrected. You must also sign your own name to the letter.

Anonymous complaints are easy to make and hard to verify. You must have the courage to sign your name. Also, ask the bishop to let you know what action he takes to resolve the issue.

6. Investigate a Mediation or Conciliation Process

Besides taking the matter up the chain of authority, any available mediation or conciliation processes could be consulted if the situation is serious enough to warrant it. The *Code of Canon Law* states:

> Whenever a person considers himself or herself aggrieved by a decree, it is particularly desirable that the person and the author of the decree avoid any contention and take care to seek an equitable solution by common counsel, possibly using the mediation and effort of wise persons to avoid or settle the controversy in a suitable way [CIC 1733 §1].

Many dioceses have conciliation or mediation processes. It is a good idea to use them—not only because it might solve the problem at the local level but also because it will contribute to your "paper trail." A paper trail will be needed if more formal procedures have to be employed, and it should include copies of all correspondence to and from Church officials you have contacted trying to get the abuse corrected, including your local priest. If you wish to pursue local conciliation or mediation, you should consult someone competent to give advice in how to handle it, such as a canon lawyer.

7. Determine Whether Formal Procedures Are Needed

In most cases, the bishop's office is likely to be your last resort in trying to get the abuse corrected. You could write to the apostolic nuncio in Washington, D.C., or to the Congregation for Divine Worship and the Discipline of the Sacraments. But you should not expect a visible result from doing so. Understand that both the pro-nuncio and the Holy See's congregations receive a great deal of mail, and personal responses are not always possible.

> Most Rev. Pietro Sambi
> Apostolic Nunciature
> 3339 Massachusetts Ave., N.W.
> Washington, DC 20008

> Most Rev. Antonio Cañizares Llovera
> Congregation for Divine Worship and the
>   Discipline of the Sacraments
> Piazza Pio XII, 10
> 00193 Roma
> Italia

The names given above are accurate at the time of this writing, but the heads of these groups change from time to time, so check the Internet for the name of the current nuncio or head of the Congregation for Divine Worship.

If you write, you should use the opening salutation "Your Excellency" instead of "Dear Archbishop" and the closing salutation "I have the honor to be, Your Excellency," instead of "Sincerely." You should also be aware that in almost all cases the correspondence will end up being handled by someone on staff and not by the person being addressed.

Redemptionis Sacramentum explains the way in which the Congregation for Divine Worship and the Discipline of the Sacraments handles cases of liturgical abuse:

> Whenever the Congregation for Divine Worship and the Discipline of the Sacraments receives at least a plausible notice of a delict or an abuse concerning the Most Holy Eucharist, it

informs the Ordinary so that he may investigate the matter. When the matter turns out to be serious, the Ordinary should send to the same dicastery as quickly as possible a copy of the acts of the inquiry that has been undertaken and, where necessary, the penalty imposed.

In more difficult cases the Ordinary, for the sake of the good of the universal Church in the care for which he too has a part by virtue of his sacred ordination, should not fail to handle the matter, having previously taken advice from the Congregation for Divine Worship and the Discipline of the Sacraments. For its part, this Congregation, on the strength of the faculties given to it by the Roman pontiff, according to the nature of the case, will assist the Ordinary, granting him the necessary dispensations or giving him instructions or prescriptions, which he is to follow diligently.[31]

In some situations you may have to take formal recourse to the appropriate Church authorities. This should be done only in the most serious of situations (e.g., something invalidating the Mass that is not being corrected). If things have progressed to this point, professional assistance is highly recommended. Consult a canon lawyer or the St. Joseph Foundation before deciding on or pursuing formal recourse.

Where to Go for More Help

Catholic Answers specializes in evangelization and apologetics. When we can, we try to help people with common liturgical questions, such as the ones discussed in this book. However, we do not specialize in answering detailed, technical questions on the liturgy, so it is worthwhile to mention the sources to which one should turn with detailed questions.

---

[31] RS 181–82.

The Church's liturgical worship is accomplished through the celebration of the sacraments and the Liturgy of the Hours. As a consequence, there is no one liturgical text that can serve as a source for the proper conduct for every liturgical act.

For the celebration of Mass there are two primary texts—the *Roman Missal* (the third typical edition) and the *Lectionary for Mass*. These two works contain the official rubrics for Mass, which are sufficient to answer the great majority of questions. The rubrics must be followed unless one can produce a text approved by the Holy See that suspends a particular rubric in a particular circumstance. Within the *Roman Missal*, the document known as the *General Instruction of the Roman Missal* (GIRM) is particularly important. It also contains the adaptations of the liturgy authorized for the United States. (Other countries have their own national adaptations.)

If the answer cannot be found in the GIRM or the rubrics, one might turn to a work summarizing the liturgy or to a standard collection of liturgical documents. One of the best general surveys of the liturgy is *Ceremonies of the Modern Roman Rite* by Msgr. Peter J. Elliott. Also very useful is *The Sacraments and Their Celebration* by Fr. Nicholas Halligan, which deals with all the sacraments but has helpful information on the liturgies associated with them.

Texts dealing with other forms of liturgy include the following:

The Rites of the Catholic Church (the *Roman Ritual* revised by decree of the Second Vatican Council) provides the rubrics for the administration of the sacraments, vows of religious persons, and the blessings of certain objects.

Book of Blessings provides the norms and texts for the blessings of persons and groups on special occasions and that of objects and places.

Sunday Celebrations in the Absence of a Priest provides the rubrics
for communal worship under the leadership of a deacon or
specially designated lay person.

Documents on the Liturgy: 1963–1979 contains many well-indexed
liturgical materials covering the reign of Paul VI.

Not all of these books may be in print, but they can usually
be found with ease through an online book service such as
Amazon.com, FetchBook.info, or LoomeBooks.com (which
specializes in used religious books).

The translations used in the above books tend to be those
prepared by the International Committee on English in the Liturgy (ICEL). Several years ago the Holy See reorganized ICEL
and insisted that it begin producing more accurate, literal translations. At the time the documents in these books were written, though, ICEL was producing faulty translations, and one
must be watchful. The ones in these books contain a number
of inaccurate renderings inspired by a dissident agenda (for example, "special ministers of the Eucharist" instead of "extraordinary ministers of Holy Communion").

Finally, a large number of liturgical documents can be found
on the Internet. The Holy See's Web site (www.vatican.va)
contains a large number (look in the section on the Curia, where you will find the Congregation for Divine Worship and the Discipline of the Sacraments' page), as does the
U.S. bishops' Web site (www.usccb.org). Valuable areas on
the U.S. bishops' site include the home page of the bishops'
Committee for Divine Worship (www.usccb.org/liturgy) and
the area devoted to the *Roman Missal* and its implementation
(www.usccb.org/romanmissal). Many other sites on the Internet also house liturgical documents that can be found using a
search engine.

If published resources are insufficient to find the answer, try calling the chancery of your diocese and ask to speak to a canon lawyer. Though canon lawyers are not usually experts in liturgical law, they can often be helpful.

Two excellent organizations, both well worth your support, should also be mentioned as resources. The first exists to help Catholics secure their ecclesial rights, including their liturgical rights, and the second exists to promote authentic liturgical reform in line with that envisioned by Vatican II. They are:

The St. Joseph Foundation
11107 Wurzbach Road, Suite 601B
San Antonio, TX 78230-2570
210-697-0717 (phone)
210-699-9439 (fax)
st-joseph-foundation.org

Adoremus
P.O. Box 300561
St. Louis, MO 63130
314-863-8385 (phone)
314-863-5858 (fax)
adoremus.org

Bonus Materials

I. Outline of the Mass

I. Introductory Rites

    A. Entrance
    B. Veneration of the Altar
    C. Greeting
    D. Act of Penitence
    E. Kyrie
    F. Blessing and Sprinkling
    G. Gloria
    H. Collect

II. Liturgy of the Word

    A. Scripture Readings
    B. Homily
    C. Profession of Faith
    D. Prayer of the Faithful

III. Liturgy of the Eucharist

    A. Preparation of the Offerings
    B. Prayer over the Offerings
    C. Eucharistic Prayer
        1. Thanksgiving (Preface)
        2. Acclamation (*Sanctus*)
        3. *Epiclesis*
        4. Institution Narrative and Consecration
        5. Memorial Acclamation (Mystery of Faith)

      6. Anamnesis
      7. Offering
      8. Intercessions
      9. Final Doxology
   D. Communion Rite
      1. Lord's Prayer
      2. Rite of Peace
      3. Fraction
      4. Communion
      5. Prayer after Communion

IV. Concluding Rites

   A. Announcements
   B. Greeting
   C. Blessing
   D. Dismissal
   E. Veneration of the Altar
   F. Exeunt

II. Guide to the Church's Liturgical Documents

Main Works

The weight of a particular liturgical directive varies depending on, among other things, the source in which it is found. Among the most authoritative sources is the current (1983) *Code of Canon Law* (CIC). Normally, anything that the Code says is binding on the Roman rite of the Catholic Church. However, the Code has only a small amount to say about liturgical matters, since it is not principally a book of liturgical law (see canon 2).

The primary liturgical resource for the Mass is the *Missale Romanum* (*Roman Missal*), which includes the *Lectionary* (the book of Scripture readings) and what was previously called the *Sacramentary* (the book containing the prayers of the Mass). With the new translation of the *Missale Romanum*, the second is now just called "the *Roman Missal*."[1] Whatever it directs one to do is binding unless it is modified by other law or immemorial custom.

The preface of this work is known as the *General Instruction of the Roman Missal* (GIRM), which is part of the Church's universal liturgical law and is binding on all Latin rite celebrations

---

[1] *Sacramentary* was a name used for some liturgical works in Church history, but these did not correspond fully to the modern *Sacramentary*, and so the decision was made to drop it.

of the liturgy. It gives general information about the Mass and how it is to be celebrated.

The body of the *Roman Missal*, which contains the texts of the prayers, also contains short directions printed in red ink. These are called "rubrics," from the Latin term for "red." As with everything in the *Missale Romanum*, they are binding unless modified by proper Church authority. It is to these short directions that we refer when quoting or citing "the rubrics." To find the rubric in question, turn to the section of the Mass being discussed.

The U.S. edition of the *General Instruction* contains adaptations that were proposed by the American bishops and approved by the Holy See for use in the Latin rite dioceses of the United States.

In the previous translation of the liturgy, the *Sacramentary* (which the *Roman Missal* was then called) contained a document known as the *Appendix to the General Instruction* (AGI). This document contained the adaptations of the liturgy that were approved for use in the United States. When the new edition of the *Missale Romanum* was issued, it was decided that the U.S. adaptations would be made part of the text of the *General Instruction* itself so that they would be immediately obvious and not hidden in another document. The legal authority of the AGI has lapsed, but it contains some helpful legislative history, which is why it is quoted in this book.

Copies of the *Code of Canon Law*, the *Lectionary*, and the *Roman Missal* may be obtained at any Catholic bookstore. One can also ask to examine them at any parish, either in the parish library or from a priest. They can also often be obtained from college or university libraries or ordered online. In some cases, their contents can be viewed online for free. The text of the *Code of Canon Law*, for example, can be found on the Vatican's Web site at www.vatican.va.

Additional Works by the Holy See and Second Vatican Council

This book also quotes from several other sources. They can often be found at the diocesan office, in the libraries of Catholic universities, and in collections of liturgical documents that can be purchase at Catholic bookstores (see "Where to Go for More Help" in Chapter 14). Many of them, especially the more recent ones, can be found online. Try searching on the name of the document and see what comes up.

One of the most important liturgical documents of the last fifty years is *Sacrosanctum Concilium* (SC), Vatican II's 1963 constitution on the sacred liturgy, which lays out the essential principles of the liturgical reform. However, many things in *Sacrosanctum Concilium* have been supplemented or implemented by post-conciliar legislation. This document provides valuable insight on the intention of the Council, but one must look to subsequent law to determine what is in force now.

Another key work is the *Acta Apostolicae Sedis* ("Acts of the Apostolic See," AAS), the official commentary in which the Holy See publishes the laws, decrees, and acts of congregations and tribunals in the Roman curia. This can be found online at the Vatican's Web site, though it seldom publishes articles in English (Latin and Italian are the most common languages).

Also important is the journal *Notitiae* ("Notices"), published by the Congregation for Divine Worship and the Discipline of the Sacraments (a fusion of two former bodies, the Congregation for Divine Worship and the Congregation for the Discipline of the Sacraments, which were originally united in 1975, separated in 1984, and reunited in 1988). This body has competency for matters pertaining to the liturgy—e.g., granting permission for local adaptations, issuing pronouncements on the Church's liturgical law, etc.

The Congregation for Divine Worship and the Discipline of the Sacraments has also issued a number of instructions dealing with particular matters, including *Fidei Custos* (on extraordinary ministers of Holy Communion), *Immensae Caritatis* (dealing with the reception of Communion in certain circumstances), *Paschales Solemnitatis* (dealing with the special celebrations of Holy Week), and *Inaestimabile Donum.*

Inaestimabile Donum is the Church's 1980 response to the numerous liturgical abuses occurring in the Church at the time. Some parts of it are outdated now, but we only cite those parts that remain in force. *Inaestimabile Donum* was "prepared by the Sacred Congregation for the Sacraments and Divine Worship, [and] was approved on April 17, 1980, by the Holy Father, John Paul II, who confirmed it with his own authority and ordered it to be published and to be observed by all concerned."[2]

In 2004 the congregation issued another document on liturgical abuses titled *Redemptionis Sacramentum*. It is much more extensive and is currently the Church's main document dealing with liturgical abuse. It was "prepared by the Congregation for Divine Worship and the Discipline of the Sacraments by mandate of the Supreme Pontiff John Paul II in collaboration with the Congregation for the Doctrine of the Faith, was approved by the same pontiff on the Solemnity of St. Joseph, 19 March 2004, and he ordered it to be published and to be observed immediately by all concerned."

A truly extraordinary document was released on November 13, 1997. The document, titled *Ecclesia de Mysterio*,[3] was jointly released by a group of eight dicasteries (departments) of the Holy See. This is very unusual, as most documents are issued

---

[2] ID, Conclusion.

[3] Also known by the lengthier title *Interdicasterial Instruction on Certain Questions Regarding the Collaboration of the Non-Ordained Faithful in the Sacred Ministry of the Priest.*

by a single dicastery. The joint issuing signaled the seriousness
with which the Holy See intended the document to be taken.
It states:

> The scope of this present document is simply to provide a clear,
> authoritative response to the many pressing requests which have
> come to our dicasteries from bishops, priests and laity seeking
> clarification in the light of specific cases of new forms of "pas-
> toral activity" of the non-ordained on both parochial and dioce-
> san levels. . . .
>
> [R]emedies based on the normative discipline of the Church,
> and deemed opportune to correct abuses which have been
> brought to the attention of our dicasteries, are hereby set forth.[4]

The abuses of which the document speaks are widespread
in many areas (including much of the United States), where
the laity have been assigned roles that should properly be filled
by priests, thus blurring and eroding the necessary distinction
between the priesthood and the laity. The instruction states:

> [Because the tasks of the laity in the Church] are most closely
> linked to the duties of pastors (which office requires reception
> of the sacrament of Orders), it is necessary that all who are in
> any way involved in this collaboration exercise particular care
> to safeguard the nature and mission of sacred ministry and the
> vocation and secular character of the lay faithful. It must be
> remembered that "collaboration with" does not, in fact, mean
> "substitution for."[5]

Signing the document were the presidents, prefects, pro-
prefects, and secretaries of eight dicasteries: the Congregation for the Clergy, the Pontifical Council for the Laity, the
Congregation for the Doctrine of the Faith, the Congregation
for Divine Worship and the Discipline of the Sacraments, the

---

[4] EM, Premise.
[5] EM, Premise.

Congregation for Bishops, the Congregation for the Evangelization of Peoples, the Congregation for Institutes of Consecrated Life and Societies of Apostolic Life, and the Pontifical Council for the Interpretation of Legislative Texts.

The authority of the text as a legislative document is established in its conclusion, which states:

> All particular laws, customs, and faculties conceded by the Holy See *ad experimentum* ["to experiment"] or other ecclesiastical authorities which are contrary to the foregoing norms are hereby revoked.
>
> The supreme pontiff, in audience of the 13th of August 1997 approved *in forma specifica* this present instruction and ordered its promulgation.[6]

The statement that the supreme pontiff approved the document *in forma specifica* ("in its specific form") means that its norms have the same force of law as if the Roman pontiff had issued them directly.

The declaration that "all prior laws, customs, and faculties . . . which are contrary to the foregoing norms are hereby revoked" creates a clean slate legislatively. It does not matter who may have issued a norm—offices or individuals in the Holy See, the national conference of bishops, the local bishop, or the parish priest. All previous policies contrary to the document's norms have been revoked by the authority of the pope.

Works of the U.S. Bishops

The liturgical documents issued by the Holy See are supplemented by those issued by local bishops' conferences. This book cites a number that are produced by the U.S. bishops.

---

[6] EM, Conclusion.

One is the bishops' *Committee on Divine Worship Newsletter*, which is not itself a work of liturgical law but publishes articles on the liturgy and often reprints documents that are authoritative (e.g., letters from the Holy See authorizing certain translations and adaptations).

The U.S. bishops have also issued a number of liturgical documents over the years that did obtain force of law. One such document was *This Holy and Living Sacrifice: Directory for the Celebration and Reception of Communion under Both Kinds*, which was approved by the Holy See in 1984. It was later superseded by another on the same subject titled *Norms for the Distribution and Reception of Holy Communion under Both Kinds in the Dioceses of the United States of America*, which was approved by the Holy See in 2002 and is the current document governing this subject.

Mention should be made of one document that does not have legal authority. For years a document titled *Environment and Art in Catholic Worship* (EACW) was in circulation. It was issued by the U.S. Bishops' Committee on the Liturgy and did not have authority because it had not been approved by the National Council of Catholic Bishops or the Holy See.

EACW was frequently used as a basis for major, austere, and often aesthetically displeasing renovations in parishes. When parishioners question these proposed changes, they are often told—*incorrectly*—that EACW is the Church's liturgical law and that the U.S. bishops approved it. The bishops did not. EACW was the publication of a single committee and was not law any more than a bill that had only been passed out of committee in the U.S. Congress (not approved by the whole Congress and signed by the president) would be a U.S. law.

This caution concerning the nonbinding status of this document was echoed by its critics, such as Msgr. Peter J. Elliott, a noted author on the liturgy, who stated:

Published by the U.S. Bishops' Committee on the Liturgy in 1978, this influential document seems dated—insofar as it reflects an era of austere taste. Moreover, together with useful practical advice, it includes unsound opinions regarding the altar (nos. 72–73), the tabernacle (nos. 78–80) and eucharistic vessels (no. 96).[7]

Elsewhere he wrote:

A partial reading of authorities and consequent dogmatism is evident in *Environment and Art in Catholic Worship*, 1978, nos. 78, 79. To be fair to the authors, their opinions reflect the era of the 1970s and were presented before *Inaestimabile Donum* and the new Code. But this dated document continues to circulate, endorsed and unmodified.[8]

The Jurist, the canon law journal of the Catholic University of America, published an article in 1996 by noted expert in liturgical law Msgr. Frederick R. McManus titled "Environment and Art in Catholic Worship," which stated:

[T]he [EACW] statement is not, nor does it purport in any way to be, a law or general decree of the conference of bishops, emanating from the NCCB's legislative power; neither is it a general executory decree of that body. Thus it lacks, and there is no suggestion that it has, juridically binding or obligatory force, for which both two-thirds affirmative vote of the conference's *de jure* membership and the *recognitio* of the Apostolic See are required.[9]

The controversy over EACW died down after the year 2000, when a new document, *Built of Living Stones: Art, Architecture, and Worship*, was produced. It "replaces *Environment and Art*

---

[7] CMRR 342.
[8] Ibid., 325, n. 1.
[9] *The Jurist* 55:350.

and addresses the needs of the next generation of parishes engaged in building or renovating churches."[10]

Unlike EACW, *Built of Living Stones* was approved by the full body of bishops, but it still does not count as law. It describes itself as "Guidelines of the National Conference of Catholic Bishops."[11] Guidelines are not the same thing as law. Had the document been intended as law, it would have required the approval of the Holy See. It was not submitted for this approval because of its status as a guideline that does not have the force of law.

---

[10] *Built of Living Stones* §9.

[11] In 2001 the National Conference of Catholic Bishops and United States Catholic Conference merged to become the United States Conference of Catholic Bishops.

III. *Roman Missal* Translation Highlights 1963–2010

The following timeline was prepared by Adoremus Bulletin.

Sacrosanctum Concilium—December 4, 1963

The Second Vatican Council's first document, the Constitution on the Sacred Liturgy, *Sacrosanctum Concilium*, called for the renewal of the liturgy and the reform of the liturgical books in order to promote deeper understanding of and fuller participation in the liturgy by all Catholics. It suggested use of the vernacular for some parts of the Mass while reaffirming the use of Latin.

Sacram Liturgiam Issued; the *Concilium* Is Formed—January 1964

Pope Paul VI issues *Sacram Liturgiam*, the first official implementation of the Council's Constitution on the Sacred Liturgy, on January 25. He also establishes the *Concilium*, a group of scholars, experts, and bishops, to implement the liturgical reform.

ICEL Established—October 17, 1963–April 1964

On October 17, 1963, during one of the sessions of the Second Vatican Council, the bishops of ten English-speaking countries (including the United States) agreed to form a mixed commission to aid in the work of liturgical reform. By April 1964, the International Commission on English in the Liturgy (ICEL) is formally established with its mandate to prepare English translations of liturgical texts.

Comme le Prévoit—January 25, 1969

Guidelines for translators of the new *Roman Missal* are produced by the *Concilium*, the group of experts appointed to implement the Constitution on the Liturgy. Its principle of translation was "dynamic equivalency" (also called "free translation"): to convey the essential meaning of the original text in the idiom of a modern target language. Thus the words, phrases, style, etc., of the original text may be freely altered or omitted in the translation.

Missale Romanum Issued by Pope Paul VI—April 3, 1969

By the Apostolic Constitution *Missale Romanum*, Pope Paul approves the revised *Missal*.

U.S. Bishops Approve ICEL Order of Mass—November 13, 1969

Within months after the promulgation of the *Missale Romanum*, the United States bishops approve the English translation of the Order of Mass prepared by ICEL.

New Order of Mass Mandated for Use—November 30, 1969

Introducing the new Order of Mass, Pope Paul VI said, "From now on the vernacular, not Latin, will be the principal language of the Mass."

English Order of Mass Confirmed—January 5, 1970

Holy See grants *recognitio* [official approval] to the English translation of the Order of Mass for the dioceses of the United States. When the text of the Order of Mass was completed, ICEL and the conferences of bishops began translating the other prayers of the *Roman Missal*.

Provisional Order of Mass Approved—June 1972

After consultation on a draft in 1971, in 1972 the U.S. bishops approve and publish a provisional text containing prayers for Sundays and other feast days.

U.S. Bishops Approve *Sacramentary*—November 12, 1973

The complete text of the *Sacramentary* (*Roman Missal*) translated by ICEL is approved by the U.S. bishops. *Recognitio* from the Holy See is granted immediately.

U.S. *Sacramentary* Published—February 4, 1974

Less than three months after the text is approved, the new books are published.

Missale Romanum Revised—March 27, 1975

The *Missale Romanum, editio typica altera*, is promulgated by Pope Paul VI only one year after the publication of the U.S. *Sacramentary*. The revised *Missal* contained additional prayers and modifications of existing prayers and rubrics.

U.S. *Sacramentary* Second Edition—March 1, 1985

A revised *Sacramentary* is published in the U.S., based on the 1975 edition of the *Missale Romanum*, including prayers for recently canonized saints.

Sacramentary Revision Begins—November 1987

ICEL begins a revised translation of the *Missale Romanum, editio typica altera*.

U.S. Bishops' Approval of *Sacramentary*—1993–1998

The U.S. bishops reviewed the revised *Sacramentary* prepared by ICEL—along with adaptations for the United States—in segments, beginning in November 1993 and ending in June 1997. The Holy See required many changes to the Pastoral Introduction to the Order of Mass, which the bishops approved in June 1998. The final text of the revised *Sacramentary* was sent to the Holy See for *recognitio* in June 1998.

New *Roman Missal*—April 10, 2000

The third "typical edition" of the *Missale Romanum* is announced during the Jubilee Year. The *Institutio Generalis Missalis Romani* (*General Instruction of the Roman Missal*) was released in advance as an introduction to the revised *Missal*.

The U.S. Bishops' Committee on the Liturgy released the Latin text of the GIRM, along with a study translation, on July 28, 2000.

However, the complete text of the *Missale Romanum* was not presented to Pope John Paul II until March 18, 2002.

Liturgiam Authenticam—April 25, 2001

Liturgiam Authenticam, the Fifth Instruction on the Right Implementation of the Constitution on the Liturgy, outlined principles of translation (and supplanted *Comme le Prévoit*). Signed March 28, 2001, with Pope John Paul II's effective date April 25, it was released May 7. The Instruction's guiding principle for translation is "formal equivalency," that is, translating "in the most exact manner, without omissions or additions in terms of their content, and without paraphrases or glosses."

Vox Clara Committee Established—July 19, 2001

The Vatican Congregation for Divine Worship and the Discipline of the Sacraments organized the *Vox Clara* ("clear voice") committee—bishops and consultants from English-speaking countries—to assist in the review and approval of the English translation of the *Roman Missal*. Since its initial meeting in Rome on April 22–24, 2002, *Vox Clara* met several times a year to review texts submitted to the Holy See for *recognitio*.

Sacramentary Formally Rejected—March 16, 2002

Although the revised *Sacramentary* had been considered moot following the appearance in 2000 of the new *Missale Romanum*, an explicit rejection was deemed necessary by the Holy See. The letter and accompanying observations from the Congregation for Divine Worship and the Discipline of the Sacraments expressly critiqued the ICEL translation.

U.S. Bishops Approve GIRM—November 2002

The *General Instruction of the Roman Missal* (GIRM), the basic outline and instructions for the celebration of Mass, including a number of adaptations for the dioceses of the United States, is approved by the U.S. bishops' conference.

Vatican Confirms GIRM's U.S. Adaptations—March 17, 2003

The new GIRM is put into effect in the United States.

ICEL Revised Statutes Approved—October 17, 2003

On its 40th anniversary, ICEL is formally re-established by the Holy See in accordance with the principles of *Liturgiam Authenticam*. ICEL's statutes were revised to establish a formal relationship with the Congregation for Divine Worship and the Discipline of the Sacraments.

ICEL Order of Mass Draft—February 18, 2004

ICEL presented its first draft of the first section of the *Roman Missal*, the Order of Mass, to English-speaking conferences for review and comments. Each section of the *Missal* would go through two drafts, the first of which (the "green book") would undergo review and modification. The second draft (the "gray book") would be presented for canonical vote by the conferences of bishops, then submitted to the Vatican Congregation for Divine Worship and the Discipline of the Sacraments for *recognitio*.

U.S. Bishops Approve Order of Mass—June 15–17, 2006

After more than two years of review and consultation and three drafts, the English translation of the Order of Mass, along with adaptations for the dioceses of the United States, is approved by the U.S. bishops at their Los Angeles meeting. Bishop Arthur Roche of Leeds, England, the president of ICEL, addressed the bishops.

Order of Mass Receives *Recognitio*—June 23, 2008

The English translation of the Order of Mass receives *recognitio* from the Congregation for Divine Worship and the Discipline of the Sacraments so that catechesis on the revised texts could begin and musical settings of the Mass texts could be prepared. It was not authorized for liturgical use.

U.S. Bishops Approve *Missal* Texts—November 18, 2009

The U.S. bishops complete approval of the remaining segments of the ICEL translation of the *Roman Missal*. It was anticipated that the Holy See will grant *recognitio* within a few months. The bishops determined that a year will be required for catechesis and publication of new books. The U.S. Committee on Divine Worship provided a special section on its Web site with resources for study of the new *Roman Missal*, including the texts of the Order of Mass: www.usccb.org/romanmissal/.

Vatican Approves English *Missal* Translation—March 25, 2010

Recognitio of the new translation was confirmed by a decree dated March 25, 2010 (Prot. 269/10/L), and signed by Cardinal Antonio Cañizares Llovera, prefect, and Archbishop J. Augustine DiNoia, O.P., secretary to the Congregation. The definitive version was not released to the English-speaking conferences, as the new translation is undergoing final review.

USCCB States Final *Missal* Texts Received, to Be in Use by Advent 2011—August 20, 2010

Cardinal Francis George, president of the U.S. Conference of Catholic Bishops, announces that the new English texts of the *Roman Missal*, approved by the Vatican on June 23, have been received. His August 20 statement said:

> The third edition of the *Roman Missal* enters into use in the dioceses of the United States of America as of the First Sunday of Advent, November 27, 2011. From that date forward, no other edition of the *Roman Missal* may be used in the dioceses of the United States of America.
>
> We can now move forward and continue with our important catechetical efforts as we prepare the text for publication.

IV. The Holy See's Norms Regarding Gender and Translation

The following are norms issued by the Holy See for translation of biblical texts. These prohibit the attempt to gender-revise texts in order to fit a modern social-political agenda and were sent to the U.S. bishops by then-Cardinal Joseph Ratzinger.

1. The Church must always seek to convey accurately in translation the texts she has inherited from the biblical, liturgical, and patristic Tradition and instruct the faithful in their proper meaning.

2. The first principle with respect to biblical texts is that of fidelity, maximum possible fidelity to the words of the text. Biblical translations should be faithful to the original languages used by the human author in order to be understood by his intended reader. Every concept in the original text should be translated in its context. Above all, translations must be faithful to the sense of sacred Scripture understood as a unity and totality, which finds its center in Christ, the Son of God Incarnate (see also DV [*Dei Verbum*] III and IV), as confessed in the creeds of the Church.

3. The translation of Scripture should faithfully reflect the Word of God in the original human languages. It must be listened to in its time-conditioned, at times even inelegant, mode of human expression without "correction" or "improvement" in service of modern sensitivities.

a) In liturgical translations or readings where the text is very uncertain or in which the meaning is very much disputed, the translation should be made with due regard to the Neo-Vulgate.

b) If explanations are deemed to be pastorally necessary or appropriate, they should be given in editorial notes, commentaries, homilies, etc.

4/1. The natural gender of personae in the Bible, including the human author of various texts where evident, must not be changed, insofar as this is possible in the receptor language.

4/2. The grammatical gender of God, pagan deities, and angels and demons according to the original texts must not be changed, insofar as this is possible in the receptor language.

4/3. In fidelity to the inspired Word of God, the traditional biblical usage for naming the persons of the Trinity as Father, Son, and Holy Spirit is to be retained.

4/4. Similarly, in keeping with the Church's Tradition, the feminine and neuter pronouns are not to be used to refer to the person of the Holy Spirit.

4/5. There shall be no systematic substitution of the masculine pronoun or possessive adjective to refer to God, in correspondence to the original text.

4/6. Kinship terms that are clearly gender-specific, as indicated by the context, should be respected in translation.

5. Grammatical number and person of the original texts ordinarily should be maintained.

6/1. Translation should strive to preserve the connotations as well as the denotations of words or expressions in the original and thus not preclude possible layers of meaning.

6/2. For example, where the New Testament or the Church's Tradition have interpreted certain texts of the Old Testament in a christological fashion, special care should be observed in the translation of these texts so that a christological meaning is not precluded.

6/3. Thus, the word *man* in English should as a rule translate *adam* and *anthropos* since there is no one synonym which effectively conveys the play between the individual, the collectivity, and the unity of the human family so important, for example, to expression of Christian doctrine and anthropology.

V. Low-Gluten Hosts and Mustum

The following is the text of a letter issued by the Congregation for the Doctrine of the Faith on July 24, 2003. It contains the current norms regarding the use of low-gluten hosts and mustum, which are used in the celebration of the liturgy for those who are unable to consume normal bread and wine. See also the November 2003 edition of the BCL newsletter (online at usccb.org) for additional helpful resources on this subject.

Congregation for Doctrine of the Faith

July 24, 2003

Prot. 89/78-174 98

Your Excellency

The Congregation for the Doctrine of the Faith has been for many years studying how to resolve the difficulties that some of the faithful encounter in receiving Holy Communion when for various serious reasons they are unable to consume normal bread or wine.

A number of documents on this question have been issued in the past in the interest of offering pastors uniform and sure direction (Congregation for Doctrine of the Faith, *Rescriptum*, 15 December 1980, in *Leges Ecclesiae*, 6/4819, 8095–8096; *De Celebrantis Communione*, 29 October 1982, in AAS 74, 1982, 1298–1299; *Lettera ai Presidenti delle Conferenze Episcopali*, 19 June 1995, in *Notitiae* 31, 1995: 608–610).

In light of the experience of recent years, it has been deemed necessary at this time to return to the topic, taking up the above-mentioned documents and clarifying them wherever necessary.

A. The use of gluten-free hosts and mustum

1. Hosts that are *completely* gluten-free are invalid matter for the celebration of the Eucharist.

2. Low-gluten hosts (*partially* gluten-free) are valid matter, provided they contain a sufficient amount of gluten to obtain the confection of bread without the addition of foreign materials and without the use of procedures that would alter the nature of bread.

3. Mustum, which is grape juice that is either fresh or preserved by methods that suspend its fermentation without altering its nature (for example, freezing), is valid matter for the celebration of the Eucharist.

B. Communion under one species or with a minimal amount of wine

1. A lay person affected by celiac disease, who is not able to receive Communion under the species of bread, including low-gluten hosts, may receive Communion under the species of wine only.

2. A priest unable to receive Communion under the species of bread, including low-gluten hosts, when taking part in a concelebration, may with the permission of the Ordinary receive Communion under the species of wine only.

3. A priest unable to ingest even a minimal amount of wine, who finds himself in a situation where it is difficult to obtain or store mustum, when taking part in a concelebration, may with the permission of the Ordinary receive Communion under the species of bread only.

4. If a priest is able to take wine, but only a very small amount, when he is the sole celebrant, the remaining species of wine may be consumed by a lay person participating in that celebration of the Eucharist.

C. Common norms

1. The Ordinary is competent to give permission for an indi-

vidual priest or lay person to use low-gluten hosts or mustum for the celebration of the Eucharist. Permission can be granted habitually for as long as the situation continues which occasioned the granting of permission.

2. When the principal celebrant at a concelebration has permission to use mustum, a chalice of normal wine is to be prepared for the concelebrants. In like manner, when he has permission to use low-gluten hosts, normal hosts are to be provided for the concelebrants.

3. A priest unable to receive Communion under the species of bread, including low-gluten hosts, may not celebrate the Eucharist individually, nor may he preside at a concelebration.

4. Given the centrality of the celebration of the Eucharist in the life of a priest, one must proceed with great caution before admitting to Holy Orders those candidates unable to ingest gluten or alcohol without serious harm.

5. Attention should be paid to medical advances in the area of celiac disease and alcoholism and encouragement given to the production of hosts with a minimal amount of gluten and of unaltered mustum.

6. The Congregation for the Doctrine of the Faith enjoys competence over the doctrinal aspects of this question, while disciplinary matters are the competence of the Congregation for Divine Worship and the Discipline of the Sacraments.

7. Concerned episcopal conferences shall report to the Congregation for Divine Worship and the Discipline of the Sacraments, at the time of their *ad Limina* visit, regarding the application of these norms as well as any new developments in this area.

Asking you to kindly communicate the contents of this letter to the members of your episcopal conference, with fraternal regards and prayerful best wishes, I am

Sincerely yours in Christ,

Joseph Cardinal Ratzinger
Prefect

VI. The U.S. Bishops' Guidelines for Receiving Communion

The following are the current "Guidelines for Receiving Communion" that were approved by the U.S. bishops at their fall 1996 meeting.

For Catholics

As Catholics, we fully participate in the celebration of the Eucharist when we receive Communion. We are encouraged to receive Communion devoutly and frequently. In order to be properly disposed to receive Communion, participants should not be conscious of grave sin and normally should have fasted one hour. A person who is conscious of grave sin is not to receive the body and blood of the Lord without prior sacramental confession except for a grave reason where there is no opportunity for confession. In this case the person is to be mindful of the obligation to make an act of perfect contrition, including the intention of confessing as soon as possible (canon 916). A frequent reception of the sacrament of penance is encouraged for all.

For our fellow Christians

We welcome our fellow Christians to this celebration of the Eucharist as our brothers and sisters. We pray that our common baptism and the action of the Holy Spirit in this Eucharist will draw us closer to one another and begin to dispel the sad divisions which separate us. We pray that these will lessen and finally disappear, in keeping with Christ's prayer for us "that they may all be one" (John 17:21).

Because Catholics believe that the celebration of the Eucharist is a sign of the reality of the oneness of faith, life, and worship, members of those churches with whom we are not yet fully united are ordinarily not admitted to Communion. Eucharistic sharing in exceptional circumstances by other Christians requires permission according to the directives of the diocesan bishop and the provisions of canon law (canon 844 §4). Members of the Orthodox churches, the Assyrian Church of the East, and the Polish National Catholic Church are urged to respect the discipline of their own churches. According to Roman Catholic discipline, the *Code of Canon Law* does not object to the reception of Communion by Christians of these churches (canon 844 §3).

For those not receiving Communion

All who are not receiving Communion are encouraged to express in their hearts a prayerful desire for unity with the Lord Jesus and with one another.

For non-Christians

We also welcome to this celebration those who do not share our faith in Jesus Christ. While we cannot admit them to Communion, we ask them to offer their prayers for the peace and the unity of the human family.

VII. Worthiness to Receive Holy Communion—General Principles

Cardinal Joseph Ratzinger

1. Presenting oneself to receive Holy Communion should be a conscious decision, based on a reasoned judgment regarding one's worthiness to do so, according to the Church's objective criteria, asking such questions as: "Am I in full communion with the Catholic Church? Am I guilty of grave sin? Have I incurred a penalty (e.g., excommunication, interdict) that forbids me to receive Holy Communion? Have I prepared myself by fasting for at least an hour?" The practice of indiscriminately presenting oneself to receive Holy Communion, merely as a consequence of being present at Mass, is an abuse that must be corrected (see also Instruction *Redemptionis Sacramentum*, nos. 81, 83).

2. The Church teaches that abortion or euthanasia is a grave sin. The encyclical letter *Evangelium Vitae*, with reference to judicial decisions or civil laws that authorize or promote abortion or euthanasia, states that there is a "grave and clear obligation to oppose them by conscientious objection[. . . .] In the case of an intrinsically unjust law, such as a law permitting abortion or euthanasia, it is therefore never licit to obey it, or to 'take part in a propaganda campaign in favor of such a law or vote for it'" (no. 73). Christians have a "grave obligation of conscience not to cooperate formally in practices which, even if permitted by civil legislation, are contrary to God's law.

Indeed, from the moral standpoint, it is never licit to cooperate formally in evil[. . . .] This cooperation can never be justified either by invoking respect for the freedom of others or by appealing to the fact that civil law permits it or requires it" (no. 74).

3. Not all moral issues have the same moral weight as abortion and euthanasia. For example, if a Catholic were to be at odds with the Holy Father on the application of capital punishment or on the decision to wage war, he would not for that reason be considered unworthy to present himself to receive Holy Communion. While the Church exhorts civil authorities to seek peace, not war, and to exercise discretion and mercy in imposing punishment on criminals, it may still be permissible to take up arms to repel an aggressor or to have recourse to capital punishment. There may be a legitimate diversity of opinion even among Catholics about waging war and applying the death penalty, but not however with regard to abortion and euthanasia.

4. Apart from an individual's judgment about his worthiness to present himself to receive the Holy Eucharist, the minister of Holy Communion may find himself in the situation where he must refuse to distribute Holy Communion to someone, such as in cases of a declared excommunication, a declared interdict, or an obstinate persistence in manifest grave sin (see also can. 915).

5. Regarding the grave sin of abortion or euthanasia, when a person's formal cooperation becomes manifest (understood, in the case of a Catholic politician, as his consistently campaigning and voting for permissive abortion and euthanasia laws), his pastor should meet with him, instructing him about the Church's teaching, informing him that he is not to present himself for Holy Communion until he brings to an end the

objective situation of sin, and warning him that he will otherwise be denied the Eucharist.

6. When "these precautionary measures have not had their effect or in which they were not possible," and the person in question, with obstinate persistence, still presents himself to receive the Holy Eucharist, "the minister of Holy Communion must refuse to distribute it" (see also Pontifical Council for Legislative Texts Declaration "Holy Communion and Divorced, Civilly Remarried Catholics" [2002], nos. 3–4). This decision, properly speaking, is not a sanction or a penalty. Nor is the minister of Holy Communion passing judgment on the person's subjective guilt, but rather is reacting to the person's public unworthiness to receive Holy Communion due to an objective situation of sin.

N.B.: A Catholic would be guilty of formal cooperation in evil, and so unworthy to present himself for Holy Communion, if he were to vote for a candidate precisely because of the candidate's permissive stand on abortion and/or euthanasia. When a Catholic does not share a candidate's stand in favor of abortion and/or euthanasia but votes for that candidate for other reasons, it is considered remote material cooperation, which can be permitted in the presence of proportionate reasons.

VIII. Table of Postures During Mass

Section 43 of the American edition of the General Instruction *explains the postures that the faithful adopt during Mass, but it does not offer a sequential list of them. The following presents the postures in the order they are used in Mass. It primarily uses the words of section 43, with a few interpolations in brackets. These are mostly due to the part of section 43 that states that the faithful should stand "until the end of Mass, except at the places indicated below." To make a sequential list, it was necessary to insert periods of standing between and around the places indicated for other postures late in the Mass. For a detailed discussion of the law underlying this table, see Chapter 13.*

Introductory Rites

1	STANDING	beginning of the Entrance chant, or while the priest approaches the altar, until the end of the Collect

Liturgy of the Word

2	SITTING	while the readings (and the Responsorial Psalm) before the Gospel are proclaimed
3	STANDING	for the *Alleluia* chant before the Gospel
4	STANDING	while the Gospel is proclaimed
5	SITTING	for the homily
6	STANDING	during the Profession of Faith and the Prayer of the Faithful

Liturgy of the Eucharist

7	SITTING	while the Preparation of the Gifts at the Offertory is taking place
8	STANDING	from [after[1]] the invitation *Orate, fratres* ("Pray, brethren"), before the prayer over the offerings until [the end of the *Sanctus*]
9	KNEELING	after the singing or recitation of the *Sanctus* until after the Amen of the Eucharistic Prayer
10	STANDING	[from after the Amen of the Eucharistic Prayer to after the *Agnus Dei*]
11	KNEELING	after the *Agnus Dei* unless the diocesan bishop determines otherwise
12	STANDING OR KNEELING	[to receive Communion]
13	SITTING OR KNEELING	while the period of sacred silence after Communion is observed

Concluding Rites

14	STANDING	[from after the silence after Communion to the end of Mass]

The *General Instruction* also states:

Those who do not kneel [during the Eucharistic Prayer] ought to make a profound bow when the Priest genuflects after the Consecration. . . .

The norm established for the Dioceses of the United States of America is that Holy Communion is to be received standing, unless an individual member of the faithful wishes to receive

---

[1] See pp. 135–36.

Communion while kneeling (Congregation for Divine Worship and the Discipline of the Sacraments, Instruction *Redemptionis Sacramentum*, 25 March 2004, no. 91).[2]

---

[2] GIRM 43, 160, 2011 ed.

IX. Liturgical Abuses by Severity

In 2004 the Congregation for Divine Worship and the Discipline of the Sacraments issued an instruction titled Redemptionis Sacramentum. *This document introduced a ranking of various liturgical abuses by severity. If offered a three-fold division, classifying them as "graviora delicta" (Latin, "more grave offenses"), "grave matters," and "other abuses." The ranking of abuses was not exhaustive, but it provided a good framework for the laity and clergy to help them understand the relative gravity of abuses. The document states:*

[171.] Among the various abuses there are some which are objectively *graviora delicta* or otherwise constitute grave matters, as well as others which are nonetheless to be carefully avoided and corrected. Bearing in mind everything that is treated especially in Chapter I of this Instruction, attention should be paid to what follows.

1. Graviora delicta

[172.] *Graviora delicta* against the sanctity of the Most August Sacrifice and Sacrament of the Eucharist are to be handled in accordance with the "Norms concerning *graviora delicta* reserved to the Congregation for the Doctrine of the Faith," namely:

a) taking away or retaining the consecrated species for sacrilegious ends, or throwing them away;

b) the attempted celebration of the liturgical action of the eucharistic sacrifice or the simulation of the same;

c) the forbidden concelebration of the eucharistic sacrifice with ministers of Ecclesial Communities that do not have the apostolic succession nor acknowledge the sacramental dignity of priestly Ordination;

    d) the Consecration for sacrilegious ends of one matter without the other in the celebration of the Eucharist or even of both outside the celebration of the Eucharist.

2. Grave Matters

[173.] Although the gravity of a matter is to be judged in accordance with the common teaching of the Church and the norms established by her, objectively to be considered among grave matters is anything that puts at risk the validity and dignity of the Most Holy Eucharist: namely, anything that contravenes what is set out above in nn. 48–52, 56, 76–77, 79, 91–92, 94, 96, 101–102, 104, 106, 109, 111, 115, 117, 126, 131–133, 138, 153 and 168. Moreover, attention should be given to the other prescriptions of the *Code of Canon Law* and especially what is laid down by canons 1364, 1369, 1373, 1376, 1380, 1384, 1385, 1386, and 1398.

3. Other Abuses

[174.] Furthermore, those actions that are brought about which are contrary to the other matters treated elsewhere in this Instruction or in the norms established by law are not to be considered of little account but are to be numbered among the other abuses to be carefully avoided and corrected.

[175.] The things set forth in this Instruction obviously do not encompass all the violations against the Church and its discipline that are defined in the canons, in the liturgical laws, and in other norms of the Church for the sake of the teaching of the magisterium or sound tradition. Where something wrong has been committed, it is to be corrected according to the norm of law.

Because the document used its internal numbering system to identify the offenses belonging to the middle category of "grave matters," we provide the following table, which makes these offenses explicit.

Grave Matters[1]

48. Using bread for confecting the Eucharist that is made from another substance besides wheat, even if it is grain or if it is mixed with another substance different from wheat to such an extent that it would not commonly be considered wheat bread; also other substances (such as fruit, sugar, or honey) are introduced into the bread.

49. Though section 49 of RS is listed as dealing with grave matter, the nature of the matter is unclear. The first sentence of the section merely states that it is "appropriate" that "some parts of the eucharistic bread coming from the fraction should be distributed to at least some of the faithful in Communion." Saying that something is merely "appropriate" (Latin, *convenit*) would not seem to generate a grave obligation to make sure it happens. The second sentence states that small hosts are "in no way ruled out when the number of those receiving Holy Communion or other pastoral needs require it." It also states that such hosts "ought customarily to be used for the most part." Perhaps the deliberate failure to use small hosts for the faithful, particularly when their use is required by the number of communicants—and instead insisting on quickly breaking up several large hosts and incurring a risk of profanation—is the grave offense in question, but this remains unclear.

50. The wine that is used in the celebration of the eucharistic sacrifice is not natural, from the fruit of the grape, pure and incorrupt, and not mixed with other substances (except a small quantity of water added during the celebration itself), or the wine has soured, or it is of doubtful authenticity or provenance, or other drinks of any kind are used in place of wine.

---

[1] Numbers in this section refer to the section numbers within *Redemptionis Sacramentum* where the offenses are found. These entries are paraphrased for concision.

51. Using a Eucharistic Prayer that is not found in the *Roman Missal* or legitimately approved by the Apostolic See and used according to the manner and the terms set forth by it. Also, a priest composing his own Eucharistic Prayer, changing the texts approved by the Church, or introducing others composed by private individuals.

52. The priest having some parts of the Eucharistic Prayer recited by a deacon, a lay minister, an individual member of the faithful, or all members of the faithful together instead of the priest alone.

56. Omitting the name of the supreme pontiff and the diocesan bishop in the Eucharistic Prayer.

76. Uniting the sacrament of penance to the Mass in such a way that they become a single liturgical celebration. (This is *not* the same as having non-celebrating priests hear confession during Mass.)

77. Inserting the celebration of Mass in any way into the setting of a common meal or joining it with this kind of banquet. Also, apart from cases of grave necessity, celebrating it on a dinner table or in a dining room or banquet hall or in a room where food is present or in a place where the participants are seated at tables during the celebration itself. Also, even in cases of grave necessity, failing to have an interval between Mass and the start of the meal or setting ordinary food before the participants during Mass.

79. Introducing into the celebration of Mass elements that are taken from the rites of other religions.

91. Denying Holy Communion to any of Christ's faithful on the grounds that the person wishes to receive the Eucharist kneeling or standing.

92. It is not clear what grave offense the CDW has in mind in section 92, but there seem to be four nonexclusive possibilities: (1) denying the faithful the right to receive Holy Communion on the tongue, (2) denying the faithful the right to receive Holy Communion in the hand in those regions where this is lawful, (3) allowing the communicant

to carry away the eucharistic species in his hand, and (4) giving Holy Communion in the hand if there is a risk of profanation.

94. Allowing the faithful to take the Eucharist by themselves or hand it from one to another or, during a Nuptial Mass, allowing spouses to administer Holy Communion.

96. Distributing unconsecrated hosts or other edible or inedible things during the celebration of Holy Mass, or beforehand, after the manner of Communion. Also, blessing unconsecrated hosts after Mass where there is a custom of blessing bread after Mass for distribution.

101. Administering Holy Communion under both kinds where even a small danger exists of the sacred species being profaned.

102. Ministering the chalice to the lay faithful where the number of communicants makes it difficult to gauge the amount of wine needed and there is a danger that more than a reasonable quantity of the blood of Christ will remain to be consumed at the end of the celebration. Also, ministering it wherever access to the chalice would be difficult to arrange, where such a large amount of wine would be required that its certain provenance and quality could be known only with difficulty, wherever there is not an adequate number of sacred ministers or extraordinary ministers of Holy Communion with proper formation, or where a notable part of the people continues to prefer not to approach the chalice.

104. The communicant intincts the host himself or receives the intincted host in the hand. Also, intincting anything other than a validly consecrated host.

106. Pouring the blood of Christ after the Consecration from one vessel to another. Also using flagons, bowls, or other vessels that are not fully in accord with the established norms to contain the precious blood.

109. A priest celebrating in a temple or sacred place of any non-Christian religion.

111. Failing to permit an unfamiliar priest to celebrate or concelebrate the Eucharist if he presents a *celebret* not more than a year old from the Holy See or his ordinary or superior or if it can be prudently judged that he is not impeded from celebrating.

115. Suspending the celebration of Mass for the people on the pretext of promoting a "fast from the Eucharist."

117. Using for the celebration of Mass common vessels, or others lacking in quality or devoid of all artistic merit or that are mere containers or vessels made from glass, earthenware, clay, or other materials that break easily or metals and other materials that easily rust or deteriorate.

126. Sacred ministers celebrating Holy Mass or other rites without sacred vestments or with only a stole over the monastic cowl or the common habit of religious or ordinary clothes, even when there is only one minister participating.

131. Reserving the Eucharist in a place that is not subject in a secure way to the authority of the diocesan bishop (apart from the prescriptions of canon 934 §1) or where there is a danger of profanation.

132. Carrying the Most Holy Eucharist to one's home or to any other place contrary to the norm of law (different than the *gravior delictum* mentioned above of removing or retaining the consecrated species for a sacrilegious purpose or throwing them away).

133. A priest, deacon, or an extraordinary minister failing to go as directly as possible to take the Eucharist Communion to a sick person and instead engaging in profane business. Also, failing to use the rite prescribed in the *Roman Ritual* for the administration of Communion to the sick.

138. The Most Holy Sacrament is exposed and left unattended even for the briefest space of time.

153. Laypersons assuming the role or the vesture of a priest or a deacon or other clothing similar to such vesture.

168. A cleric who has lost the clerical state celebrating the sacraments under any pretext whatsoever save in the exceptional case set forth by law (e.g., hearing the confession of one in danger of death). Also, Christ's faithful having recourse to such men for the celebration of the sacraments or one of these men giving the homily or ever undertaking any office or duty in the celebration of the liturgy.

The final category mentioned by Redemptionis Sacramentum, *"other abuses," contains too many offenses to list (which is why the document itself did not attempt to do so). As it notes, however, those things that "are contrary to the other matters treated elsewhere in this Instruction or in the norms established by law are not to be considered of little account but are to be numbered among the other abuses to be carefully avoided and corrected." To see everything provided in* Redemptionis Sacramentum, *read the document at the Holy See's Web site,* www.vatican.va.

X. Commonly Raised Issues

The following tables are based on some of the most commonly asked questions about liturgical practices. Not all of these practices are common—many of the prohibited ones are very uncommon—but people inquire about them based on reports they have heard.

Changing Words

Priest changes the words of fixed prayers (p. 218)—	Prohibited
Person doing a Scripture reading revises the text to eliminate male references (p. 109)—	Prohibited
A creed that has been stripped of male references or altered in any other way is used (pp. 109, 122)—	Prohibited
Parish announcements are made during the Concluding Rites (pp. 233–34)—	Permitted

Introductory Rites

Priest gives a general, sacramental absolution in the penitential rite (p. 100)—	Prohibited
Penitential rite and "Lord have mercy" are omitted when rite of blessing and sprinkling is used (p. 102)—	Required

Liturgy of the Word

Lector uses a translation that has not been approved by both the bishops and the Holy See for liturgical use in the United States (pp. 108–109)—	Prohibited
Homily is omitted on a Sunday or holy day of obligation (p. 119)—	Prohibited
Homily is omitted on weekday (p. 119)—	Permitted
Someone other than a bishop, priest, or deacon gives the homily at Mass (p. 114)—	Prohibited
Someone gives a talk in place of the homily on a Sunday or holy day of obligation (p. 62)—	Prohibited
The Creed is not said on a Sunday or solemnity (p. 120)—	Prohibited
The Apostles' Creed is used in place of the Nicene Creed (p. 278)—	Permitted

Liturgy of the Eucharist

Priest does not wash his hands at the beginning of the Liturgy of the Eucharist (p. 133)—	Prohibited
Female altar servers are used (p. 72)—	Permitted
A bell is not rung during the Eucharistic Prayer (p. 145)—	Permitted

People say parts of the Eucharistic Prayer that are reserved to the priest, such as the *Per Ipsum* ("Through him, and with him, and in him . . .") (p. 46)—	Prohibited
Priest uses an unapproved Eucharistic Prayer or changes an approved one (p. 147)—	Prohibited
Priest alters the words of Consecration (pp. 147–48)—	Prohibited
In a Latin rite parish, the recipe for altar bread includes ingredients other than flour and water (p. 91)—	Prohibited
Communion hosts that leave many crumbs are used (p. 90)—	Prohibited
People hold hands during the Our Father (p. 281)—	Not authorized
Priest omits the exchange of an individual sign of peace (p. 212)—	Permitted
Exchange of an individual sign of peace is relocated to another part of the Mass (p. 213)—	Prohibited
During the sign of peace the priest leaves the sanctuary to shake hands with the congregation (p. 211)—	Prohibited[1]

---

[1] On special occasions such as weddings and funerals, however, he may exchange the sign of peace with some of the faithful who are standing near the sanctuary.

Communion

People at the altar receive Communion at the same time as the priest (p. 219)—	Prohibited
Extraordinary ministers of Holy Communion are used excessively or unnecessarily (p. 198)—	Prohibited
Minister or priest refuses a person the right to choose whether to receive the host on the tongue or in their hands (except in case of Communion by intinction) (p. 194)—	Prohibited
Priest refuses extraordinary ministers and altar servers the right to receive on the tongue (p. 194)—	Prohibited
Communion under both kinds is given at all Masses where it is permitted (p. 196)—	Preferred
The chalice is handed to the communicants (p. 192)—	Generally Preferred
The communicants pick up the chalice from a table (p. 191)—	Prohibited
Communion is given to Protestants apart from the special circumstances indicated in the *Code of Canon Law* (p. 176)—	Prohibited
Communion is given to Protestants at weddings and funerals (p. 177)—	Prohibited
Children are not allowed to have first confession before First Communion (p. 187)—	Prohibited

Purification of Vessels

Unless it is being taken to the sick, all of the precious blood is consumed after Mass rather than reserved (p. 230)—   Required

The precious blood is poured down a sink or sacrarium (p. 228)—   Prohibited

Vessels are purified by a deacon or an instituted acolyte rather than by the priest (p. 224)—   Permitted

Vessels are purified by an extraordinary minister of Holy Communion or other lay person (p. 224)—   Prohibited

Vessels are purified after Mass (p. 223)—   Permitted

Vessels are purified at a side table (p. 223)—   Preferred

Liturgical Articles and Furnishings

Eucharistic vessels are made of materials other than metal (pp. 252–54)—   Permitted

The inside of the chalice is made of an absorbent material, such as unglazed clay, or an ungilded and corrosion-prone material, such as silver (p. 253)—   Prohibited

Baskets are used to hold consecrated hosts (p. 253)—   Prohibited

The altar is used exclusively for divine worship (p. 250)—   Required

There is a cross on or near the altar during Mass (p. 251)—	Required
The altar cross has an image of the crucified Christ on it (p. 251)—	Required
The tabernacle is located in the sanctuary on the central axis of the nave (p. 255)—	Permitted
The tabernacle is located in a hard-to-find, out-of-the-way chapel (p. 255)—	Prohibited
A parish has kneelers or kneeling cushions (p. 274)—	Preferred
A parish has no kneelers or kneeling cushions (p. 274)—	Discouraged
There are no images of the saints in the church (p. 243)—	Prohibited

Postures and Actions

People genuflect when passing in front of the Eucharist, whether in the tabernacle or publicly exposed, unless they are moving in procession (p. 276)—	Required
Ministers carrying the processional cross or candles bow their heads instead of genuflecting (p. 276)—	Preferred
People kneel after the end of the *Sanctus* and remain kneeling through the Consecration until after the Great Amen (p. 266)—	Required
People remain standing during the Consecration because there are no kneelers (p. 273)—	Prohibited

People stand around the altar holding hands during
the Consecration (pp. 265–66)—   Prohibited

People assume any posture that is helpful to them
—standing, sitting, or kneeling—as soon as they return from Communion (pp. 270–73)—   Permitted

People imitate gestures made by the priest that are
appropriate to his role (p. 46)—   Prohibited

Dancing of any kind is performed during a liturgical
service (pp. 282–83)—   Prohibited

Acolytes, altar servers, lectors, and other lay ministers wear the alb or other suitable vesture (p. 258)— Permitted

These same ministers wear other appropriate and
dignified clothing (p. 258)—   Permitted

Seasonal Practices

Blue is used as a liturgical color in Advent or Lent
(p. 263)—   Prohibited

Crosses are veiled the Saturday before the fifth Sunday of Lent (p. 84)—   Permitted

Crosses are veiled following the close of the Mass
of the Lord's Supper on Holy Thursday (p. 84)—   Permitted

Women have their feet washed on Holy Thursday
at the discretion of the bishop (p. 58)—   *De Facto*
                                                   Permitted

Holy water fonts are refilled with water blessed at
Easter Vigil (p. 238)—   Required

XI. *Summorum Pontificum*

In 2007, Pope Benedict XVI issued the following motu proprio *dealing with the celebration of the Mass according to the form it had prior to the Second Vatican Council. This document, which had long been anticipated, was much commented on in the media and was hotly debated, as some saw in it an effort to "turn back the clock," liturgically speaking. To address the criticism he knew it would be met with, Pope Benedict also issued an accompanying letter (see next section). The following is an unofficial translation of the original Latin provided by the Vatican Information Service.*

Pope Benedict XVI
Apostolic Letter Given *Motu Proprio*
Summorum Pontificum

Up to our own times, it has been the constant concern of supreme pontiffs to ensure that the Church of Christ offers a worthy ritual to the divine majesty, "to the praise and glory of his name," and "to the benefit of all his Holy Church."

Since time immemorial it has been necessary—as it is also for the future—to maintain the principle according to which "each particular church must concur with the universal Church, not only as regards the doctrine of the faith and the sacramental signs, but also as regards the usages universally accepted by uninterrupted apostolic Tradition, which must be observed not only to avoid errors but also to transmit the integrity of the faith, because the Church's law of prayer corresponds to her law of faith."[1]

---

[1] General Instruction of the Roman Missal, 3rd ed., 2002, no. 397.

Among the pontiffs who showed that requisite concern, particularly outstanding is the name of St. Gregory the Great, who made every effort to ensure that the new peoples of Europe received both the Catholic faith and the treasures of worship and culture that had been accumulated by the Romans in preceding centuries. He commanded that the form of the sacred liturgy as celebrated in Rome (concerning both the sacrifice of Mass and the Divine Office) be conserved. He took great concern to ensure the dissemination of monks and nuns who, following the Rule of St. Benedict, together with the announcement of the Gospel, illustrated with their lives the wise provision of their Rule that "nothing should be placed before the work of God." In this way the sacred liturgy, celebrated according to the Roman use, enriched not only the faith and piety but also the culture of many peoples. It is known, in fact, that the Latin liturgy of the Church in its various forms, in each century of the Christian era, has been a spur to the spiritual life of many saints, has reinforced many peoples in the virtue of religion and fecundated their piety.

Many other Roman pontiffs, in the course of the centuries, showed particular solicitude in ensuring that the sacred liturgy accomplished this task more effectively. Outstanding among them is St. Pius V who, sustained by great pastoral zeal and following the exhortations of the Council of Trent, renewed the entire liturgy of the Church, oversaw the publication of liturgical books, amended and "renewed in accordance with the norms of the Fathers," and provided them for the use of the Latin Church.

One of the liturgical books of the Roman rite is the *Roman Missal*, which developed in the city of Rome and, with the passing of the centuries, little by little took forms very similar to that it has had in recent times.

"It was towards this same goal that succeeding Roman pontiffs directed their energies during the subsequent centuries in order to ensure that the rites and liturgical books were brought up to date and when necessary clarified. From the beginning of this century they undertook a more general reform."[2] Thus our predecessors Clement VIII, Urban VIII, St. Pius X,[3] Benedict XV, Pius XII, and Blessed John XXIII all played a part.

In more recent times, Vatican II expressed a desire that the respectful reverence due to divine worship should be renewed and adapted to the needs of our time. Moved by this desire our predecessor, the supreme pontiff Paul VI, approved in 1970, reformed, and partly renewed liturgical books for the Latin Church. These, translated into the various languages of the world, were willingly accepted by bishops, priests, and faithful. John Paul II amended the third typical edition of the *Roman Missal*. Thus Roman pontiffs have operated to ensure that "this kind of liturgical edifice . . . should again appear resplendent for its dignity and harmony."[4]

But in some regions, no small numbers of faithful adhered and continue to adhere with great love and affection to the earlier liturgical forms. These had so deeply marked their culture and their spirit that in 1984 the supreme pontiff John Paul II, moved by a concern for the pastoral care of these faithful, with the special indult *Quattuor Abhinc Anno*, issued by the Congregation for Divine Worship, granted permission to use the *Roman Missal* published by Blessed John XXIII in the year 1962. Later, in the year 1988, John Paul II, with the Apostolic Letter given as *motu proprio Ecclesia Dei*, exhorted bishops to

---

[2] John Paul II, Apostolic Letter "Vicesimus quintus annus," 4 December 1988, 3: AAS 81 (1989), 899.

[3] Ibid.

[4] St. Pius X, Apostolic Letter Motu propio data, "Abhinc duos annos," 23 October 1913: AAS 5 (1913), 449–50; cf John Paul II, Apostolic Letter "Vicesimus quintus annus," no. 3: AAS 81 (1989), 899.

make generous use of this power in favor of all the faithful who so desired.

Following the insistent prayers of these faithful, long deliberated upon by our predecessor John Paul II, and after having listened to the views of the cardinal fathers of the Consistory of 22 March 2006, having reflected deeply upon all aspects of the question, invoked the Holy Spirit and trusting in the help of God, with these Apostolic Letters we establish the following:

Art 1. The *Roman Missal* promulgated by Paul VI is the ordinary expression of the *lex orandi* (law of prayer) of the Catholic Church of the Latin rite. Nonetheless, the *Roman Missal* promulgated by St. Pius V and reissued by Bl. John XXIII is to be considered as an extraordinary expression of that same *lex orandi* and must be given due honor for its venerable and ancient usage. These two expressions of the Church's *lex orandi* will in no way lead to a division in the Church's *lex credendi* (law of belief). They are, in fact two usages of the one Roman rite.

It is, therefore, permissible to celebrate the sacrifice of the Mass following the typical edition of the *Roman Missal* promulgated by Bl. John XXIII in 1962 and never abrogated as an extraordinary form of the liturgy of the Church. The conditions for the use of this *Missal* as laid down by earlier documents *Quattuor Abhinc Annis* and *Ecclesia Dei* are substituted as follows:

Art. 2. In Masses celebrated without the people, each Catholic priest of the Latin rite, whether secular or regular, may use the *Roman Missal* published by Bl. Pope John XXIII in 1962 or the *Roman Missal* promulgated by Pope Paul VI in 1970 and may do so on any day with the exception of the Easter Triduum. For such celebrations, with either one *Missal* or the other, the priest has no need for permission from the Apostolic See or from his Ordinary.

Art. 3. Communities of institutes of consecrated life and of societies of apostolic life, of either pontifical or diocesan right, wishing to celebrate Mass in accordance with the edition of the *Roman Missal* promulgated in 1962, for conventual or "community" celebration in their oratories, may do so. If an individual community or an entire institute or society wishes to undertake such celebrations often, habitually or permanently, the decision must be taken by the Superiors Major, in accordance with the law and following their own specific decrees and statutes.

Art. 4. Celebrations of Mass as mentioned above in art. 2 may—observing all the norms of law—also be attended by faithful who, of their own free will, ask to be admitted.

Art. 5. §1 In parishes, where there is a stable group of faithful who adhere to the earlier liturgical tradition, the pastor should willingly accept their requests to celebrate the Mass according to the rite of the *Roman Missal* published in 1962 and ensure that the welfare of these faithful harmonizes with the ordinary pastoral care of the parish, under the guidance of the bishop in accordance with canon 392, avoiding discord and favoring the unity of the whole Church.

§2 Celebration in accordance with the *Missal* of Bl. John XXIII may take place on working days, while on Sundays and feast days one such celebration may also be held.

§3 For faithful and priests who request it, the pastor should also allow celebrations in this extraordinary form for special circumstances such as marriages, funerals, or occasional celebrations, e.g., pilgrimages.

§4 Priests who use the *Missal* of Bl. John XXIII must be qualified to do so and not juridically impeded.

§5 In churches that are not parish or conventual churches, it is the duty of the rector of the church to grant the above permission.

Art. 6. In Masses celebrated in the presence of the people in accordance with the *Missal* of Bl. John XXIII, the readings may be given in the vernacular, using editions recognized by the Apostolic See.

Art. 7. If a group of lay faithful, as mentioned in art. 5 §1, has not obtained satisfaction to their requests from the pastor, they should inform the diocesan bishop. The bishop is strongly requested to satisfy their wishes. If he cannot arrange for such celebration to take place, the matter should be referred to the Pontifical Commission *Ecclesia Dei*.

Art. 8. A bishop who, desirous of satisfying such requests, but who for various reasons is unable to do so may refer the problem to the Commission *Ecclesia Dei* to obtain counsel and assistance.

Art. 9. §1 The pastor, having attentively examined all aspects, may also grant permission to use the earlier ritual for the administration of the sacraments of baptism, marriage, penance, and the anointing of the sick, if the good of souls would seem to require it.

§2 Ordinaries are given the right to celebrate the sacrament of confirmation using the earlier Roman pontifical if the good of souls would seem to require it.

§3 Clerics ordained *in sacris constitutes* may use the Roman breviary promulgated by Bl. John XXIII in 1962.

Art. 10. The ordinary of a particular place, if he feels it appropriate, may erect a personal parish in accordance with canon 518 for celebrations following the ancient form of the Roman rite, or appoint a chaplain, while observing all the norms of law.

Art. 11. The Pontifical Commission *Ecclesia Dei*, erected by

John Paul II in 1988,[5] continues to exercise its function. Said commission will have the form, duties, and norms that the Roman pontiff wishes to assign it.

Art. 12. This commission, apart from the powers it enjoys, will exercise the authority of the Holy See, supervising the observance and application of these dispositions.

We order that everything we have established with these Apostolic Letters issued as *motu proprio* be considered as "established and decreed" and to be observed from 14 September of this year, Feast of the Exaltation of the Cross, whatever there may be to the contrary.

From Rome, at St. Peter's,
7 July 2007, third year of Our Pontificate

Pope Benedict XVI

---

[5] Cf. John Paul II, Apostolic Letter *motu proprio data Ecclesia Dei*, July 2, 1988, 6: AAS 80 (1988), 1498.

XII. Letter of Pope Benedict Accompanying *Summorum Pontificum*

Pope Benedict XVI foresaw that the release of Summorum Pontificum *would cause a great deal of controversy. Indeed, there was controversy even before it was released. He also knew that many bishops would have concerns about it. To deal with these problems, he accompanied its release with the following letter to the bishops.*

LETTER OF HIS HOLINESS BENEDICT XVI
TO THE BISHOPS ON THE
OCCASION OF THE PUBLICATION
OF THE APOSTOLIC LETTER *MOTU PROPRIO DATA*
SUMMORUM PONTIFICUM
ON THE USE OF THE ROMAN LITURGY
PRIOR TO THE REFORM OF 1970

My Dear Brother Bishops,

With great trust and hope, I am consigning to you as pastors the text of a new Apostolic Letter *motu proprio data* ["given on one's own initiative"] on the use of the Roman liturgy prior to the reform of 1970. The document is the fruit of much reflection, numerous consultations, and prayer.

News reports and judgments made without sufficient information have created no little confusion. There have been very divergent reactions ranging from joyful acceptance to harsh opposition about a plan whose contents were in reality unknown.

This document was most directly opposed on account of two fears, which I would like to address somewhat more closely in this letter.

In the first place, there is the fear that the document detracts from the authority of the Second Vatican Council, one of whose essential decisions—the liturgical reform—is being called into question.

This fear is unfounded. In this regard, it must first be said that the *Missal* published by Paul VI and then republished in two subsequent editions by John Paul II obviously is and continues to be the normal form—the *forma ordinaria*—of the eucharistic liturgy. The last version of the *Missale Romanum* prior to the Council, which was published with the authority of Pope John XXIII in 1962 and used during the Council, will now be able to be used as a *forma extraordinaria* of the liturgical celebration. It is not appropriate to speak of these two versions of the *Roman Missal* as if they were "two Rites." Rather, it is a matter of a twofold use of one and the same rite.

As for the use of the 1962 *Missal* as a *forma extraordinaria* of the liturgy of the Mass, I would like to draw attention to the fact that this *Missal* was never juridically abrogated and, consequently, in principle, was always permitted. At the time of the introduction of the new *Missal*, it did not seem necessary to issue specific norms for the possible use of the earlier *Missal*. Probably it was thought that it would be a matter of a few individual cases which would be resolved, case by case, on the local level. Afterward, however, it soon became apparent that a good number of people remained strongly attached to this usage of the Roman rite, which had been familiar to them from childhood. This was especially the case in countries where the liturgical movement had provided many people with a notable liturgical formation and a deep, personal familiarity with the earlier form of the liturgical celebration. We all know that, in the movement led by Archbishop Lefebvre, fidelity to the old *Missal* became an external mark of identity; the reasons for the break which arose over this, however, were at a deeper level. Many people who clearly accepted the binding character of the Second Vatican Council, and were faithful to the pope and the bishops, nonetheless also desired to recover the form of the sacred liturgy that was dear to them. This occurred above all because in many places celebrations were not faithful to the prescriptions of the new *Missal*, but the latter actually was understood as authorizing or even requiring creativity, which frequently led to deformations of the liturgy which were hard to bear. I am speaking from experience, since I too lived through that period with all its hopes and its confusion. And I have seen how arbitrary deformations of the liturgy caused deep pain to individuals totally rooted in the faith of the Church.

Pope John Paul II thus felt obliged to provide, in his *motu proprio Ecclesia Dei* (2 July 1988), guidelines for the use of the 1962 *Missal*; that document, however, did not contain detailed prescriptions but appealed in a general way to the generous response of bishops toward the "legitimate aspirations" of those members of the faithful who requested this usage of the Roman rite. At the time, the pope primarily wanted to assist the Society of Saint Pius X to recover full unity with the Successor of Peter and sought to heal a wound experienced ever more painfully. Unfortunately this reconciliation has not yet come about. Nonetheless, a number of communities have gratefully made use of the possibilities provided by the *motu proprio*. On the other hand, difficulties remain concerning the use of the 1962 *Missal* outside these groups because of the lack of precise juridical norms, particularly because bishops, in such cases, frequently feared that the authority of the Council would be called into question. Immediately after the Second Vatican Council it was presumed that requests for the use of the 1962 *Missal* would be limited to the older generation which had grown up with it, but in the meantime it has clearly been demonstrated that young persons too have discovered this liturgical form, felt its attraction, and found in it a form of encounter with the mystery of the Most Holy Eucharist, particularly suited to them. Thus the need has arisen for a clearer juridical regulation which had not been foreseen at the time of the 1988 *motu proprio*. The present norms are also meant to free bishops from constantly having to evaluate anew how they are to respond to various situations.

In the second place, the fear was expressed in discussions about the awaited *motu proprio* that the possibility of a wider use of the 1962 *Missal* would lead to disarray or even divisions within parish communities. This fear also strikes me as quite unfounded. The use of the old *Missal* presupposes a certain degree of liturgical formation and some knowledge of the Latin language; neither of these is found very often. Already from these concrete presuppositions, it is clearly seen that the new *Missal* will certainly remain the ordinary form of the Roman rite, not only on account of the juridical norms, but also because of the actual situation of the communities of the faithful.

It is true that there have been exaggerations and at times social aspects unduly linked to the attitude of the faithful attached to the ancient Latin liturgical tradition. Your charity and pastoral prudence will be an incentive and guide for improving these. For that matter, the two forms of the usage of the Roman rite can be mutually enriching: new saints and some of the new prefaces can and should be inserted in the old *Missal*. The *Ecclesia Dei* Commission, in contact with various bodies devoted to the *usus antiquior* ["older usage"], will study the practical possibilities in this regard. The celebration of the Mass according to the *Missal* of Paul VI will be able to demonstrate, more powerfully than has been the case hitherto, the sacrality which attracts many people to the former usage. The most sure guarantee that the *Missal* of Paul VI can unite parish communities and be loved by them consists in its being celebrated with great reverence in harmony with the liturgical directives. This will bring out the spiritual richness and the theological depth of this *Missal*.

I now come to the positive reason which motivated my decision to issue this *motu proprio* updating that of 1988. It is a matter of coming to an interior reconciliation in the heart of the Church. Looking back over the past, to the divisions which in the course of the centuries have rent the body of Christ, one continually has the impression that, at critical moments when divisions were coming about, not enough was done by the Church's leaders to maintain or regain reconciliation and unity. One has the impression that omissions on the part of the Church have had their share of blame for the fact that these divisions were able to harden. This glance at the past imposes an obligation on us today: to make every effort to enable for all those who truly desire unity to remain in that unity or to attain it anew. I think of a sentence in the Second Letter to the Corinthians, where Paul writes: "Our mouth is open to you, Corinthians; our heart is wide. You are not restricted by us, but you are restricted in your own affections. In return . . . widen your hearts also!" (2 Cor. 6:11–13). Paul was certainly speaking in another context, but his exhortation can and must touch us too, precisely on this subject. Let us generously open our hearts and make room for everything that the faith itself allows.

There is no contradiction between the two editions of the *Roman Missal*. In the history of the liturgy there is growth and progress but no rupture. What earlier generations held as sacred remains sacred and great for us too, and it cannot be all of a sudden entirely forbidden or even considered harmful. It behooves all of us to preserve the riches which have developed in the Church's faith and prayer and to give them their proper place. Needless to say, in order to experience full communion, the priests of the communities adhering to the former usage cannot, as a matter of principle, exclude celebrating according to the new books. The total exclusion of the new rite would not in fact be consistent with the recognition of its value and holiness.

In conclusion, dear brothers, I very much wish to stress that these new norms do not in any way lessen your own authority and responsibility either for the liturgy or for the pastoral care of your faithful. Each Bishop, in fact, is the moderator of the liturgy in his own diocese (see also *Sacrosanctum Concilium* 22: *"Sacrae Liturgiae moderatio ab Ecclesiae auctoritate unice pendet quae quidem est apud Apostolicam Sedem et, ad normam iuris, apud Episcopum"* ["Regulation of the sacred liturgy depends solely on the authority of the Church, that is, on the Apostolic See and, as laws may determine, on the bishop"]).

Nothing is taken away, then, from the authority of the Bishop, whose role remains that of being watchful that all is done in peace and serenity. Should some problem arise which the parish priest cannot resolve, the local Ordinary will always be able to intervene, in full harmony, however, with all that has been laid down by the new norms of the *motu proprio*.

Furthermore, I invite you, dear brothers, to send to the Holy See an account of your experiences three years after this *motu proprio* has taken effect. If truly serious difficulties come to light, ways to remedy them can be sought.

Dear brothers, with gratitude and trust, I entrust to your hearts as pastors these pages and the norms of the *motu proprio*. Let us always be mindful of the words of the apostle Paul addressed to the presbyters of Ephesus: "Take heed to yourselves and to all the flock, in which the Holy Spirit has made you overseers, to care for the Church of God which he obtained with the blood of his own Son" (Acts 20:28).

I entrust these norms to the powerful intercession of Mary, Mother of the Church, and I cordially impart my apostolic blessing to you, dear brothers, to the parish priests of your dioceses, and to all the priests, your co-workers, as well as to all your faithful.

Given at Saint Peter's, 7 July 2007

Benedictus PP. XVI

XIII. Glossary

The following are terms commonly used in discussion of the liturgy. Terms that are printed in small capitals have their own entry (e.g., the entry ACCLAMATION *mentions the* EUCHARISTIC PRAYER, *which is in small capitals to indicate that it also has an entry).*

ACCLAMATION: In general, an expression of praise, approval, or assent. Commonly used in the liturgy to describe the responses said by the faithful at Mass. More specifically: one of two parts of the EUCHARISTIC PRAYER. The first is simply called "the Acclamation," but it is better known as the *Sanctus*. It follows the THANKSGIVING and precedes the *EPICLESIS*. The second is known as "the MEMORIAL ACCLAMATION," but it is better known as the Mystery of Faith or *Mysterium Fidei* (p. 144).

ACOLYTE: "The acolyte is instituted to serve at the altar and to assist the priest and deacon. In particular, it is his responsibility to prepare the altar and the sacred vessels and, if it is necessary, as an extraordinary minister, to distribute the Eucharist to the faithful" (GIRM 98). This office is not the same as that of ALTAR SERVER, which developed later in Church history to allow boys to substitute for and perform most of the functions of acolytes. While females are now also permitted to be altar servers, only men can be instituted acolytes (CIC 230 §1) (p. 62).

ACT OF PENITENCE: One of the INTRODUCTORY RITES. In it the priest invites the faithful to recall their sins, there is a moment of silence, and then there is a general confession and a non-sacramental absolution. It follows the GREETING and precedes the *KYRIE* (p. 103).

ADORATION: The worship owed to God. Eucharistic adoration is the adoration of Christ in the EUCHARIST. Note: Sometimes people speak of the exposition of the Eucharist as "adoration," though they are not the same thing. One can adore the Eucharist whether it is exposed or not. During adoration various devotions—including the rosary[1]—are used (p. 26).

ADVENT: The liturgical season that precedes and prepares for Christmas. Although purple is its liturgical color, it is not a penitential season. "Advent begins with evening prayer I of the Sunday falling on or closest to 30 November and ends before evening prayer I of Christmas."[2]

AGNUS DEI: Latin, "Lamb of God." A prayer that is sung or recited during the FRACTION in the COMMUNION RITE. It begins, "Lamb of God, you take away the sins of the world, have mercy on us" (p. 214).

ALB: A long-sleeved white linen robe that reaches the ankles. It is worn by ministers of the altar over their ordinary clothes and may be decorated in a variety of ways (pp. 258–61).

ALLELUIA: Hebrew, *hallelujah*, "Praise the Lord!" One of the chants performed during the SCRIPTURE READINGS. It occurs immediately before the reading of the GOSPEL, except in the season of Lent, when it is not used (p. 112).

ALTAR CLOTH: A large piece of linen used to cover the altar (p. 250).

ALTAR SERVER: A person, typically a boy or girl, appointed to perform the functions of an instituted ACOLYTE when an

---

[1] RS 137.
[2] GNLC 40.

acolyte is not present. Altar servers (also known as *altar boys* and *altar girls*) typically can perform most of the functions of an acolyte but not all. For example, they are not generally empowered to function as extraordinary ministers of Holy Communion, while an acolyte is (cf. GIRM 191) (p. 72).

AMBO: Furnishing used for the proclamation of the SCRIPTURE READINGS, the RESPONSORIAL PSALM, the HOMILY, and the intentions during the PRAYER OF THE FAITHFUL. Ambos are stationary, in contrast with movable LECTERNS. They are also typically blessed before being put into use (p. 246).

AMBROSIAN RITE: A variant of the Latin rite that is used in the liturgy of Milan, the former see of St. Ambrose.

AMICE: A rectangular piece of linen with two long strips attached to two of its corners. It is worn under the ALB and is optional if the alb is made in such a way as to cover the wearer's street clothing at the neck (p. 260).

ANAMNESIS: Greek, "remembrance." Part of the EUCHARISTIC PRAYER in which the priest, following the commandment of Christ to "do this in memory of me," recalls the passion, resurrection, and ascension of Christ. It follows the MEMORIAL ACCLAMATION and precedes the OFFERING (p. 159).

ANAPHORA: Greek, "carrying back, offering." Term used in Eastern liturgies for the EUCHARISTIC PRAYER (see also CANON OF THE MASS) (p. 153).

ANNOUNCEMENTS: Typically, items of parish news. They may be given at the beginning of the CONCLUDING RITES, following the PRAYER AFTER COMMUNION and before the GREETING (p. 233).

ANTIPHON: Greek, *anti-* "opposite" + *phonē* "voice." A short text, typically from Scripture and often used as a refrain said by the congregation (e.g., during the RESPONSORIAL PSALM), though it has other uses in the liturgy.

ANTIPHONAL: A responsorial style in which two individuals or groups alternate, with one person or group saying one part of the text and another saying the antiphon.

ASPERGES: Another name for the RITE OF BLESSING AND SPRINKLING (p. 102).

BASILICA: Originally, a kind of large public building used for certain civic and commercial functions. Today, a title bestowed on certain church buildings of special significance.

BENEDICTION: In general, a blessing. More specifically, a ceremony in which exposition of the Eucharist occurs and a priest uses the MONSTRANCE to make the sign of the cross to bless the people.

BIDDING PRAYERS: See PRAYER OF THE FAITHFUL (p. 402).

BLESSING AND SPRINKLING: See RITE OF BLESSING AND SPRINKLING (p. 405).

BLESSING: In general, an occurrence in which the priest or other qualified minister invokes God's favor on another. More specifically, part of the CONCLUDING RITES in which the priest blesses the people in the name of the Father, the Son, and the Holy Spirit. On certain days this is preceded by an additional solemn form of blessing. The Blessing of the Concluding Rites follows the GREETING and precedes the DISMISSAL.

BURSE: Case used to hold the CORPORAL—folded—when not in use. Alternately, a small leather container used to hold a PYX.

CANON: Greek, *kanon*, "measuring rod, standard, rule." In general, a rule or standard. The term also has more specific meanings.

CANON LAW: The internal legal system of the Catholic Church. Notable works of canon law include the *CODE OF CANON LAW* (CIC) and the *Code of Canons of the Eastern Churches* (CCEO). Canon law involves liturgical law but also deals with other subjects.

CANON OF THE MASS: Another name for the EUCHARISTIC PRAYER, especially Eucharistic Prayer I (the Roman Canon). See also *ANAPHORA* (p. 137).

CANTOR: Latin, "chanter, singer." Person who performs or leads the performance of the chants and songs at Mass (p. 61).

CASSOCK: Form of clerical dress consisting of an ankle-length robe. Typically black in color. While a priest may wear one during Mass under the approved liturgical vestments, it is not specifically a liturgical vestment (p. 260).

CELEBRANT: The priest who says Mass. Alternately, the main priest celebrating Mass when other priests concelebrate with him.

CELIAC DISEASE: A condition caused by a reaction to the gluten found in wheat and certain other grains. Special provisions are made for those with this condition as they usually cannot digest ordinary hosts (p. 91).

CENSER: Liturgical furnishing used for holding burning incense. Typically attached to a chain so that it can be swung during the process of incensation, though chainless "hand censers" are used in some Eastern liturgies. See also THURIBLE.

CHANCEL: Another (and uncommon) term for the SANCTUARY (p. 277).

CHASUBLE: The outermost vestment of the celebrating priest at Mass and reflecting the liturgical color of the day or season.

Though different styles have been used, the most common today is that of a large piece of cloth with a hole in the center for the priest's head (p. 258).

CHRISMATION: A term used for the sacrament of CONFIRMATION in Eastern rite Catholic churches (p. 190).

CHRISTMAS: The day on which the birth of the Lord is celebrated (December 25). Alternately, the liturgical season inaugurated by Christmas. "The Christmas season runs from Evening Prayer I of Christmas until the Sunday after Epiphany or after 6 January, inclusive."[3]

CHURCH *SUI IURIS*: A church with its own law. There are over twenty churches *sui iuris* in the Catholic Church, the largest of which is the Latin Church. Sometimes a church *sui iuris* is incorrectly referred to as a "rite." See *RITE, EASTERN RITE*.

CIBORIUM: A vessel used to hold many hosts; it may be shaped either like a chalice or like a dish (one deeper than patens usually are).

CINCTURE: A cord used to gather the ALB at the waist. It may be white or the liturgical color of the day.

CLERIC: A person who is an ordained deacon, priest, or bishop.

COLLECT: One of the INTRODUCTORY RITES. It is a prayer that varies depending on the liturgical day. It follows the *GLORIA* and concludes the Introductory Rites. The former translation of Mass referred to it as the "opening prayer," but its historical name is restored in the new translation.

COMME LE PRÉVOIT: French, "As [it] provides." Document produced by the CONCILIUM in 1969 on the translation of liturgical texts. It encouraged the translation philosophy known

---

[3] GNLC 33.

as DYNAMIC EQUIVALENCE or "free translation." It was replaced in 2001 by the document *LITURGIAM AUTHENTICAM*, which mandated formal equivalence or a "literal translation (p. 330)."

COMMENTATOR: An individual, including a lay person, "who provides the faithful, when appropriate, with brief explanations and commentaries with the purpose of introducing them to the celebration and preparing them to understand it better"[4] (p. 61).

COMMINGLING: The point at which the priest drops a fragment of his host into the precious blood (p. 214).

COMMUNION ANTIPHON: An ANTIPHON that may be said just before the distribution of Holy Communion to the faithful (p. 223).

COMMUNION RITE: The fourth part of the LITURGY OF THE EUCHARIST, in which those participating in the Mass prepare to and then receive COMMUNION. It follows the EUCHARISTIC PRAYER and concludes the Liturgy of the Eucharist (p. 207).

COMMUNION: Latin, *communio*, "participation." In general, mutual participation. More specifically, ecclesial communion (mutual participation in or union with the Church) and eucharistic Communion (mutual, sacramental participation in the body and blood of Christ). The latter is also called Holy Communion. More specifically still, the part of the COMMUNION RITE in which Holy Communion is distributed. It includes the second elevation of the elements and is often accompanied by a chant, hymn, or song. It follows the FRACTION and precedes the PRAYER AFTER COMMUNION.

CONCELEBRANT: A priest who celebrates Mass along with the main priest CELEBRANT.

---

[4] GIRM 105b.

CONCELEBRATE: To join in the celebration of Mass together; concelebration occurs when a group of priests share or divide the priestly prayers and actions among them in the manner laid down in the *ROMAN MISSAL*.

CONCILIAR: In general, having to do with a council. More specifically, having to do with the Second Vatican Council or VATICAN II, which was held from 1962 to 1965.

CONCILIUM: In general, the Latin term for a council or advisory group. More specifically, shorthand for the Concilium for the Implementation of the Constitution on the Sacred Liturgy, a group tasked by Pope Paul VI with overseeing the liturgical reform called for by VATICAN II. It later became the Congregation for Divine Worship.

CONCLUDING RITES: The fourth and final part of the Mass. They include ANNOUNCEMENTS (if there are any), the GREETING, the BLESSING, the DISMISSAL, the VENERATION OF THE ALTAR, and the *EXEUNT*. The Concluding Rites follow the LITURGY OF THE EUCHARIST unless there is another liturgical action immediately following, in which case they are omitted (p. 233).

CONFITEOR: Another name for the prayer of the PENITENTIAL ACT that begins "I confess" (p. 31).

CONSECRATION: In general, an act of making something sacred or the event at which something is made sacred. More specifically: The point in the Mass when the bread and wine are transformed into the body and blood of Christ (p. 146).

COPE: A floor-length vestment resembling a cloak. It is worn at various rites, including eucharistic BENEDICTION, and is usually highly decorated (p. 258).

CORPORAL: A square, white piece of linen on which the paten, CIBORIUM, and chalice are placed during Mass. Not the same as the ALTAR CLOTH. See also BURSE (p. 126).

COWL: A hood or hooded robe worn by monks and other men religious (p. 258).

CREDENCE TABLE: A table used to hold various liturgical articles until they are needed during the MASS. The previous translation of the *Roman Missal* referred to it as the "side table" (p. 64).

CRUETS: Small vessels used to hold the wine and water used at Mass. Typically they are glass and have a flat bottom, narrow neck, handle, stopper, and indented lip or spout for pouring (p. 82).

CURIA: Group of individuals who participate in the governance of a church (e.g., diocesan curia, the Roman Curia).

DALMATIC: A tunic of varying lengths and decorative style that is worn over other liturgical vestments, especially by deacons. It reflects the liturgical color of the day.

DEANERY: Group of neighboring parishes joined together to foster pastoral care. Also called a vicariate forane. It is headed by a dean, also known as a vicar forane. In Eastern Catholic churches the dean is known as an archpriest.

DELICT: A canonical crime. Specifically, "an external and morally imputable violation of a law to which a canonical sanction, at least an indeterminate one, is attached"[5] (p. 357).

DICASTERY: A department in the ROMAN CURIA. For example, the Congregation for Divine Worship and the Discipline of the Sacraments, the Congregation for the Doctrine of the Faith, and the Pontifical Commission for Legislative Texts (note: Many dicasteries have had name changes in recent years, so do not be surprised if you see a dicastery going under a somewhat different name).

---

[5] CIC (1917 edition) 2195 § 1.

DISMISSAL: Part of the CONCLUDING RITES in which the deacon or priest dismisses the people using one of the approved formulas (e.g., "Go forth, the Mass is ended"). It follows the BLESSING and precedes the VENERATION OF THE ALTAR.

DIVINE LITURGY: A common term for the Mass in Eastern rite liturgies (p. 169).

DOXOLOGY: Greek, *doxa*, "glory" + *logion*, "a speech." A prayer that praises God's glory.

DUBIUM: Latin, "doubt" or "question." Often used as shorthand for *responsum ad dubium* ("response to a doubt," "answer to a question"). A type of reply in question-and-answer format typically given by a DICASTERY of the Holy See to clarify or settle an issue.

DYNAMIC EQUIVALENCE: A translation philosophy in which the translator tries to express the thoughts that are in the original but having significant liberty in the way in which they are expressed. Also called "free translation." Compare with FORMAL EQUIVALENCE.

EASTER: The Sunday on which the Resurrection of the Lord is celebrated (i.e., the first Sunday following the first full moon following the vernal equinox, based historically on the timing of Passover, when the Lord was crucified). Alternately, the liturgical season that follows the TRIDUUM, consisting of the fifty days from Easter Sunday to PENTECOST.

EASTER PROCLAMATION: The hymn of praise used in the Easter Vigil, typically performed by the deacon. Also called the *EXSULTET.*

EASTERN RITE: A liturgical tradition used by one of the Eastern Catholic Churches *sui iuris.* There are five Eastern rites: the Alexandrian, the Antiochene, the Armenian, the Chaldean, and the Constantinopolitan. These are used by more than twenty Eastern churches *sui iuris.* Note: Sometimes these Eastern Catholic churches are referred to incorrectly as "the Eastern rites" or—worse—simply as "the Eastern rite." Properly speaking, the rite refers to the form of liturgy, etc., that these churches use (see RITE), not to the churches themselves. The LATIN RITE is the only major liturgical tradition that does not belong to the Eastern rites.

ECCLESIA DEI: A 1988 document issued *MOTU PROPRIO* by John Paul II to deal with the schism of the Society of St. Pius X. It mandated the creation of the Pontifical Commission *Ecclesia Dei* to oversee its application.

EMBER DAY: See ROGATION AND EMBER DAYS.

EMBOLISM: Greek, *embolismos* = "insertion." A liturgical insertion that occurs at the end of the LORD'S PRAYER in the COMMUNION RITE. At this point the priest says the prayer beginning, "Deliver us, Lord, we pray, from every evil." It follows the recitation of the Lord's Prayer and precedes the people's DOXOLOGY, "For the kingdom, the power, and glory are yours, now and forever" (p. 206).

ENCHIRIDION: Greek and Latin, "handbook" or "manual." Thus the *Enchiridion of Indulgences* is also known as the *Handbook of Indulgences.*

ENTRANCE ANTIPHON: An ANTIPHON that may be spoken or sung during the ENTRANCE procession. Also called the INTROIT.

ENTRANCE CHANT: A chant or song accompanying the ENTRANCE in the INTRODUCTORY RITES (p. 30).

ENTRANCE: The first part of the INTRODUCTORY RITES, in which the priest and other ministers approach the altar. It precedes the VENERATION OF THE ALTAR (p. 96).

EPICLESIS: The third part of the EUCHARISTIC PRAYER. In it, by
means of particular invocations, the Church implores the
power of the Holy Spirit that the gifts offered by human
hands be consecrated. It follows the ACCLAMATION (*SANC-
TUS*) and precedes the INSTITUTION NARRATIVE AND CONSE-
CRATION (p. 144).

EUCHARISTIC PRAYER: The third part of the LITURGY OF THE EU-
CHARIST. In it the bread and wine are transformed into the
body and blood of our Lord. It follows the PRAYER OVER THE
OFFERINGS and precedes the COMMUNION RITE.

EXEUNT: Latin, "they exit." The part of the CONCLUDING RITES
in which the priest, deacon, and other ministers process away
from the altar. It follows the VENERATION OF THE ALTAR (p.
41).

EXPOSITION: A ceremony in which the Eucharist is exposed
for the adoration of the people, typically in a MONSTRANCE.
See also ADORATION, BENEDICTION.

EXTRAORDINARY FORM: A form according to which Mass is celebrated in the Latin Church. It is celebrated in Latin according to the 1962 *Missal*, which was the last before the liturgical reform initiated by Vatican II. It was given this name
by Benedict XVI in his *MOTU PROPRIO SUMMORUM PONTI-
FICUM*, in which he gave regulations concerning its use.

EXTRAORDINARY MINISTER OF HOLY COMMUNION: A person authorized to distribute Holy Communion, either for a particular occasion or in a more stable fashion, due to extraordinary circumstances such as lack of ordinary ministers of
Holy Communion. The ordinary ministers of Holy Communion are bishops, priests, deacons, and instituted acolytes.
All others are extraordinary. Note that the term *extraordinary
minister of Holy Communion* is the correct term. Terms such

as *extraordinary minister of the Eucharist, eucharistic minister*, and *special minister* are all incorrect.

EXSULTET: Another name for the EASTER PROCLAMATION. This name derives from the first word of the hymn in Latin, which means "May it [i.e., the angelic multitude] exult".

FEAST: Liturgical day that has less gravity than a solemnity but more than a memorial. "Feasts are celebrated within the limits of the natural day and accordingly do not have evening prayer I. Exceptions are feasts of the Lord that fall on a Sunday in Ordinary Time and in the CHRISTMAS season and that replace the Sunday office."[6]

FINAL DOXOLOGY: The final part of the EUCHARISTIC PRAYER, in "which the glorification of God is expressed and is confirmed and concluded by the people's ACCLAMATION, Amen."[7] It follows the INTERCESSIONS. Also known as the *PER IPSUM* from its opening words in Latin ("Through him"). The people's amen that concludes it is sometimes called the GREAT AMEN (p. 139).

FONT: Vessel used for containing holy water. This may be the small kind also called a STOUP ("holy water font") or a larger kind at which or in which baptisms are performed ("baptismal font") (p. 238).

FORMAL EQUIVALENCE: Translation philosophy in which the translator tries not only to express the thoughts in the original but to also follow closely the wording, syntax, and other features of the original. Also called "literal translation." Compare with DYNAMIC EQUIVALENCE (p. 21).

---

[6] GNLC 13.
[7] GIRM 79h.

FRACTION: Latin, *fractio*, "act of breaking." Part of the COMMU-
NION RITE in which the priest breaks a piece of the host and
drops it into the precious blood, "to signify the unity of the
body and blood of the Lord in the work of salvation, namely,
of the living and glorious body of Jesus Christ."[8] "Christ's
gesture of breaking bread at the Last Supper, which gave the
entire eucharistic action its name in apostolic times, signifies
that the many faithful are made one body (1 Cor. 10:17) by
receiving Communion from the one Bread of Life which
is Christ."[9] During the Fraction the AGNUS DEI is sung or
recited. It follows the RITE OF PEACE and precedes the distribution of COMMUNION (p. 214).

GAUDETE SUNDAY: Third Sunday of Advent. The name comes
from the Latin word meaning "rejoice"—the first word of
the INTROIT of the day's Mass. Rose-colored vestments may
be used on this day and on *LAETARE* SUNDAY (p. 262).

GENERAL INTERCESSIONS: See PRAYER OF THE FAITHFUL.

GENUFLECT: To bend the right knee to the ground, signifying
adoration. It is reserved for the Eucharist and for the VEN-
ERATION OF THE CROSS on Good Friday up to Easter Vigil[10]
(p. 275).

GLORIA: Prayer in the INTRODUCTORY RITES that begins "Glory
to God in the highest, and on earth peace to people of good
will." It follows the *KYRIE* and precedes the COLLECT (p. 103).

GRADUAL: Term formerly used for the RESPONSORIAL PSALM,
based on the fact that in the Tridentine Mass the psalm was
said on one of the steps (Latin, *gradus*) leading to the altar.
Also, one of two books containing musical settings of the

---

[8] GIRM 83.
[9] Ibid.
[10] GIRM 274.

psalms and other texts used in the Mass. (See ROMAN GRADUAL, SIMPLE GRADUAL.)

GRADUALE: Latin term for the GRADUAL.

GREAT AMEN: The people's ACCLAMATION Amen at the end of the FINAL DOXOLOGY of the EUCHARISTIC PRAYER. Often given a musical setting (p. 267).

GREETING: Liturgically speaking, a dialogue in which the priest greets the people ("The Lord be with you") and the people respond ("And with your spirit"). It appears several times in the Mass: In the INTRODUCTORY RITES (before the ACT OF PENITENCE), in the LITURGY OF THE WORD (before the Gospel reading), in the LITURGY OF THE EUCHARIST (at the beginning of the EUCHARISTIC PRAYER), and in the CONCLUDING RITES (before the BLESSING).

HOMILY: The second part of the LITURGY OF THE WORD. The homily is a form of preaching in which the priest or deacon provides "an exposition of some aspect of the readings from Sacred Scripture or of another text from the Ordinary or from the Proper of the Mass of the day." Homilies are mandatory on Sundays and holy days of obligation, though they can be omitted for a serious reason. The homily follows the SCRIPTURE READINGS and precedes the PRAYER OF THE FAITH (or the PROFESSION OF FAITH, when it is used) (p. 113).

INSTITUTION NARRATIVE AND CONSECRATION: The part of the EUCHARISTIC PRAYER in which the priest recites the account of Jesus instituting the Eucharist at the Last Supper, including the words of CONSECRATION that transform the elements into the body and blood of Christ. It follows the EPICLESIS and precedes the MEMORIAL ACCLAMATION (Mystery of Faith) (p. 146).

INTERCESSIONS: In general, acts of prayer on behalf of another. More specifically: part of the EUCHARISTIC PRAYER in which "expression is given to the fact that the Eucharist is celebrated in communion with the entire Church, of heaven as well as of earth, and that the offering is made for her and for all her members, living and dead, who have been called to participate in the redemption and the salvation purchased by Christ's body and blood."[11] It follows the OFFERING and precedes the FINAL DOXOLOGY (p. 160).

INTINCTION: Practice of administering COMMUNION under both kinds by dipping the host in the precious blood and then placing it on the tongue of the communicant (p. 202).

INTRODUCTORY RITES: The first part of Mass, which begins with the ENTRANCE and runs through the COLLECT. They precede the LITURGY OF THE WORD.

INTROIT: Another term for the ENTRANCE ANTIPHON.

KYRIE: One of the INTRODUCTORY RITES. Involves the saying of the prayer that begins "*Kyrie, eleison*" or its English equivalent, "Lord, have mercy." It follows the ACT OF PENITENCE and precedes the *GLORIA* (p. 103).

LAETARE SUNDAY: Fourth Sunday of Lent. The name comes from the Latin word meaning "Be glad"—the first word of the INTROIT of the day. Rose-colored vestments may be worn on this day and on *GAUDETE* SUNDAY (p. 262).

LAITY: People who have not received holy orders and so are not bishops, priests, or deacons.

LATAE SENTENTIAE: Latin, "(already) given sentence." Manner in which a penalty is incurred automatically. Crimes that have a *latae sententiae* penalty do not have to have the penalty

---

[11] GIRM 79g.

declared by a judge. The penalty is incurred by the commission of the act itself. For example, using the sacred species for a sacrilegious purpose (such as in a "black Mass") incurs a *latae sententiae* excommunication that is reserved to the Holy See—that is, an excommunication that only the Holy See can lift under ordinary circumstances.

LATIN CHURCH: The largest church *sui iuris* in the Catholic Church. Its principal liturgical form is the LATIN RITE, though it also hosts smaller liturgical traditions such as the AMBROSIAN RITE. The Latin Church is distinguished from the Eastern Catholic churches *sui iuris* that are also in communion with the pope.

LATIN RITE: The liturgical tradition that is used in the LATIN CHURCH. See CHURCH *SUI IURIS*, EASTERN RITE, LATIN CHURCH, RITE.

LAVABO: (Latin, "I will wash") Part of the PREPARATION OF THE OFFERINGS in which the priest washes his hands and asks to be cleansed of his sins (p. 132).

LECTERN: A movable furnishing that can be used for the proclamation of the SCRIPTURE READINGS, etc., in the same way as a stationary ambo. LITURGICAL LAW expresses a preference for the use of an AMBO over a lectern[12] (p. 246).

LECTIONARY: The book containing the SCRIPTURE READINGS used at Mass (p. 312).

LECTOR: Properly speaking, a person who is formally instituted to proclaim the Scripture readings at Mass. In casual speech, a person who is not formally instituted as a lector but who performs this function by temporary deputation.

---

[12] GIRM 309.

LENT: The liturgical season that precedes and prepares for TRIDUUM and EASTER. It is a penitential season. "Lent runs from Ash Wednesday until the Mass of the Lord's Supper [on Holy Thursday] exclusive."[13]

LICIT/LICEITY: *Licit* means "in conformity with the law," "lawful." Liceity is the quality of being licit. Contrast with VALID/VALIDITY.

LITURGIAM AUTHENTICAM: Instruction produced in 2001 by the Congregation for Divine Worship and the Discipline of the Sacraments. It dealt with the translation of liturgical texts and mandated a FORMAL EQUIVALENCE or "literal translation" philosophy. It replaced the 1969 document *COMME LE PRÉVOIT,* which had mandated a DYNAMIC EQUIVALENCE philosophy.

LITURGICAL LAW: The body of laws that the Church has established dealing with the LITURGY. Although liturgical law is dealt with in some portions of the *CODE OF CANON LAW* and the *Code of Canons of the Eastern Churches,* it is principally dealt with in the Church's liturgical books, such as the *MISSALE ROMANUM* or *ROMAN MISSAL.*

LITURGICAL REFORM: Attempt to improve the liturgy and its celebration. While small steps concerning the reform of the liturgy occur frequently with the approval of the Holy See, a major liturgical reform followed VATICAN II.

LITURGY OF THE EUCHARIST: The third part of Mass, in which the Eucharist is celebrated and Holy COMMUNION is given. It runs from the PREPARATION OF THE OFFERINGS through the PRAYER AFTER COMMUNION. It follows the LITURGY OF THE WORD and precedes the CONCLUDING RITES.

---

[13] GNLC 28.

LITURGY OF THE WORD: The second part of Mass, in which God's word in Scripture is proclaimed. It runs from the SCRIPTURE READINGS to the PRAYER OF THE FAITHFUL. It follows the INTRODUCTORY RITES and precedes the LITURGY OF THE EUCHARIST (p. 105).

LITURGY: The official worship of the Church as expressed through the sacraments and the LITURGY OF THE HOURS.

LORD'S PRAYER: The first part of the COMMUNION RITE, in which the Lord's Prayer or Our Father is recited in preparation to receive Communion. "In the Lord's Prayer a petition is made for daily food, which for Christians means preeminently the eucharistic bread, and also for purification from sin, so that what is holy may, in fact, be given to those who are holy."[14] It also contains the EMBOLISM and concludes with the doxology, "For the kingdom, the power, and the glory are yours, now and forever." It follows the FINAL DOXOLOGY of the EUCHARISTIC PRAYER and precedes the RITE OF PEACE (p. 207).

MAGISTERIUM: The teaching authority of the Church, exercised by the bishop of Rome and the bishops of the world teaching in union with him.

MAJOR ORDERS: The offices of subdeacon, deacon, priest, and bishop. Compare with MINOR ORDERS.

MASS OF THE CATECHUMENS: Term used for the first part of the Mass in the EXTRAORDINARY FORM. It corresponds to the INTRODUCTORY RITES and the LITURGY OF THE WORD. The name derives from the fact that the unbaptized were once dismissed before the celebration of the EUCHARIST.

MASS OF THE FAITHFUL: Term used for the second part of the Mass in the EXTRAORDINARY FORM. It corresponds to the

---

[14] GIRM 81.

LITURGY OF THE EUCHARIST and the CONCLUDING RITES. The name derives from the fact that once only the baptized were present for the celebration of the EUCHARIST.

MAUNDY THURSDAY: The Thursday of Holy Week. More commonly called Holy Thursday.

MEMORIAL: A liturgical day that has less gravity than a SOLEMNITY or FEAST. "Memorials are either obligatory or optional. Their observance is integrated into the celebration of the occurring weekday in accord with the norms set forth in the *General Instructions of the Roman Missal* and the Liturgy of the Hours."[15]

MEMORIAL ACCLAMATION: The part of the EUCHARISTIC PRAYER in which the priest or deacon says, "Let us proclaim the mystery of faith," and the people respond with one of the approved ACCLAMATIONS. It follows the INSTITUTION NARRATIVE AND CONSECRATION and precedes the *ANAMNESIS*. Better known as the MYSTERY OF FAITH (Latin, *Mysterium Fidei*) (p. 157).

MENSA: Latin, "table." The top surface of an altar.

MINISTER: A person performing a particular service or function in the LITURGY. Ministers may be clerics or lay, depending on the ministry in question.

MINOR ORDERS: Series of stages or offices that historically preceded the reception of the MAJOR ORDERS of deacon, priest, and bishop. The minor orders included porter, lector, exorcist, and acolyte. In 1972 the law governing them was reordered and they came to be called "ministries" and were no longer reserved for those preparing to receive holy orders. Two such ministries—LECTOR and ACOLYTE—were re-

---

[15] GNLC 14.

tained in the whole Latin Church. Local conferences of bishops could request the institution of other ministries in their area, including porter, exorcist, and catechist.

MISSAL: Book containing the texts (prayers and readings) used at Mass. See MISSALE ROMANUM, ROMAN MISSAL.

MISSALE ROMANUM: Latin, "*Roman Missal.*" Technically, a work containing both the SCRIPTURE READINGS and the prayers used at Mass. More commonly, the work containing the prayers used at Mass. Contrast with LECTIONARY.

MISSALETTE: An abbreviated missal, often provided in pews for the use of the faithful. It commonly contains the SCRIPTURE READINGS for the current liturgical season, the order of Mass, and some hymns.

MONSTRANCE: A larger eucharistic vessel used for the exposition and adoration of the Blessed Sacrament. It often takes the form of a stand with a circular metal design atop it. During exposition the host is placed at the center of the design to honor and call attention to it.

MOTU PROPRIO: A kind of papal letter issued on the pope's own initiative. *Motu propria* are often used to clarify or change norms. One of the most famous *motu propria* was Benedict XVI's 2007 document SUMMORUM PONTIFICUM, which clarified the status of the extraordinary form of Mass and gave norms regarding its use.

MUSTUM/MUST: "Grape juice that is either fresh or preserved by methods that suspend its fermentation without altering its nature (for example, freezing)"[16] (p. 95).

MYSTERIUM FIDEI: See MEMORIAL ACCLAMATION.

---

[16] CDF, *Letter to the Presidents of Bishops' Conferences*, July 24, 2003.

MYSTERY OF FAITH: See MEMORIAL ACCLAMATION.

NAVE: "The space within the church building for the faithful other than the priest celebrant and the ministers is sometimes called the *nave*."[17]

NORM: A rule, a law.

NOTITIAE: The journal published by the Congregation for Divine Worship and the Discipline of the Sacraments (p. 323).

NOVUS ORDO: Latin, "new order." Term sometimes used for what is properly called the ordinary form.

NUNCIO: A papal envoy who heads a diplomatic mission of the Holy See to a particular nation or international organization. Functions as an ambassador as well as performing certain other duties for the Holy See.

OFFERING: The part of the EUCHARISTIC PRAYER in which "the Church—and in particular the Church here and now gathered—offers in the Holy Spirit the spotless victim to the Father. The Church's intention, however, is that the faithful not only offer this spotless victim but also learn to offer themselves, and so day by day to be consummated, through Christ the mediator, into unity with God and with each other, so that at last God may be all in all."[18] It follows the *ANAMNESIS* and precedes the INTERCESSIONS.

OFFERTORY: The name given in the extraordinary form to the first part of the MASS OF THE FAITHFUL. It corresponds to the PREPARATION OF THE OFFERINGS and the PRAYER OVER THE OFFERINGS in the LITURGY OF THE EUCHARIST.

OFFERTORY CHANT: A chant or song performed during the PREPARATION OF THE OFFERINGS.

---

[17] *Built of Living Stones* 51.
[18] GIRM 79f.

OPENING PRAYER: See COLLECT.

ORANS: Latin, "praying." A posture in which one prays with arms outstretched. Used by the priest in the PRESIDENTIAL PRAYERS and during the LORD'S PRAYER (p. 280).

ORATIONS: In general, formal speeches or prayers. In the liturgy, the PRESIDENTIAL PRAYERS except for the EUCHARISTIC PRAYER. In other words, the COLLECT, the PRAYER OVER THE OFFERINGS, and the PRAYER AFTER COMMUNION.[19]

ORDINARY FORM: The form according to which Mass is ordinarily celebrated in the Latin Church. This is the form that developed from the liturgical reform that followed VATICAN II. The name "ordinary form" was given to this type of Mass by Benedict XVI in his *MOTU PROPRIO SUMMORUM PONTIFICUM.* See also EXTRAORDINARY FORM.

ORDINARY OF THE MASS: Those parts of the Mass that do not change based on the liturgical day. Also called the ordinary. Compare with PROPER OF THE MASS.

ORDINARY TIME: "Apart from those seasons having their own distinctive character, thirty-three or thirty-four weeks remain in the yearly cycle that do not celebrate a specific aspect of the mystery of Christ. Rather, especially on the Sundays, they are devoted to the mystery of Christ in all its aspects. This period is known as Ordinary Time. Ordinary Time begins on Monday after the Sunday following 6 January and continues until Tuesday before Ash Wednesday inclusive. It begins again on Monday after Pentecost and ends before evening prayer I of the First Sunday of Advent."[20]

PASCHAL: Having to do with EASTER.

---

[19] GIRM 30.
[20] GNLC 43-44.

PATEN: Typically a flat plate or shallow dishlike vessel used to hold hosts—especially the priest's host—both before and after CONSECRATION. It is also used during COMMUNION as a precaution in case a host is accidentally dropped. It may be large enough to hold all of the hosts that will be used at Mass (GIRM 331).

PER IPSUM: Latin, "Through him." Prayer said by the priest in the FINAL DOXOLOGY of the EUCHARISTIC PRAYER. It begins "Through him, and with him, and in him" (p. 161).

PONTIFICAL COMMISSION *ECCLESIA DEI:* A DICASTERY in the RO-MAN CURIA tasked with overseeing the implementation of John Paul II's 1988 *MOTU PROPRIO* Ecclesia Dei. This included outreach to certain traditionalists no longer in full communion with the Church as well as oversight of what is now known as the extraordinary form of the Mass. Originally a freestanding commission, during the reign of Benedict XVI it was attached to the Congregation for the Doctrine of the Faith (p. 367).

POSTCOMMUNION: Another term for the PRAYER AFTER COMMU-NION.

PRAYER AFTER COMMUNION: The final part of the COMMUNION RITE. In it, the priest says a prayer that varies depending on the liturgical day and the people respond, "Amen." It follows the distribution of Holy COMMUNION and precedes the CONCLUDING RITES.

PRAYER OF THE FAITHFUL: The fourth part of the LITURGY OF THE WORD. In it prayer intentions are announced "for the holy Church, for civil authorities, for those weighed down by various needs, for all men and women, and for the salvation of the whole world,"[21] and the people typically re-

---

[21] GIRM 69.

spond with an invocation such as "Lord, hear our prayer." It follows the PROFESSION OF FAITH and concludes the LITURGY OF THE WORD. Also called the UNIVERSAL PRAYER and BIDDING PRAYERS. The former translation referred to this as the GENERAL INTERCESSIONS.

PRAYER OVER THE OFFERINGS: The second part of the LITURGY OF THE EUCHARIST. In it the priest says a prayer that changes based on the liturgical day. The Prayer over the Offerings follows the PREPARATION OF THE OFFERINGS and precedes the EUCHARISTIC PRAYER. The previous translation of the Mass referred to this as the PRAYER OVER THE GIFTS. See also SECRET.

PREFACE: A prayer that the priest says during the THANKSGIVING of the EUCHARISTIC PRAYER. It varies by the liturgical day or by which Eucharistic Prayer is being said.

PREPARATION OF THE OFFERINGS: The first part of the LITURGY OF THE EUCHARIST. In it the bread and wine that will be used for the Eucharist, as well as other offerings, are brought forward. Also, the altar is prepared, the bread and wine are placed on the altar, and the priest washes his hands (see LAVABO). The Preparation of the Offerings occurs after the PRAYER OF THE FAITHFUL, which concludes the LITURGY OF THE WORD, and precedes the PRAYER OVER THE OFFERINGS.

PRESBYTER: Latin, "elder." A person who has the second degree of holy orders, that is, a priest. It excludes deacons and bishops. Compare with SACERDOS.

PRESBYTERIUM: A group of priests (e.g., those of a particular diocese). In the liturgy, another name for the SANCTUARY.

PRESIDENTIAL PRAYERS: Those prayers assigned to the priest that "are addressed to God in the name of the entire holy people and all present."[22] They include the EUCHARISTIC PRAYER and the ORATIONS. "The nature of the presidential texts demands that they be spoken in a loud and clear voice."[23] Other prayers, which the priest says in his own name, are said quietly.

PROFESSION OF FAITH: The third part of the LITURGY OF THE WORD. The Profession of Faith involves the proclamation of either the Nicene Creed or the Apostles' Creed. It is done on Sundays, solemnities, and other solemn occasions. It follows the HOMILY and precedes the PRAYER OF THE FAITHFUL.

PROFOUND BOW: A bow made with the body rather than just the head (p. 266).

PROPER OF THE MASS: Those parts of the Mass that change based on the liturgical day. Also called the proper or the proper of the day. Compare with ORDINARY OF THE MASS.

PSALMIST: A person who sings the psalm or other biblical canticle that comes between the readings.

PURIFICATOR: A small linen cloth used to purify the sacred vessels and to wipe the lip of the chalice after a person has drunk from it (p. 204).

PYX: A small container typically used to bring COMMUNION to the sick. It is often shaped like a small, short, cylindrical box, just large enough to hold a few hosts.

RECOGNITIO: The official recognition or approval of the Holy See. This is required for changes in the liturgy that go beyond the competence of the local bishop or conference of bishops (p. 291).

---

[22] GIRM 30.
[23] GIRM 32.

REFORM: An attempt to improve or otherwise correct something. See also LITURGICAL REFORM.

REPROBATED: Something that is condemned. A practice that has been expressly reprobated by the Holy See is prohibited and cannot become a legitimate custom.

RESPONSORIAL PSALM: One of the chants that occurs between readings in the SCRIPTURE READINGS. The Responsorial Psalm follows the first reading. It is typically performed in a responsorial or antiphonal style in which one person or choir sings or proclaims parts of the psalm and the rest of the congregation provides responses. See ANTIPHON.

RESPONSUM: Latin, "response" or "answer." Often used as shorthand for *responsum ad dubium* ("response to a doubt," "answer to a question")—a type of reply in question-and-answer format typically given by a DICASTERY of the Holy See to clarify or settle an issue.

RITE: A specific ritual action (e.g., the RITE OF BLESSING AND SPRINKLING, the COMMUNION RITE). Alternately, the liturgical, theological, spiritual, and disciplinary patrimony, culture, and circumstances of history of a distinct people.[25] There are six such rites in the Church: the Alexandrian, Antiochene, Armenian, Chaldean, Constantinopolitan, and Roman rites. Compare with CHURCH *SUI IURIS.*

RITE OF BLESSING AND SPRINKLING: One of the INTRODUCTORY RITES, in which holy water is blessed and then used to sprinkle the people. It occasionally occurs on Sunday, especially in EASTER. It follows the GREETING and precedes the *KYRIE,* taking the place of the ACT OF PENITENCE (pp. 102, 209)

---

[25] CCEO 28 §1.

RITE OF PEACE: Part of the COMMUNION RITE. In it, "the Church asks for peace and unity for herself and for the whole human family, and the faithful express to each other their ecclesial communion and mutual charity before communicating in the sacrament."[24] The Rite of Peace may also include an individual exchange of a sign of peace among the faithful. It follows the LORD'S PRAYER and precedes the FRACTION.

ROGATION AND EMBER DAYS: "On rogation and ember days the practice of the Church is to offer prayers to the Lord for the needs of all people, especially for the productivity of the earth and for human labor, and to give him public thanks. In order to adapt the rogation and ember days to various regions and the different needs of the people, the conferences of bishops should arrange the time and plan for their celebration."[26] The term *rogation* is from the Latin *rogare*, "to ask." The term *ember day* is from the *ymbrendaeg*, meaning "circuit day" or "anniversary day." Formerly ember days were held at the change of seasons.

ROMAN CANON: Another name for EUCHARISTIC PRAYER I (p. 141).

ROMAN CURIA: "The complex of dicasteries [DICASTERY] and institutes which help the Roman pontiff in the exercise of his supreme pastoral office for the good and service of the whole Church and of the particular Churches."[27] It includes the Congregation for Divine Worship and the Discipline of the Sacraments and the Congregation for the Doctrine of the Faith.

ROMAN GRADUAL: Latin title, *GRADUALE ROMANUM.* The book containing musical settings for the psalms and other parts

---

[24] GIRM 82.
[26] GNLC 45–46.
[27] John Paul II, *Pastor Bonus* art. 1.

of the Mass. It uses more complex chants than those in the SIMPLE GRADUAL.

ROMAN MISSAL: Another way of referring to the *MISSALE ROMANUM*. Alternately, the English translation of that part of the *Missale Romanum* that contains the prayers used at Mass.

ROMAN RITE: The form of liturgy used at Rome and elsewhere in the Latin Church.

RUBRICS: Instructions printed in red in a liturgical book (e.g., the ROMAN MISSAL) that direct the actions of those participating in a liturgical celebration. Rubrics are typically scattered among the text of the prayers (which are printed in black).

SACERDOS: Latin, "priest," pronounced: "sa-CHAIR-dos." A term used in ecclesiastical documents to indicate a person who is either a priest or a bishop. It is commonly translated into English simply as "priest." It does not include deacons. When a person is a priest but not a bishop, the Latin word *presbyter* is used.

SACRAMENTAL: When used as an adjective, having to do with the sacraments. When used as a noun, a rite or thing that is not a sacrament but is a sacred sign instituted by the Church to prepare men to receive the fruit of the sacraments and sanctify different circumstances of life. Examples include blessings and holy water.

SACRAMENTARY: Historically, a book containing the prayers used by the priest at Mass and certain other rites. More recently this term was used for the book containing the prayers used by the priest and people at Mass. Because this did not correspond fully to the historic use of the term, when the current translation of the liturgy was produced, it was decided that the book formerly called the *Sacramentary* would now simply be called the ROMAN MISSAL.

SACRARIUM: A special basin or sink, typically found in a SAC-
RISTY, that drains into the earth rather than the sewer system. It is used to dispose of water that has been used for
a sacred purpose (e.g., cleaning altar linens or eucharistic
vessels) and similar functions (e.g., disposing of the ashes
of blessed objects that have been burned). It is altogether
forbidden to pour the precious blood into the sacrarium (p.
227).

SACRED SPECIES: Another way of referring to the consecrated
elements. They are referred to in this way because after the
CONSECRATION only the "species" (appearances) of bread and
wine remain, the substance having become Jesus Christ (p.
228).

SACRIFICE: Latin, *sacer* = "holy, sacred" + *facere* "to make." To
make something holy by giving it to God in worship.

SACRISTAN: An individual who "carefully arranges the liturgical books, the vestments, and other things necessary in the
celebration of Mass."[28]

SACRISTY: A room used to house the articles needed for Mass
when not in use. These include vestments, altar furnishings,
and liturgical vessels. It also typically contains a SACRARIUM
and is usually the place where priests and other ministers
vest for Mass.

SACROSANCTUM CONCILIUM: The document issued by VATICAN
II on the liturgy; it provided the initial impetus for the LITUR-
GICAL REFORM that followed (p. 323).

SANCTUARY: "The sanctuary is the space where the altar and
the ambo stand," and "where the priest, deacon and other
ministers exercise their offices. The special character of the

---

[28] GIRM 105a.

sanctuary is emphasized and enhanced by the distinctiveness of its design and furnishings, or by its elevation."[29] Also called the CHANCEL or PRESBYTERIUM.

SANCTUS: The more common name for the ACCLAMATION that follows the THANKSGIVING in the EUCHARISTIC PRAYER. From its opening word, *Sanctus* (Latin, "holy"). Also called the Trisagion. Sometimes colloquially called the "Holy, Holy, Holy," from its opening words (p. 144).

SCRIPTURE READINGS: The first part of the LITURGY OF THE WORD, in which various readings from Scripture are proclaimed, along with chants (such as the RESPONSORIAL PSALM) inserted between them. They precede the HOMILY.

SECRET: A prayer said inaudibly in the extraordinary form, shortly before the *SURSUM CORDA*. It changes based on the liturgical day and corresponds to the PRAYER OVER THE OFFERINGS in the ORDINARY FORM. Unlike the Secret, the PRAYER OVER THE OFFERINGS is said audibly and does not change.

SIMPLE GRADUAL: Latin title, *GRADUALE SIMPLEX*. The book containing musical settings for the psalms and other parts of the Mass. It uses simpler chants than those of the ROMAN GRADUAL.

SOLEMNITY: A liturgical day of the highest significance, more solemn than a FEAST or MEMORIAL. "Solemnities are counted as the principal days in the calendar, and their observance begins with Evening Prayer I of the preceding day. Some also have their own vigil Mass for use when Mass is celebrated in the evening of the preceding day. The celebration of Easter and Christmas, the two greatest solemnities, continues for eight days, with each octave governed by its own rules."[30]

---

[29] *Built of Living Stones* 54.
[30] GNLC 11–12.

STOLE: A long strip of cloth worn around the neck as a symbol of office by a bishop, priest, or deacon. Its color matches the liturgical color of the day.

STOUP: A small vessel containing holy water, typically placed at the entrances to a church. Also called a holy water FONT (p. 238).

SUBDEACON: Historically, one of the MAJOR ORDERS. It preceded ordination to the diaconate. In 1972 the office was abolished in the Latin Church, though Paul VI stated that there was "no reason why the acolyte cannot be called a subdeacon in some places, at the discretion of the conference of bishops"[31] (p. 52).

SUMMORUM PONTIFICUM: A 2007 Apostolic Letter issued *MOTU PROPRIO* by Benedict XVI to clarify the status of the EXTRAORDINARY FORM of Mass and establish rules regarding it use (p. 365).

SURPLICE: A loose-fitting vestment made of cotton or linen that typically reaches just below the hips. Often worn by laymen over a cassock when serving at liturgies.

SURSUM CORDA: Latin, "Hearts up!" Part of the THANKSGIVING of the EUCHARISTIC PRAYER in which the priest invites the people to rejoice by saying, "Lift up your hearts."

SYMBOLUM: Another name for the PROFESSION OF FAITH.

THANKSGIVING: In general, the act of giving thanks to God. More specifically, the first part of the EUCHARISTIC PRAYER. In it the priest offers thanks to God, especially in the prayer known as the PREFACE. The *SURSUM CORDA* also occurs in the THANKSGIVING.

---

[31] *Ministeria Quaedam.*

THURIBLE: A censer that is suspended by a chain so that it can be swung (p. 88).

THURIFER: A minister who carries the THURIBLE.

TONSURE: The ceremonial cutting of hair to indicate entrance into the clerical state. Also, the hairstyle that resulted from this cutting. Historically, tonsure was administered when one entered the MINOR ORDERS. It was abolished in 1972, and subsequently entrance into the clerical state has occurred upon ordination to the diaconate (p. 51).

TRADITIONAL LATIN MASS: Another term for what is properly called the EXTRAORDINARY FORM. The word *traditional* is used because the ORDINARY FORM of Mass can be celebrated in Latin, so "the Latin Mass" would not refer to the extraordinary form in particular. Often abbreviated to "TLM" and sometimes called the TRIDENTINE MASS.

TRADITIONALIST: In a liturgical context, one who has a preference for the LITURGY as it was celebrated prior to the LITURGICAL REFORM that followed VATICAN II.

TRANSUBSTANTIATION: The transformation of the substance of bread and wine into the body, blood, soul, and divinity of the Lord Jesus Christ. After transubstantiation, the appearances of bread and wine remain, but the reality is Jesus Christ (p. 137).

TRENT: An ecumenical council held from 1545 to 1563. It dealt principally with the Protestant Reformation and the internal reform of the Church. Following it the *Roman Catechism* (or *Catechism of Pius V*) and a revised *Missal* were released. This gave rise to the so-called TRIDENTINE MASS. It was revised over the years until the *Missal* of 1962, which is now used to celebrate the EXTRAORDINARY FORM of the Mass.

TRIDENTINE MASS: Another term for what is properly called the EXTRAORDINARY FORM. Also called the TRADITIONAL LATIN MASS.

TRIDENTINE: Having to do with the Council of Trent.

TRIDUUM: The liturgical season that follows Lent. "The Easter triduum begins with the evening Mass of the Lord's Supper, reaches its high point in the Easter Vigil, and closes with Evening Prayer on Easter Sunday."[32]

TRISAGION: Greek, "Thrice holy." Another name for the *SANCTUS.*

TROPE: In current liturgical law, a phrase or sentence that may be injected into the *KYRIE* before each petition. For example, "You were sent to heal the contrite of heart," "You came to call sinners," and "You are seated at the right hand of the Father to intercede for us" are tropes that the priest may say before "Lord have mercy" (p. 103).

TYPICAL EDITION: The authoritative edition of a liturgical book, whether in Latin or another language. From the Latin *editio typica*, translations into vernacular languages are made. The current English-language *Roman Missal* is a translation of the *editio typica* of the Latin *Missale Romanum*.

UNIVERSAL PRAYER: See PRAYER OF THE FAITHFUL.

VALID/VALIDITY: Having efficacy, force, or soundness; having its intended effect. For example, the Eucharist is celebrated validly if TRANSUBSTANTIATION occurs. Validity is the state or quality of being valid. Note that, properly speaking, Masses are not valid or invalid; they are licit or illicit. It is the sacraments themselves, such as the Eucharist, that are valid or invalid. See also LICIT/LICEITY.

---

[32] GNLC 19.

VATICAN II: An ecumenical council held from 1962 to 1965. It dealt principally with the pastoral challenges of the modern world. Following it the *Catechism of the Catholic Church* (1992) was published. Also following it was a LITURGICAL REFORM that resulted in the *Missal* of 1970, which was modified in 1975 and again the early 2000s. The most recent edition represents the ORDINARY FORM of celebration for the Mass.

VENERATION OF THE ALTAR: An act performed both during the INTRODUCTORY RITES and the CONCLUDING RITES. The priest, deacon, and other ministers make a profound bow to the altar and the priest and deacon kiss it. In the Introductory Rites it precedes the GREETING. In the Concluding Rites it precedes the *EXEUNT*.

VERNACULAR: A language spoken by a particular group of people; a local native language. English, Spanish, French, and German are vernacular languages. They contrast with Latin, which is no longer a local or native language but an international one that is spoken only as a second language (p. 15).

VESTMENT: A special article of clothing worn by a minister at Mass. Examples include ALBS, CHASUBLES, STOLES, COPES, and others (pp. 256ff.).

VIATICUM: The reception of Holy COMMUNION by a person in danger of death. Intended to be the final sacramental reception of the Lord Jesus, who accompanies one through death and into the next life. Catholic Tradition places great importance on the administration of *viaticum* (p. 167).

VIR: Latin, "man." The term used to indicate an adult of the male gender. Plural: *viri* (p. 54).

VULGATE: A Latin edition of Scripture, initially translated and compiled by St. Jerome. It has been recently revised, and the new edition is sometimes referred to as the Neo-Vulgate. The Vulgate is used as a reference point for settling certain questions regarding the translation of the Scripture into vernacular languages (p. 338).

WESTERN RITE: Another term for the Latin rite.

Bibliography

Book of Blessings. Collegeville, Minn.: Liturgical Press, 1989.

Canon Law Digest, vol. 10. Mundelein, Ill.: 1986.

Ceremonies of the Modern Roman Rite. (Elliott, Msgr. Peter J.) San Francisco: Ignatius Press, 1995.

Documents on the Liturgy: 1963–1979. Collegeville, Minn.: Liturgical Press, 1982.

Eucharistic Prayer for Masses for Various Needs and Occasions. Totowa, N.J.: Catholic Book Publishing Co., 1996.

Fundamentals of Catholic Dogma. (Ott, Ludwig.) Rockford, Ill.: TAN, 1974.

The Rites of the Catholic Church. Collegeville, Minn.: Liturgical Press, 1990.

The Sacraments and Their Celebration. (Halligan, Fr. Nicholas.) New York: Alba House, 1986.

Sunday Celebrations in the Absence of a Priest. Collegeville, Minn.: Liturgical Press, 1997.

Index